T0044329

Karolinum Press

Jiří Přibáň & Karel Hvížďala

In Quest
of History

On Czech Statehood
and Identity

VÁCLAV HAVEL SERIES

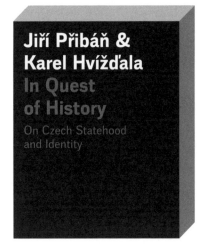

Jiří Přibáň &
Karel Hvížďala
In Quest
of History
On Czech Statehood
and Identity

KAROLINUM PRESS

KAROLINUM PRESS is a publishing department of Charles University
Ovocný trh 560/5, 116 36 Prague 1, Czech Republic
www.karolinum.cz

Originally published in Czech as *Hledání dějin. O české státnosti a identitě*,
Prague: Karolinum Press, 2018.

Reviewed by Pavel Kolář (European University Institute, Fiesole)
Jan Kuklík (Charles University, Prague)
Cover and graphic design by /3.dílna/
Typeset and printed by Karolinum Press

ISBN 978-80-246-4267-3
ISBN 978-80-246-4288-8 (pdf)
ISBN 978-80-246-4290-1 (epub)
ISBN 978-80-246-4289-5 (mobi)

Let us then seek as those who would find, and find as those who would seek.
ST AUGUSTINE OF HIPPO

The purpose of history as a science is to enrich and expand human consciousness.
ZDENĚK KALISTA

CONTENTS

PREFACE

That we are experiencing a cultural watershed is growing into a refrain for our times. Globalisation has assimilated individual national societies into a single world society that we all share. There is no escape from this society; it has become our destiny. We share hopes and fears, technological advances that are groundbreaking and unprecedented in human history, and the classic political, economic and ecological crises that have been dogging us since the dawn of history.

In this global society, modern nations and their states are rapidly and radically evolving, yet remain, in the minds of those who belong to them, an imaginary community where moral ideals and political goals are pursued and attained. For some, the nation state is a tool of globalisation; others see it as a last-chance emergency brake before we crash into globalisation's calamitous fallout.

People are clamouring against the march of global civilisation, but are forced to react to it both within and outside their national cultures because it cannot be pushed aside or sidestepped. We can also see this in the emerging generation's protests and political engagement: unlike the older generation of rapidly globalising professional classes, they believe that global risks are just as serious as the local defence of democracy in their own country. Similar threads run throughout our civilisation: in France and Germany there are the Greens, in the Czech Republic the Pirates and A Million Moments for Democracy, in Hong Kong the student movement, and so on.

Central Europe is a place whose modern history has spawned more cultural watersheds than its inhabitants have been able to cope with by civilised means. The history of the Czech nation and its statehood is no exception. Historians and politicians, idealists and realists, democrats and their enemies all seek to understand these watersheds. Everyone is on a quest for history, even if their minds are set on the present and future. This is also true of our dialogue between a legal philosopher living in Cardiff and a probing journalist from Prague.

While the internet has foisted this idea on today's globalised humanity that speed and concise communication are paramount, we have headed in the opposite direction in this book: we try to amplify the context both territorially and temporally. In our republic's centenary year, we concentrated on key points in our history, ranging from the 9th to the 21st century. This allowed us to peer into the past and ask ourselves how we perceived and understood our history at different times, why this was so, and what it means for our present and future.

In certain respects, this is a quest to stop history from being reduced to a screen on which we project our frustrations. We were keen to return to the public arena those issues that tend to be contained within the walls of academia or that we generally steer clear of.

We extend our gratitude to Pavel Kolář, a comparative historian from the European University Institute in Florence, and Jan Kuklík, a legal historian and the dean of the Faculty of Law at Charles University in Prague, for their valuable advice and comments on the manuscript.

We would like to thank Petr Valo, the director of the Karolinum Press, and his deputies Martin Janeček and Milan Šusta for giving us the impetus to write this book.

KH and JP, 2018

History and National Identity

Karel Hvížďala: Czechoslovakia was proclaimed an independent state on 28 October 1918, yet in the century since there have been only two periods when it was truly master of its own fate: from the time it came into being until 1938, and then post 1989. At the end of 1992, it split into two separate states. If we are serious about discussing the history of Czech statehood and Czech identity, we should perhaps start by taking a look at the first historically documented beginnings of the Bohemian medieval state, which would take us back to the 9th century and the baptism of Duke Bořivoj. I firmly believe that our current gripes and grumbles are rooted far in the past. Can this be attributed to historical events and facts per se, or rather to how they have been interpreted in the accounts we call history?

Jiří Přibáň: National identity, its historical origins, and the political autonomy of each of these themes would make for a work spanning numerous volumes. And each of those volumes could stir up untold heated debates. Nationalism, for instance, can be defined quite simply as an ideology that demands the reconciliation of ethnic and political boundaries and legitimises power via the principle of popular sovereignty, in which the rulers and the rest of society together shape their integral national unity. Note, though, how many political and cultural ideals and disputes hide behind this definition and how this definition has been manifested in the history of various nations. History, including national history, then primarily becomes a matter of storytelling about the past. Through those narratives and stories, we pass on everything that we consider important in our history and that we believe gives it meaning. I am fond of the puristically conceived word *dějepis* [loosely "event-writing"] that we use in Czech to translate *historia*, the Greek term that originally meant a general capacity to become cognisant, through a narrative, of what has been learned. *Histor* generally designated a learned or wise man.

The Czech *dějepis* mirrors that original inner dynamic, where the historian's task is to write down past events and the expectation is that this very description, in itself, is an event and hence forms part of the history from which we should learn and enlighten ourselves. Consequently, unlike Latin's neutralised *historia*, the Czech *dějepis* continues to remind us that every historical narrative is self-referential, by which I mean that, ultimately, it always folds back on itself as part of history, the historical narrative, and the wisdom attached to history. History is the process of hauling yesteryear into the present so that past events acquire meaning and purpose for the current generation. National history has that and more: it is imbued with numerous existential questions such as "who are we?", "where do we come from?", and "where are we going?", which are pivotal, and all the more dangerous for it, because they also conjure up the illusion that nations are special, chosen to take on humanity's historical tasks, and that they have been here since time immemorial as natural groupings of people whose claim to their own existence takes precedence over any other right of an individual or group, or even of any other nation. Likewise, history routinely creates the illusion that the state is some sort of eternal political institution in which a nation finds and confirms its own existence and identity. In point of fact, the state is a product of modern politics, and the nation is an imaginary community devised by political romantics in the modern industrial age. Were every nation to exercise an unconditional right to self-determination in its own state, total political chaos and anarchy would ensue on a global scale.

To be sure, we tend to forget that today's nations are a product of the 19th century, and yet we see politicians in the Czech Republic and surrounding countries increasingly talking about the nation, national interests and national sovereignty as though this were something eternal, ancient beyond memory. What are our chances of extracting ourselves from this trap?

If we are to understand the historical processes behind the formation of the state and the birth of modern nations organising themselves politically into nation states, we must dispense with grand ideologies and established doctrines and, instead, study the specific language and lexicon used by society to describe its own history. Rather than concentrating on general patterns and abstract concepts, we should turn our attention to the specific speech that has been employed and the peculiar forms of power that are associated with it. Words are weapons and the past is littered with countless examples of how historical narratives become battlefields. The modern history of nation states eloquently documents this knack of bygone times to fashion myths and, by then invoking them, to foment wars and mobilise entire populations. This is precisely why we need to stop trying to find any objective rhyme or reason in the course of history, to stop searching for some *Weltgeist* of humanism manifesting itself in the process of human civilisation, or any other straitjackets laced up by philosophy as it seeks to understand human history. The idea that, in history, we will discover some transcendental principle in the form of progress, freedom, reason or humanity is untenable. Instead of the speculative philosophy of history familiar, say, to 19th-century national revivalists or revolutionary Marxists, we need to ponder particular historical situations and periods that may be construed as significant junctions where various relations between the structure of society and its semantics intersect. In other words, it is necessary to understand the processes underlying how society both organises and describes itself. Observe, for example, how modern Western societies describe their structures in crystal-clear terms, such as the state, the nation or sovereignty, while at the same time infusing them with equally clean-cut ideals, such as freedom, equality and fraternity. Our job is to peel back this "clean" description to lay bare the "dirty" and intricate world of economic, pedagogical, moral or legal structures and the most diverse technologies of power. This distinction between "clean" and "dirty" history cannot be viewed in any moral or philosophical sense, by which I mean we cannot uncover any true essence of history and figure out how it works and where it's headed. That sort of moralism would be as unseemly as any speculative philosophy of history. What we do need to do, though, is expose even the contemporary "dirty" language and lexicon within the seemingly "clean" structures and concepts we use to describe our history. The aim is to grasp how, even under the surface of apparently unambiguous, accepted concepts in the history of modern society and politics, there are always specific conflicts with smudged contours and historically haphazard processes and consequences.

But such considerations are too complicated. Politicians and the media shun them, afraid of alienating voters, readers or listeners. And that flings the door open wide to power-hungry populists and fabulists who have simple pre-cooked solutions for any problem. The internet has helped this shift and decay by marginalising debate with a barrage of emotionally-charged sound bites. Instead of the collective, it gives life to the connective...

The paradox of modern society is that its life is influenced far more by future expectations than past experience and tradition, yet its hunger for historical stories, and thirst for their moral significance, continues to mount. The social predominance of expectations over experience, then, also increases the specific expectation that history has answers to the questions posed by the present. Even the famous end-of-history thesis written by the Russian-born French philosopher Alexandre Kojéve and retold by the American political scientist Francis Fukuyama after 1989 as a historic victory of liberal democracy is nothing more than an attempt to decipher the definitive meaning of human history. Although Fukuyama's thesis provoked the ire of both the left and the right, blazing from their respective ideological positions, I think its most problematic factor is that, in Popper's words, it is merely another example of the "poverty of historicism". Nevertheless, if we were to say that there are no metaphysical or dialectical laws concealed in history, that does not necessarily mean that they are entirely meaningless for us. On the contrary, historical narratives retain importance even in our post-traditional age, with its fixation on future expectations. At the same time, however, these narratives are evidently unable to guarantee the validity of any social contract or general consensus. Has history been relegated to a social pastime, meaning that, in reality, the numbers of books, journals and other periodicals devoted to history paradoxically document the ascent of a post-historical age? Can we even question whether history has meaning if teachers and their pupils, as every generation passes, attach so little importance to historical knowledge? What do we actually expect from "history" teaching?

I think that might be oversimplifying things...
I take your point because, in historical science, sociology and the philosophy of history these days, extreme views denying history *per se* are coming to light. The entirely correct and necessary criticism of the former social-Darwinist or Marxist concept of history as a linear time in which the objective law of human progress and the supremacy of modern times over all past experience and tradition has now been repeatedly turned into a nihilistic assertion that every historical narrative is merely a form of cultural hegemony and elitism, ethnocentric supremacy or political ideology and oppression by the powers that be. This is particularly true of national history, where the original Romantic apotheosis of nations has given way to an equally passionate hatred of any manifestation of national culture. It is as though fanatical nationalism has been replaced by an equally fanatical struggle against everything that has something to do with the nation as a social group and the sense of belonging it engenders. Admittedly, historians have helped to shape the collective memories of modern nations and their myths, but that does not mean that history is "just" a handmaiden in the service of political leaders and elitist interests. Nor does it suggest, in the slightest, that we could

say that nations – because they are "imaginary", or "invented", communities formed in modern times – are only a plaything and consequence of those interests. The imaginariness of nations in no way implies that these communities did not actually exist and that we can shrug them off as the product of a "false" consciousness. The sociological term "imagined communities", encompassing not only the nation, but also, for instance, religious communities and economic classes, certainly doesn't mean that such communities do not exist or are based on ideological lies. It simply denotes large social groups that we, as individuals, can never see in their entirety in our lifetime, but we can imagine them all too well through various symbols, feel a strong bond with them, and share a collective identity with others. What we imagine, and what is therefore imagined, is simultaneously very real and has a major impact on our social life. We must realise that society itself is one such imagined community, and yet, in a very real sense, we experience its existence every day. We need to adopt the same approach to nations and their history, as well as to their very specific forms of social organisation and life, which includes not only the national economy and art, but also the state. Quite a few people these days may feel that this opinion is nothing to wonder at, but in the first half of the 20th century it was routine for many historians, sociologists and ethnologists to adhere to the naturalistic notion that social and cultural differences between various ethnicities and nations were the legacy of biological disparities and inherited characteristics established by a shared biological – read "racial" – origin. When the German sociologist Max Weber claimed that ethnic groups were actually artificial social creations, that is, that they were not *natürlich* but *künstlich*, and that they were based on subjective beliefs about a shared community and its fate, he wasn't exactly voicing the view of the majority. What is more, Weber argued that it was not beliefs that make a community, but that a community forms its own system of beliefs. He also argued that creating a community such as a nation always results in efforts to monopolise power within it and to secure status. So when we talk of the nation, we have to look not for its natural foundations, but for the socially moulded power constellation and privileges within its political organisation.

This is why we manufactured the Czechoslovak nation, so that we could proclaim a state. But can we then really talk about history as a scientific discipline? Is not this, too, largely just a construct, a fiction, as we have seen it increasingly being discussed?
Some historians really are fighting doggedly against their own scientific discipline, labelling it a science in the service of political power and its ideology, the worst specimen of which is nationalism justifying the repressive policy pursued by nation states and imperial superpowers alike. For example, the controversial Israeli historian Shlomo Sand has recently described history, in his *Twilight of History*, as a science that has always served the nation state and its interests, and calls historians "priests of this official cult", tasked with shaping national identity and maintaining the collective memory in various forms, starting with history lessons at school, then museum exhibitions and, ultimately, all manner of academic institutions and historical institutes.

Essays in the same vein can also be found in our country...
This harsh condemnation of history and historians exemplifies more than historical relativism; it is a form of intellectual reduction and moral blindness that sees only power-driven and ideological context behind every text while completely overlooking the fact that, say, national history these days is typically studied in a global context in which national political interests are just one of many variables. Similarly, the relationship between history and state power is not merely servile, but also critical. For instance, a historian or sociologist who studies police or ministerial statistics does not automatically accept the official interpretation of the data. Historical and social

sciences have their own methods, which are far from just "mythologising"; they are also critical and, above all, independent. Those who assume the mantle of "myth-busters" paradoxically claim that history does not exist, yet they themselves are devising a canon of critical historical science that defines how history is to be written. For example, Sand's conclusion that the rise and fall of modern history is linked to the nation state turns a blind eye not only to the long line of historical studies that do not address the history of the nation state at all, but also ignores the internal disputes and conflicts within historical science that confirm its relative independence of the primarily political creation of national monuments, cults and myths. History, then, does not exist solely to legitimise the myths of a nation state, just as the nation state is not just a perverse institution of mass extermination and ethnic cleansing. This intellectual nihilism masquerading as a myth-buster's pseudo-Romantic moral mission must be rejected along with all self-absorption in national history and the glorification of nations as the only historically natural group for which there is an absolute *raison d'être* in the architecture of the state. Crowding out national identity in the name of universal ideals is just another form of the same fanaticism that once stoked national hatred. Today, that very same hatred is reserved for all those who do not prescribe horror of the nation *comme il faut* and do not regard the nation state as the source of all political evil. A high degree of intellectual balance and civic courage is still required today in order to sidestep these fanaticisms and simplifications.

My generation came of age in the Stalinist 1950s and, without even telling ourselves how important history was, we methodically sought it out in our families' bookcases, in witness accounts and in second-hand bookshops. What we really wanted to know was what was going on in Czechoslovakia between 1918 and 1938 and from 1945 to 1948, and what had been wrongly defamed or glorified. How did your generation view history?

History isn't what it used to be! This is how we might flip a sentence by the poet Paul Valéry, who more than a hundred years ago remarked that "the trouble with our times is that the future is not what it used to be". It would be unthinkable to claim offhand that history doesn't exist, but its intrinsic value, importance and narrative styles do appear to be evolving to the extent that, for example, the political and pedagogical influence of history is steadily waning. Nevertheless, there are historical points of intersection, key events, fateful decisions and protagonists that, for individuals, social groupings, and political communities and clans, such as nations, give meaning to their own existence. Our two bouts of autonomy that you mentioned are, timewise, entirely negligible periods which, put together, make up less than half a century in one nation's history. Yet note the swelling pride (whether or not it is justified is irrelevant) in the First Republic or dismay at the disintegration of the shared state of Czechs and Slovaks in 1992. For my generation, which grew up in the "normalisation" period of the 1970s and 1980s, history was an intellectual alternative to the ideological ballast of the present and also a form of moral resistance, a way of manifesting our contempt for the current situation. History can play an exceptional role of this nature only in historically exceptional times. Today, however, we are faced with the completely opposite question, namely whether history, which is no longer a fateful alternative for present generations, can survive as a literary and moral story. In other words, in this day and age the question is not only "what is the meaning of history?", but also "what is the point of narrating past events – history – at all?"

I'm afraid that, before we consider your question, we will have to go back to what the historians Josef Pekař and his teacher Jaroslav Goll started at the turn of the 20th century, by which I mean take our leave of the revivalist programme and the entrenched stereotypes and symbols that peep out at us from all manner of widely distributed papers.

I agree that we need to deal critically with historical stereotypes and symbols, including those that historians used to – and still do – devise about themselves, referring to themselves as "Masarykians" or "Pekařians", or when someone invokes Rádl's moralist diction in his philosophy of national history. If we remove ourselves from this contemporary tribal warfare between historians and their schools, we find that what interests us today about Pekař's famous 1928 lecture *The Meaning of Czech History* is not so much the dispute over Palacký or Masaryk's concept of national history, as the assertion that our history has the meaning that it has fashioned for itself and that has been imprinted on it by the historiography of one time or another, whether that be the *Chronicle of Dalimil*, the work of Václav Hájek of Libočany, or the writings of Balbín or Palacký. In this respect, the meaning of history lies in its active creation, and we cannot exclude from that Hanka and Linda's forged *Manuscripts* or the modern-day national myths conjured up by Zdeněk Nejedlý or, on film, Otakar Vávra. Pekař was lambasted for his positivist and empirical method and "science for science's sake" or "history for history's sake". However, he wanted to extricate history from the philosophy of history, where Masaryk was containing it by subordinating empirical methods to teleological judgements on the Czech nation's roles in human history and to metaphysical notions that our national history had a profound religious meaning. Besides the important idea that the meaning of history is determined solely by history, i.e. that historical science can rely only on its own methods and observations, rather than on metaphysical ideas and ideals, Pekař's lecture contains another very important and critical idea – that no nation is a chosen people or has a particular historical purpose. The notion that national history has meaning is inextricably linked to belief in the fact that a nation is chosen, i.e. that each nation has a different historical purpose and hence different historical tasks and meaning within human history. This idea can be found, for example, in Hegel's *Philosophy of History* and in certain later works by Romantic philosophers, who attributed various ideas and creative acts to various nations in various periods of history. It was as though every nation had been chosen by a historical spirit for various tasks, and the purpose of its existence was to accomplish those tasks and thus contribute to the absolute development of humanity. Pekař rejected philosophical speculation in his criticism of both Palacký and Masaryk's concepts of national history, but he realised that national patriotism cannot get by without historical science and that this science contributes to the defence of national existence, even though this is never just a matter of will and decision, but the product of much more complicated contexts derived from historical development.

We have to expound on that a little. In *The Czech Question* (1895), Masaryk criticised the ideological vacuity of Czech politics and pitted the religiously founded humanity of the 15th-century Bohemian Reformation against its pragmatism. Pekař countered that Hussitism and the Unity of the Brethren were purely medieval phenomena that could not be conflated with the later formation of a modern nation steeped in the Enlightenment and liberalism. However, I would say that both stances have remained very important for us to this day. How do you feel about this?
There is a disparity between Masaryk's concept of national history and its historical significance. Masaryk's critical and rational approach to Czech history at a time when many viewed history as the mythologising justification of national existence was of utmost importance for the modern formulation of the Czech question and both the political and cultural programme. Masaryk definitely didn't see the Czech nation as a historically chosen people representing a unique meaning in history or of history *per se*. Eschewing this notion of a culturally or racially chosen people, Masaryk probes the question of meaning as a matter of the political and moral shepherding of national life. The meaning of historical purpose is thus

imposed on a nation on the basis of its present situation and its future direction. In *The Czech Question*, Masaryk literally writes: "We are rising from the dead and the world expects words of redemption from us." The national revival therefore had the historical task of contributing to the moral and political revolution of the modern world. Imposing on the Czech nation the moral task of fulfilling the universal religious ideals of Christianity and embracing it in politics as a mission to establish a democratic society as part of the world revolution – this was indeed Masaryk's revolutionary vision. It contributed, among other things, to the criticism of politics and national identity derived from Slavophile tribal affiliation. However, it should be noted that Pekař criticised Palacký's concept of national history more generally for being based on the idea of autonomous historical development taking place in clashes and struggles with the outer Germanic world. In this historical narrative, the Czechs became the bearers of a higher culture that, in the face of violence and the warlike German spirit, historically advocated freedom and peace, which was supposedly characteristic not only of the Czechs, but of all Slavs. Pekař countered this with the idea that the historical development of the Czech nation was not decided by any original high Old Slavonic culture, but by the ability to open up to foreign influences and to accept them as its own. Pekař also pointed out that the millennium of Czech history from the 10th to the 20th centuries was determined primarily by the extent to which we, too, participated in broader European history. In this sense, for instance, he viewed Hussitism as a period in which the Czech nation was Europeanised to such a degree that it felt so culturally strong that "we ourselves wanted to give guidance to Europe, our teacher and governess". Needless to say, for Pekař this governess was not a chosen continent with an autonomous and historically unique culture and role. Rather, this was a culture whose origins "were shaped enormously by the Orient, Antiquity and the Arab world". Although Masaryk and Pekař's philosophy of history and historical methods are markedly different from each another, in principle both men were able to dispel strong contemporary prejudices implying that our history was a constant conflict with the world around us, in the face of which we had to distinguish and define our own uniqueness if we were to have any success in defending our right to national existence. In contrast to this, both Masaryk and Pekař agree that the meaning of our national existence is not determined by the nation as an ethnic or racial community, but as a historically formed community that is constantly mutating just as history itself is reshaped. In other words, every era creates its own Czechs, setting them very specific tasks and ascribing specific meaning to their existence.

The historian Dušan Třeštík also drew attention to this in the 1990s when he said that we need to reinvent the Czech nation. What he actually meant was that history is not just positivist knowledge, but also comprises constantly changing value judgements.

I agree entirely that history's job is to explore the past, but the story and narrative are always loaded with a specific value-charged bullet that we use to shape our present and find our bearings in the future. There are moments in the collective memory of any modern nation in which national identity is inherent. It is not important in the slightest whether these events really happened or have been thought up by historians and national revivalists. They may be tragic or heroically celebrated. Through them, modern nations come up with answers to the question of where they come from, what they are, and where they are heading, and, out of these historical events, they compose their own meaningful narratives of history and try to cobble together universally valid canons from them. Historical texts pile up and often contradict each other, but, most of all, they assure us that even products of social imagination, such as modern nations, can share a very specific historical experience and thus confirm that they have a right to exist. As the French sociologist Maurice Halbwachs said: collective memory is our lived history. Rather than start at the beginning, which always gives the illusion of a fixed point from which we can move through the universe of history, it is important – as we have already mentioned – to enquire into the nodal points and key events that still make sense and have somehow left their mark on historical developments or the present. And we need to keep revisiting them with the same tenacity with which, for example, the Czech novelist and dissident Ludvík Vaculík wrote his feuilletons *Spring is Here* and *A Day in August* every year. I would even say that history only makes sense if we put up historical resistance to it. In this context, I am particularly fond of a sentence Vaculík wrote in *A Day in August* in 1985, during the normalisation era: "The situation is numbing me; it looks like I'm not resisting enough."

How would you define what has been termed "the Czech question"? As we know all too well, Masaryk formulated the Czech question in his work of the same title as a response to the *Manuscripts* debate. In doing so, he freed history once and for all from its servility to the political mythologisation of national history. At the same time, however, this question had a purely political slant because Czech national politics had to react to the social, economic, and even constitutional and political changes sweeping through the Habsburg monarchy in the second half of the 19th century. That is why we must always read Masaryk's *The Czech Question* together with his reflective *Our Current Crisis*, and place both of these works in the context of a time when Hubert Gordon Schauer, now barely remembered, asked a fundamental question about the meaning and purpose of our historical right and struggle to preserve our national identity and language in a lopsided battle with the Germanic environment around us.

Begging your pardon, but perhaps we ought to recall how Gordon Schauer articulated his questions. He was asking whether Czech society was big enough and morally strong enough to build a cul-

ture of its own, and whether the efforts put into the national revival might not be better invested in general cultural pursuits within the framework of German culture. His text was published in the magazine *Čas* in 1886. At the time, there were even rumours that the essay had been initiated by Masaryk himself.

More's the shame that, in this "dispute" over the meaning of Czech history, we tend to stick to subsequent polemics from the first half of the 20th century. Schauer's reflective essay *Our Two Questions* embraces the general and yet utterly crucial dilemma of any national revival and self-determination, as you have quoted in your question: whether the efforts and energies devoted to preserving national identity and the language are exhausting the domestic elite and intelligentsia, which could otherwise directly target universal goals such as scientific or political progress and the moral rebirth of society. Masaryk viewed this sceptically formulated question as a challenge to the political advancement of his philosophy of history, where there is no place for fabricated myths, but where historical events and the course of history carry higher metaphysical meaning. For Masaryk, the universal "ideals of humanity" were to form the bedrock for the continuity of Czech history, from Hussitism and the Unity of the Brethren to the idea of national revival formulated by Palacký. According to Masaryk, the purpose of Czech politics was to spiritually and morally "awaken" the nation. As you have said, this metaphysical concept of history was opposed by Pekař and other adherents of Goll's positivist school in historiography, who rejected not only the culturally mythologising, but also political function of historical science. The Czech question, then, was more than half a century's conflict that was not so much about the meaning of Czech history as it was – much more – about the status and autonomy of historical science. In other words, history can only have scientific responsibility; it cannot be assigned the cultural task of bolstering national identity or the metaphysical task of political and moral rebirth based on philosophical and religious ideals. When we explore the historical significance of that dispute about the Czech question and the meaning of Czech history, waged by historians, and also among the broader public and politicians, from the final decades of the 19th century until the turn of 1939, when, in the wake of Munich, it was brought to a definitive end by the Nazi occupation (which paradoxically returned the whole saga to square one and to the plane of the existential struggle for bare survival), our understanding of the whole controversy should be that an emancipated nation can only ask history to deliver history, not national mythology or political metaphysics.

In your opinion, this is the answer to the question of the meaning of Czech history and the meaning of narratives about historical events, from which we have digressed. But does this question of meaning, as you yourself say, also affect the political, cultural and social present?

Yes, this is the second and more general plane of the whole dispute, namely that the Czech question, no matter how it is formulated by historical language and lined with historical events and quarrels, always also affects the national present and future expectations in both a good and a bad way. In this sense, every generation is compelled to ask its own "Czech question". Zdeněk Nejedlý placed it in the service of communist ideology and power, while Karel Kosík formulated it in the context of critical Marxist philosophy as a general struggle against the bureaucratic alienation of modern humankind. Kosík's *Our Current Crisis* of spring 1968 returned the topic of national and political crisis to a philosophical context by construing the question of the meaning of Czech history as part of a general question about the meaning of human existence. That text repeats the well-known themes of the geography and heritage of Central Europe as a space where there are cultural and political clashes between East and West, Rome and Byzantium, individualism and collectivism, and so on. At this point in time, Kosík viewed the Czech question as a challenge to engage in the active and distinct synthesis of all the contradictions and the various influences mentioned – an active search for true human existence, thereby making a stand against the indifference and superficiality of life. As we know, the August occupation transformed this question of "crisis" into a question of "Czech destiny" and saw Milan Kundera and Václav Havel clash in late 1968 and the months that followed. In his *Czech Destiny*, Kundera regarded this destiny as a historical dispute between alliance and sovereignty, the latter of which the Czech nation aspired to but was being denied. He was actually elaborating on an original proposition from a speech he had delivered at the Fourth Congress of the Union of Czechoslovak Writers in June 1967, in which he contrasted the mentality of large nations with the mentality of small nations, who must steadfastly struggle for their existence and the historical significance of that existence, as though theirs was the pursuit of something non-axiomatic that needed to be moulded anew constantly and every day. While Kundera thought that the Soviet occupation of 1968 was fated to happen as part of this historical destiny, it is interesting how actively Václav Havel embroiled himself in the entire conflict in his rejoinder *Czech Destiny?*, the question mark in the title doubling up as an exclamation mark warning against the very notion of "national destiny". Havel went in very hard and very personally for the time, generalising Kundera's view as a classic way in which a political situation was translated into a *fatum*, thus inhibiting not only critical assessment of the real causes of the crisis, but also opportunities to resolve it. Havel then pitted specific historical responsibility against general historical parallels and abstract context.

Paradoxically, as Václav Havel later told me in *Disturbing the Peace*, Kundera's attitude galvanised the first large-scale writers' petition at the dawn of the normalisation era, challenging the sentences handed down to dissidents and demanding a Christmas amnesty.

And that's not all. It is interesting how this dispute subsequently fringed historical and ethical discussions of Czech dissent and how it informed, say, Patočka's reflections on Czech history and Czechness, and Pithart's *Sixty-Eight*, in which the author describes the political debacle of reformist communism, in its broader historical and cultural context, as an example of traditional Czech inability to pursue a practical policy and shoulder responsibility for it. We need only dwell a little on these historical disputations and reflections on modern Czech history, of which – because they themselves shape it – they also happen to be a quite fundamental part, to realise that the Czech question is also a question of the political role of erudition and intellectuals in modern Czech history! It combines intellectual doubts, moral imperatives and cultural stereotypes. The Czech nation was originally formed as a cultural community that had to codify its own language, which it then used as a vehicle to establish its own educational attainment. Only after language, science and modern culture have been "constituted" can we address the question of political constitution. This means, among other things, that the national revivalists and their education and knowledge were of huge importance. As the political responsibility of Czech intellectuals has always reached very high, it is hardly surprising that the first president of the Czechoslovak Republic was a philosopher and that his closest associate and successor was a sociologist and political scientist. In this context, Havel's more recent presidency also appears to be a paradoxical fusion of a quite exceptional historical situation and cultural tradition. Here, Czech society places on its intellectuals unrealistic political expectations that usually give way to traditional mistrust and loathing, sometimes mutating into outright hatred. From the perspective of social psychopathology, it was also fascinating to observe the narrowly technocratic Václav Klaus as, exhibiting the traditional posturing of the Czech petty bourgeois, he attacked the intellectuals while securing a professorship for himself at Charles University, pointedly insisting on being addressed as "professor", and scooping up honorary doctorates from the regional universities of post-Soviet countries. And the original purpose of Miloš Zeman's once-famous quips was also to demonstrate the general knowledge of their progenitor at a time when he had not yet sunk to the bottom of his linguistic, political and cultural cesspool. This is precisely why the scandal surrounding his "quote" from Peroutka's non-existent article was so important to him that he felt no sense of shame or embarrassment about it, nor did he baulk at the prospect of an ignominious lawsuit. I think that, even taking into account these cultural and political traditions and historical disputes playing out at crucial points in Czech national history, it is now relevant to ask ourselves, once more, the Czech question about the meaning of history. As in the past, this question can broach fundamental topics of the present and the problems of our national future. And I hope that we get to discuss some of these themes and issues in our conversations here.

What, then, do we need to resist in 2018 if we are to take a more accurate and bolder look at ourselves and not succumb to fatalism? Neither of us is a historian, so let's keep the focus throughout our talks on exploring what makes up the living history of a nation. This concerns the relationship between structures and semantics, that is, between how society is shaped and how it describes itself, including the constant permeation of seemingly pure and clear historical concepts with their dirty and opaque historical background. We also have the tremendous historical advantage and the truly social and political luxury of having been governed, over the last three decades, by people we have freely and democratically elected as our representatives, and no foreign power poses a direct threat to us. Consequently, we might end up being our own worst enemy, but the reality is that we do not have to constantly defend and justify our bare existence and independence as the world crowds around. We do not need Masaryk's index finger raised in guidance to a young and immature nation. Nor do we need fists clenched as the only and futile response to the occupation of our country. And we have no need at all for any "official interpretations" of history, or the branding of history as "good" or "bad" according to some moral distinction, where historically variegated narratives are typically reduced to black-and-white images of national history. That is the domain not only of ever-popular efforts to guard our precious little national pond, but also of the simplifying criticism of political scientists who reconstruct Czech history as a place of permanent backwardness and the inability to be a part of "Europe", "the West", and the like.

But this hinges on learning to live without an official interpretation of history and on seeking its meaning over and over again, i.e. on learning to think of and rethink history. What questions should we be asking ourselves in this context?
An official interpretation of history makes no sense in a free society because, among other things, we do not discover history as a set of objective laws underpinning humanity's development. Instead, every piece of historical and empirically verifiable knowledge is always subject to a certain means of interpretation. Notice how contemporary historians often talk about the need for critical discussion, review or re-evaluation of past knowledge, and the reconstruction of historical interpretations. Today's historians routinely and fondly "reject ideological clichés", "critically discern the past" and "critically contemplate historical periods", seeing themselves as scientists who, sure of the solid knowledge of present-day historical science, reshape the general historical consciousness of society. Critical reflection of history has paradoxically been transformed into the highly popular *history of historians*. Yet when we say that there is a need for a critical discovery of the past or a re-evaluation of historical narratives, we do not have in mind the possibility of arbitrarily making up stories about history. On the contrary, it is intellectually challenging not to fabricate history, but to think of and rethink it.

If we narrate our history while having our own experience of it, we are exposed to the need to constantly determine its significance and meaning from a specific perspective and in specific situations. History is nothing but hermeneutics of the past, where each account of the past is simultaneously an interpretation. We need to keep our heads all the more in order to understand the meaning of the Czech state a hundred years on from its modern democratic and liberal foundation within the common Czechoslovak Republic, and to grasp what being a mature European and democratic nation means to us today. These questions and answers are directly related to the changes that the nation state, as a political institution, has gone through in Europe and across the world over the last fifty years, and to the process generally referred to as the globalisation of society.

The Formation of Nations and Nationalism

I would like to start this chapter by recalling Dušan Třeštík's claim that history is a projection of the past that leads not to the present, but to the future…

… and so we will explore everything that gives meaning to our common present and moulds the collective memory of the historically established social group known as the Czech nation, and how the notion of the Czech state and its actual historical creation and present form and attendant ideals have impressed themselves in that memory. Let's look into the points of intersection we have mentioned, as well as events, documents and other texts, and most of all the political and constitutional contexts, which can offer us an answer to the question of the historical meaning of Czech statehood and the way it has been transformed in today's globalised society. When I say that, I do not just have in mind the historical nodal points and watershed events that we accept almost without thinking, such as the founding of Charles University in 1348, the formation of an independent Czechoslovakia in 1918, the Munich Agreement of 1938, the Communist takeover in February 1948, and the August occupation in 1968. We should also be asking ourselves, for instance, about the historical significance of Wenceslas II's monetary reform, the work done by Italian craftsmen in the Czech Lands in the 18th century, the establishment of Masaryk's Realist Party, and the mutual influence of Czech and French Surrealism. And these questions should be a form of intellectual resistance to what is presented to society as either the trivialisation or heroisation of national history. History, in my view, is the ability to put up intellectual resistance to the historical events that bear down on us, be they wars, revolutions, or scientific discoveries and the technical transformation of our civilisation. I think, for example, that Bořivoj's baptism in around 883 should be regarded first and foremost as an important moment when the Czechs – as pointed out by our expert on the Early Middle Ages,

Dušan Třeštík – made history. They made history because Bořivoj, who lived from about 852 to 890, is the first historically documented Czech ruler and Přemyslid, mentioned in the *Chronica Boemorum*, in the *Legend of Christian* and in *Fuit in provincia Boemorum*, the legend about his wife, St Ludmila. Going down in history means becoming a part of historical documents and the stories that are told in them. It is not so much whether this is sooner or later than other nations; what is important is that, at that moment, political events in the territory of what is now our state become historically not only important, but also documented. The seat of the ruling power moves from Levý Hradec to Hradčany, the marriage to Ludmila unites the prominent Pšovans and Přemyslids, who are ruling over the territory of our country, and baptism by Archbishop Methodius in Great Moravia weakens the influence wielded by the monarchs of East Francia. These are undoubtedly big events at the time. They profoundly defined the early medieval politics subsequently applied in the territory of our state. The figure of Bořivoj, then, is associated not only with political control of this area, but also with the House of Přemyslids and the laying of the cultural, religious and dynastic foundations of society at that time. What's more, I have a very personal relationship with Bořivoj and Ludmila because Odolena Voda, where I come from, is located directly on the route between Mělník and Levý Hradec, so I could always see the very earliest topography and formation of the Přemyslids' power and social influence before my very eyes, and literally feel it in my bones.

Today, though, we can feel something else in our thinking because our historically formed group, the Czech nation, has firmly established itself in modern European history.

We have the advantage today that, unlike the historians of the national revival period, we do not have to constantly preoccupy ourselves with distinctions between West and East, Germans and Slavs, or Latin and Old Church Slavonic, and use them to show where we should belong in the present, against whom we should be taking a stand, and how we should perceive ourselves. These distinctions are, in fact, merely reductive devices that helped to mould modern nations, when in reality early medieval society was a lot more kaleidoscopic. There were no homogeneous national collectives. While we are at it, it would also be misguided to view the state as a political organisation because, again, this is something that does not emerge until a lot later, when the Middle Ages were drawing to a close.

Even so, it has been said that we have survived major threats on at least two occasions in European history. First of all when, after 800, the idea of a universal Roman Empire was reborn with Charlemagne's coronation as Emperor. It was at this point that most of the tribes living alongside the Elbe and the Danube suddenly disappeared from history. And the second time was when we revived our language in the latter half of the 19th century.

It wasn't just the tribes living in Central Europe. The Muslim conquest of the Iberian Peninsula in the early eighth century, for example, wiped Visigothic Hispania off the face of the earth. This was a kingdom that had existed for three centuries and, unlike most of the territory of the former Western Roman Empire, had managed to maintain deep-rooted continuity with classical culture, including law. The seventh-century *Lex Visigothorum*, while drawing on Roman law, was imbued with Christian ethics and, in a diversion from the ancient principle of personality, promoted the territoriality of law. The code also forbade masters from executing their slaves without public trial, which did much to change the latters' status. And let's not forget that, parallel to this, the Frankish merchant Samo was establishing a Central European empire that doubled up as a military and trade alliance of Slavic tribes. When Charlemagne had himself crowned by the Pope at Christmas in 800, he too was clearly aiming for continuity in a highly unstable and politically impetuous world. He was keen to restore the Roman Empire in the sense of reviving social order and borders that could be effectively protected and controlled. Yet, at the same time, he was establishing it as a new empire of Christian spiritual culture. His support for the monasteries helped to create a much more educated, more united and more organised clergy, which was also responsible for organising all inhabitants' social life and nurturing their souls. In this respect, Charlemagne was pursuing a vision of a society that was much larger and more organised politically and culturally than any in existence at that time anywhere in the western part of the European continent. It is sometimes said that, in this respect, his reign squeezed a last gasp out of antiquity and laid the first foundations of the Europe we know today. And, in the period that followed, it is historically remarkable how adroit the Czechs' tribal politics was and how it was able not only to stand up to all of those shifts in power and culture, but also to capitalise on them for its own ends. We could pick out hundreds of such political manoeuvres in that period and beyond, but they could hardly be hailed as the beginnings of modern statehood.

Should we perhaps mention the change in liturgical language from Old Church Slavonic to Latin in this respect? Dušan Třeštík, for example, claimed that there was no document from that period that had been written in Glagolitic script, whereas, in the first few decades of the ninth century, the local aristocracy in Moravia was building churches and inviting priests there from Bavaria, Italy and Dalmatia.

Notice that, hardly have we started discussing national history, and we are already talking about the early history of political geography, language and religion. The clear lesson we can learn from this is that the nation is not some sort of naturally formed group whose existence is in any way more authentic or more real than other groups. We need to emphasise, again and again, that everything which seems "natural" or even part of a certain "national spirit" to us actually often has random historical and political roots. All nations have to have a history from which they derive their own identity, but that is not to say that nations need to be connected by blood bonds or that this sense of tribal belonging is at their core. What seems to be natural is really a historical attachment and an affinity to past generations that, apart from nations, could quite easily apply, for example, to religious groups, universities or professional organisations. We also think of language as natural, but it is a highly complex system of rules, symbols and meanings, which even Saints Cyril and Methodius knew very well long before the structuralists. It comes as no surprise, then, that these days there are countries with a strong sense of national identity despite their linguistic diversity, such as Switzerland. Similarly, you can share a national identity even in a religiously very diverse and divided society – witness the United States of America. We could go on and on listing examples confirming that, when examining any national history, including our own, we should always steer clear of the temptation to lay bare the "true substance" of our national identity or our "naturalness" and what is specific to us Czechs. Conversely, we should always stress how our current identity is often moulded by historically haphazard events and more general processes at points in the past, such as the missions in the Early Middle Ages and the attendant linguistic codification. By accentuating such historical arbitrariness and peculiarities, however, we are in no way casting doubt on the power of national identity and the sense of belonging that binds the members of a nation to one another and to their shared collective. Modern nations are typified by two seemingly contradictory tendencies. The first is the yearning for vertical political organisation, such as a state founded on sovereign power, before which everyone must bow down. The second aspiration, by contrast, is to fashion a horizontally organised community in which the shared sense of belonging creates a strong collective bond. Common to both of these desires is a hint of inevitability, constancy and naturalness, enabling the members of one nation to accept social inequality, even if it runs deep, and circumstances that they would find offensive individually and unbearable personally. In other words, if anyone speaking your own language or perhaps even a local dialect thereof tells you to do something in the name of your faith and conviction, that command somehow seems more legitimate and acceptable.

Since we have mentioned Old Church Slavonic and its gradual displacement, how important is this history of languages to a modern national revival.
The significance of Old Church Slavonic as a liturgical language that was subsequently squeezed out by Latin following the fall of the Great Moravian Empire should not be overstated in this respect because it was not the everyday language spoken by the population at the time. This language, its script and the texts written in it are of immeasurable historical value and provide us with fascinating proof of the cultural diversity of Europe at the time, as well as of political rivalries and the forging of allegiance through the pursuit of contemporary cultural politics. And yet, for the modern Czech identity, this historical episode with Old Church Slavonic carries little more than token value. Having said that, the fact that the Romantics succeeded in reviving the Czech language in the modern era is a cultural miracle, of course. In fact, there were many such miracles across the European continent in the 19th century. There was the Finnish and Norwegian national revival in the north of Europe, the formation of the Flemish identity and language, and the *Risorgimento*, where unified culture, history and language provided the political spark for revolution and wars to unify the Italian peninsula. Stark interregional cultural and social differences in what is now Italy or Germany and, equally, the ethnic and national diversity of Spain and the United Kingdom just go to show that the nationalist notions of "every nation a state" and "only one state for the entire nation", as espoused by Giuseppe Mazzini in

the 19th century, can never come to fruition in *realpolitik* in Europe or anywhere else in the world.

And what do you say about the disputes over the existence of Great Moravia in our territory?
Historians have long wrangled over this but, these days, such an issue makes sense only for a very weak and young nation that is still looking to somehow prove itself and justify its own existence. As a rule of thumb, the younger the nation, the older the history. I realised this, for example, in Norway, where quite a few people will tell you that they are the true descendants of the Vikings. Why is that? Because, politically, Norwegian society is still in its infancy and, until recently, before it made its fortune from oil, it was an impoverished backwater of Scandinavia whose inhabitants had an inferiority complex in relation to the imperial Danes and Swedes. Anyone who claims today that they are the true heir of Svatopluk the Great would be exhibiting much the same complex. At the time, Europe was clearly a melting pot of religious, political, legal and linguistic influences. Looking at the Hiberno-Scottish missions, for example, we can see their impact in many parts of the British Isles and continental Europe between the sixth and ninth centuries, stretching from the south of Wales down to Fiesole in Tuscany, and then back up to Würzburg, Salzburg and Regensburg. Incidentally, about 25 km west of Cardiff, where I live, there is a small town called Llantwit Major where a Celtic monk from Brittany, St Illtud, founded a monastery and divinity school, Cor Tewdws, in the sixth century. This is thought to be the oldest centre of university-type learning in the British Isles. Students included both St Patrick, the patron saint of Ireland, and St David, the patron saint of Wales. I occasionally wonder whether the graduates of that school could have travelled to us here in Central Europe, with the Welsh consequently Christianising the Czech Lands. However, the importance of this to today's national identity is probably akin to asking our-

selves whether the Vikings, who, in their day, plundered Europe, raping and pillaging its population, and destroyed Cor Tewdws in 987, were the forefathers of current Norwegians, who take pride in their own political correctness and view themselves as being at the vanguard of global civilisation.

But there are two types of nationalism: territorial and linguistic.
I'm sure you're alluding to Jan Patočka's comparison of Josef Jungmann's concept of national revival, which places language in the spotlight, and Bernard Bolzano's concept of the territorial nation, which is defined by constitutional history, patriotism, the social question and the need to address oppression, conflicts and the problems of modern society.

Yes, because Bernard Bolzano advocated Bohemism: one nation speaking two languages. Jungmann borrowed his concept from Johann Gottfried von Herder, a contemporary of Bolzano. Was that a mistake?
Patočka precisely described Bolzano's concept of the nation, which is not based solely on shared feelings of provincial patriotism and is not shrouded in references to tradition and political history, but draws on a utopian vision of society that criticises societal schisms, including linguistic ruptures. Entirely in keeping with the spirit of the Enlightenment, then, Bolzano made the problem of the nation a moral issue that could be resolved with instruction and education. Jungmann, on the other hand, emphasised another aspect underpinning the modernisation of society at the time, specifically the dominance of German, occasioned by the Josephine reforms and the administrative centralisation of the country. In such a situation, provincial patriotism becomes a relic of the past, a moribund tradition, replaced by rising economic and power-driven interests advocated in German. At the time, Czech, too, was at risk of turning into a dying tradition that placed farmers and the petty bourgeoisie at

a social and political disadvantage compared to the German-speaking population. Jungmann, unlike Bolzano, but entirely in the spirit of many other political movements of the time, paired the social issue with the linguistic issue and viewed the nation as a community that spontaneously formed itself and gained self-awareness through a shared language. Patočka rather brusquely dismissed this central role of language in Jungmann's concept of the nation as a "shibboleth" purportedly detaching the nation from the then multilingual state. Yet this underestimates the cultural hegemony engineered by the official German language from the late 18th century and the rapidly vanishing possibility of sticking to a territorial concept of nation in a situation where, courtesy of its economic and political predominance, one linguistic culture starts to devour and menace other cultures and, being dominant, defines them as the remnants of traditions that need to stop obstructing society's modernisation. It should be pointed out that the linguistic concept of nation espoused in Bohemia by Jungmann and across Europe by many other revivalists was not a clash between (linguistic) tradition and (territorial) modernity. It was another way of looking at modernity. Although the nation was regarded as a natural social group, much like a family, this "natural" unit, entirely in the Romantic-cum-Enlightenment-cum-Herderian spirit you mentioned, went beyond cultural and territorial boundaries and, via historical differences and peculiarities, was related to the universal ideals of humanity. This is a typically Romantic paradox in which universal ideals take on a particular form. It is interesting how Patočka, for example, turns a blind eye to this fundamental paradox of Herder's philosophy. He pits Herder's universal reciprocity of nations against Jungmann and Kollár's ideology of the nation, accusing the latter, furthermore, of entrenching the Czech nation in the concept of Slavdom as a natural community of national tribes. Patočka's argument is that, rather than latching on to some older historical and cultural identification, such as the Cyril-and-Methodius tradition or Old Church

Slavonic liturgy, Jungmann and, later, Kollár and others come up with this flawed naturalistic justification for our sense of belonging to this peculiar cultural and civilisational group.

But, in his thinking, there is a logic to this criticism. Patočka was wont to advertise that national politics cannot limit itself to searching for such a sense of belonging.

Patočka's criticism of Jungmann's linguistic concept of the nation has the same basis as Bolzano's utopian concept of the "best state", i.e. the conviction that politics' primary role is to remove social inequality and bridge gaps typically thought to be "natural", such as linguistic differences. Bolzano's essay *On the Best State* may be utopian in genre but, unlike Thomas More's early modern work, it takes the need for social reform – which has always required political decisions – much more seriously and, in many respects, it is closer than Renaissance literature to modern manuals on how to change political and social circumstances, the content of which is driven by the poverty of human existence in real conditions and the opportunities that exist to eradicate such abjection. In his utopia, Bernard Bolzano formulated the fundamental moral principle that the political constitution should champion universal well-being and happiness to the fullest possible extent. To that purely modern utilitarian notion of the utmost happiness for the entire community, he then adds the egalitarian demand for real social inequality to be stamped out. Patočka was acutely aware of this accent, and his concept of nation, averse to an exclusive community with a shared language, draws on the assumption of political, economic and social inclusion. To that effect, Patočka forged a direct link to Bolzano's moral philosophy and elaborated on the moral concept of the nation as an intellectual community shaped by its level of education and capable of overcoming social disparities and inequalities in the political community. In this context, it is important to remind ourselves that Patočka, in his concept of Czech history and national identity, also embraced radical democrats from the revolutionary events of 1848, whose movements were to pave the way for Czech social democracy and socialism as both an ideology and political agenda. He did so in the deep-seated knowledge that we cannot grasp the meaning of Czechness unless we understand that spiritual and political history. Here he was fully aligned with Masaryk, for whom the Czech question and social question also formed a single intellectual, cultural and political whole. In other respects, Patočka was mainly following in the footsteps of Bolzano and Rádl in that he viewed patriotism as collectiveness, i.e. as a nation that was not divided, but unified by cultural and civilisational aspirations, and that was focused on the future, and the tasks and challenges that would arise, more than on its own past. Patočka's concept of Czechness is citizens' capacity to share and make sacrifices for political ideals, rather than a bastion of tribesmen fighting off anything that might approach from outside and poke holes in the supposedly infallible points of reference they had established for themselves through national culture and historical myths.

That's why I brought up Herder. His definition of a nation is determined by ethnic characteristics and awareness of a historical sense of belonging.
And yet Jungmann and other language revivalists pick up on Herder's philosophical concept of culture and history, which contrasts natural creations and mechanical artefacts of humanity. Language is just as natural as, say, the family, which spontaneously grows out of a world of nature, and, according to Herder, the nation is just as organic as, perhaps, flora, with differences apparent only in complexity and the rate of growth. As such, Herder establishes an important difference between culture's mechanical and organic forms. That difference has profoundly informed the way we think about society. Its most diverse adaptations can be found in historical, sociological, political and philosophical writings. For Herder, the nation is a naturally evolving organism, while the state is nothing but

a mechanism used by the political powers to organise society. Without this viewpoint put forward by Herder, Tönnies' fundamental sociological work *Gemeinschaft und Gesellschaft*, Durkheim's concept of social solidarity, Popper's criticism of Plato, and Hegel and Hayek's concept of spontaneous order would all have been inconceivable. It comes as no surprise, then, that the contradiction of a naturally self-organising nation, as a community of language, and a state, which may also be a multinational society mechanically organised by political coercion, was also adopted by national revivalists and Romantics across Europe at the time.

For the same reasons, it is evidently no coincidence that nationalism became one of Romanticism's key ideas and its most enduring legacy. In the Romantic era, the emphasis was on developing national languages and folklore, and on local customs and traditions, i.e. the spiritual heritage of nations. Was anything else playing a central role here?

Romanticism really triggered a sea-change in what we consider to be natural. The Enlightenment's rationalism had continued the long-running tradition of ancient philosophy that, though making a distinction between nature and human culture, also worked on the assumption that human endeavours to safeguard peace and security, justice, wisdom and happiness, were essentially universal. In other words, there are universal laws and objectively applied rules of thought and action which are inherent in everyone without discrimination and in defiance of natural diversifications, such as climate, landscape, and the sources and availability of subsistence. Romanticism dismantled this belief in the universal currency of reason and intellectual order, replacing it with a stress on the diversity, uniqueness and differences of human cultures. Universality took on particular forms favoured by the Romantics. Going forward, they wanted diversity and differences to function as a starting point in the search for humanity's shared roots. Instead of a reign of reason, there was a revolt of will, both individual and collective. Where the Enlightened seeks the rationality of the universal text, the Romantic explores the vitality of particular contexts. While will was reason in action for Immanuel Kant, for Fichte, Schiller and Lessing the idea of freedom meant the ability to shake off the shackles of rationalism and achieve true being by harnessing the senses, emotions and, most of all, will. Henceforth it is not reason, but will, that elevates humankind above nature, but also that makes us the tragic hero of our own fate. Schiller even discusses the divine lawmaker in us and the proud demon lurking inside humans, defying the outside pressure. Sensibility versus sense, subjective passion versus objective reason, will versus nature. The tragic hero takes a stand against the elements and, revolting against the world, discovers his new naturalness.

Do you think that, behind this, we can make out the ideas of Rousseau and Herder, who argued that geography moulded people's natural economy and formed their customs and society?
Rousseau still conflated nature with the objective order and eternal values that culture stultified in people and trampled in society. Herder, on the other hand, augurs a shift towards the uniqueness of culture as the source of all humanity and towards cultural differences providing a basis on which to classify the status of individual nations and ethnicities and to gauge their civilisation and maturity. A key difference between the Enlightenment and Romanticism, then, is the turn away from the idealistic and universal humanism of reason towards the humanism of the real differences and particularisms of culture and history, through which individuals and entire nations can find and confirm their own identity. A golden age of humanity was meant to return to Earth and, all of a sudden, it could be achieved by turning to history, customs, language, religion, and the like. Within the scope of this self-affirmation, however, there is another important concept besides will preceding reason: the objective spirit, capable of subjugating the diversity that the Romantics had discovered

to new laws of reality. In this context, Isaiah Berlin claimed that Romanticism was tantamount to the coronation of both individual and collective will and the rejection of the order of reason because the human spirit was imprisoned in it. We can see that those great Romantic metaphors about "dungeons of the spirit" and "gaols of nations" originate in this superiority of spirit over reason and the acceptance of will as a fundamental way of seizing and moulding the world. Nationalism is merely one of the many consequences of this Romantic turn towards the real diversity of the world and the human will to recognise and overcome that diversity. Nationalism was originally meant to be a liberal and revolutionary idea, not collectivist and reactionary.

Perhaps it's not that simple. After all, nationalism heralded the idea of nation states, which continues to underpin how the states of the world are arranged. And it was logical because the nation state relies on the constantly recurring political choices of its members, but at the same time that choice requires a firmer social and historical bond.

My observation that the gun of nationalism was originally loaded with a liberating, revolutionary and democratising political bullet was in no way intended to defend it. Nor was it meant in the slightest as an example of objective historical developments in a humankind that is bound to evolve towards democracy and political freedoms and, at a certain stage in its historical development, used nationalism as an ideology and nation states as a political organisation facilitating such advancement. I simply wanted to accentuate certain historical antecedents and political circumstances linked to national revival and national movements across Europe in the first half of the 19th century. And, in this respect, I always remember my colleague and friend, one of the most prominent European legal philosophers of the past half-century, Neil MacCormick, who, besides his numerous other academic and public activities, was a member of the European Parliament for the Scottish National Party. Not only was Neil one of the most talented students of the Oxford theoretician H. L. A. Hart, but he was also a dyed-in-the-wool liberal pursuing a socially democratic political agenda while simultaneously espousing Scottish independence. When we first met at a conference in Edinburgh in 1994 and he found out that I was from Prague, he questioned me long and hard about the minutest constitutional details surrounding Czechoslovakia's breakup. It took me a while to realise that he was interested in how a state union could be constitutionally divided without a referendum by the will of representative legislative bodies. We found a surprisingly large number of parallels with the United Kingdom's constitutional fabric, but democracy in that country enjoys a longer tradition than in the former Czechoslovakia or in today's Spain, hence the referendum on Scottish independence took place 20 years later. Neil and I went on to see each other many times and when, before his death in 2009, we were chatting one summer's evening at Ross Priory on the banks of Loch Lomond, he gradually switched from legal and political philosophy to a description of the landscape and the lake's surface as the twilight transformed them, and suddenly, glass of whisky in hand, I had this feeling as though Karel Hynek Mácha and Lord Byron were standing alongside us, while behind us sat Walter Scott, who, during the time he spent time at Ross Priory, wrote several works and pondered further verses of *The Lady of the Lake*. This original ethos of nationalism is frequently buried under the silt of modern Europe's political tragedies, but as our Cypriot colleague noted that evening: "If you have to be a nationalist in this day and age, make sure you're also a liberal and a democrat!"

I'd like to stick with the nationalism for a bit longer. The nature of nationalism has changed over the course of history, most of all following the French Revolution. Napoleonic nationalism and republicanism initially served as inspiration for nationalist move-

ments in other countries. Self-determination and the recognition of national unity were thought to be the two reasons why France was capable of defeating other countries. However, as soon as the French Republic made the transition to Napoleon's empire, Napoleon was no longer inspirational for nationalism and, instead, became a target of the struggle waged by nations that refused to submit themselves to that empire.

It is probably worth remembering that the political concept of the nation, *demos* – the people, is the inner spring that unleashed modern political revolutions in America in 1776 and in France in 1789. The American Revolution sought the self-determination of a highly diverse population of colonies who, having experienced economic and political injustice at the hands of the imperial centre, declared their political independence first, and only afterwards, during the war for that independence, formed together as a constitutional and political nation of peoples. Similarly, the French Revolution was only set in motion when the Third Estate became politicised...

... a process already helped along by the Encyclopédistes Diderot and d'Alembert, as well as other figures of the Enlightenment.

... and in January 1789, half a year before the revolution, Abbé Sieyès published his famous pamphlet *What is the Third Estate?*, which starts with these questions and answers: 1. What is the Third Estate? *Everything*; 2. What has it been hitherto in the political order? *Nothing*; 3. What does it desire to be? *Something*. That "something" is a complete and sovereign nation as a source of all power in what was then an absolute monarchy. So we can see that the political idea of the nation and modern nationalism are two different and yet intertwined historical phenomena. Napoleon sighed that he may have France, but he found it lacking in French people. As late as the mid-19th century, Parisian officials were still complaining that the population did not identify enough with the French state and that local identities were stronger than the shared national identity. Napoleon and all others holding the reins of power therefore did their utmost to Frenchify the inhabitants of France. In his external sorties, occupations and wars, Napoleon was ever the war criminal, so the backlash against his conquering troops was also articulated as national opposition to foreign occupiers. The mutual history of Spain and Britain is bristling with sensitive points and issues, but if you go, say, to towns in the north of Spain, you will see memorials on the main squares commemorating the Duke of Wellington and his triumph in curbing Napoleonic terror in Spain. Incidentally, the term "guerrilla" is essentially Romantic, hailing from the period when Spanish patriots refused to lie down and be civilised by the bayonets of Napoleon's army, and instead launched the first modern asymmetric war against it. The imperial *guerra*, so regular and symmetric, often had no chance against this partisan irregular guerrilla warfare. *Guerra* versus guerrilla, that's also the difference between the Enlightenment and Romanticism. And it is still going on, as we can see in the most diverse corners of the world to this day.

While we're at it, let's remember that the term "nationalism" is said to have first appeared in a work by the anti-Jacobin French priest Augustin Barruel, before the Germans got their hands on it. Every nation has a history of nationalism. Barruel used this term in response to the emergence of the French nation state, but nationalist ideas were just as spirited in the early days of the 19th century in South America, for example. German nationalism, for its part, was formed in opposition to the Napoleonic dictatorship and, to take one example, Friedrich Carl von Savigny's entire school of legal history, which placed a stress on the importance of legal traditions and local customs over the general reason represented in the law, and which built on the typically Romantic concept of *Volksgeist*, or spirit of the nation, was a response to French expansion and an attempt to truss the legal order with codified law and statute books. We are also familiar with Beethoven's initial enthusiasm for Napoleon the liberator, who was going to fulfil the Republican and Enlightenment ideals of the French Revolution, thereby elevating Germans and other European nations and their cultures from local backwardness, and we remember how this enthusiasm dissipated when Napoleon had himself anointed emperor in 1804, which dismayed Beethoven so much that he ditched the original dedication of his Third Symphony ("Eroica"), replacing Napoleon with a Bohemian aristocrat, Prince Joseph Franz Maximilian Lobkowitz.

The German word *Volkstum* (national characteristics) was first used as part of this opposition to the conquering French emperor. The philosopher Johann Gottlieb Fichte formulated the unity of language and nation in his Addresses to the German Nation in 1808 and decided that Napoleon himself was the greatest evil in the world. We need to add to our talk on that frequently mythicised concept of *Volksgeist*, the spirit of the nation. It tends to be attributed to Herder, but he himself never used it, despite the fact that we could well imagine it popping up in his works. Philosophers, lawyers, ethnographers, psychologists and many others have built their own theories around it, but the first to use it, just as the 19th century was dawning, was Hegel. In doing so, it was as though he had symbolically charted the course that would be followed by this century, in which nations first found and invented themselves in order to seek self-determination and the revolutionary ideals of liberty, equality and fraternity therein, but ultimately lost their way in the traps of national prerogatives and expansionist policies which, in the century to come, would develop into utterly racist totalitarian ideologies of the nation and state. The Romantic spirit of the nation should not be confused with Montesquieu's spirit of the laws or Rousseau's concept of the nation as the unity of general will. The *Volksgeist* envisages the unity of a community and the collective will with which it performs its historical role and becomes a vehicle for the *Weltgeist*. Consequently, Hegel is a much more significant philosopher for Romanticism, with all of its excesses, than Herder. Obviously, there is no direct path from Romanticism to brutal irrationalism and collectivist totalitarian ideologies such as fascism and Nazism. Even so, there is quite plainly a link between these and the Romantic adulation of heroes and leaders, and of will as the primary source and self-affirmation of humankind.

You recently mentioned that European nationalisms have different roots, but also very much in common, regardless of whether we are talking about the Czech national revival or the Greek struggle for national independence, in which Byron also participated. What's more, Byron's work is of particularly profound significance for Bohemia because it heavily inspired Karel Hynek Mácha, who gave us our first true Romantic poetry. How important was culture for us at this time?

Romanticism was a pan-European movement and Mácha's work is a shining example of this. Art, poetry and literature have always provided a platform for freedom and self-expression, but suddenly we see the fates of writers and artists and their individual genius tied a lot more to the *genius loci* of everyone who shares that place, its history and lives, and language with them, and who lives here and creates the collective *Volksgeist*. Greek nationalism was more than a national revival. It was also heavily republican and, as such, attracted freedom-loving souls from across Europe, including – as we have mentioned – Byron. This liberal element was just as important for Romanticism as the fight against monarchism and conservative politics, which was attempting to restore pre-revolutionary order.

Is there any connection between the poetic imagination of Romanticism and political imagination?

Definitely! Like philosophers, Romantic poets believed that humans were not only beings who rationally recognised objective and eternally valid laws, but also that they were engineers of their own fate and the world. The English Romantic poet and radical thinker Percy Bysshe Shelley, whose work inspired all manner of people, including Karl Marx, Leo Tolstoy and Mahatma Gandhi, even proclaimed that poets were the "unacknowledged legislators of the world".

He perhaps was drawing on the Irish tradition where, about halfway through the first millennium, poetry was regarded as the highest form of public language.

Human history is not merely a subject to be narrated and understood, but also a call to action and to recreate that history. Imagination becomes more important than memory in a world where the only objective rules are those we devise ourselves. Politics, like art, is not just an image of the external world and its laws, but is becoming much more a form of self-expression for the individual and collective spirit. The question of the Greek national revival is also a question of universal revolution and specific struggle, becoming involved in which means helping to build a new world. Enlightenment philosophy is dominated by a constant war between people's innate naturalness and external form, forced on them by culture and convention. The Rousseauistic ideal of natural humanity which is concealed within the noble savage and is being corrupted by human civilisation was transformed into the idea of the Romantic hero for whom, as for Byron, freedom means opposing and revolting against rules and conventions, even if this requires crimes to be committed. The Enlightenment notion of an ideal world is replaced by the Romantic idea of the world as a work of art fashioned by human genius. Naturally, this aesthetic model of the world was also applied to politics, which, courtesy of Romanticism, became an area dominated by the individual will of the politician and the collective will of the sovereign people, which all modern nations without fail – although each in its own way – considered (and still consider) themselves to be. The upshot was that politics became both art and a test of will no longer beholden to the Enlightenment ideals of truth, justice and prudence, and, with them, the possibility of forming a perfect, conflict-free and harmonious society guided by reason. This is why Romantic poets were simultaneously political revolutionaries and visionaries who saw themselves as new-age leaders. It was not until the civil revolutions in the first half of the 19th century and, most prominently, the pan-European revolutionary year of 1848 that, paradoxically, the social authority they wielded was weakened by the fact that the democratic public slowly started to come to life. Post-Romantic poets and writers turned not to lawmakers in the service of providence, but to the inner self and social mores. And yet that original creative force of the lawmakers of humanity was not lost because, for example, Victor Hugo was convinced that true knowledge and justice could be achieved through poetry, not politics. On the other hand, at the time of the Paris Commune and in the face of political developments, Rimbaud stopped grooming himself and started to rid himself of senses and reason so that, in his own words, he would gain visionary power and work his way to poetic transcendence. Against this cultural and historical background, Marxism, for example, was peculiar by dint of its heroic attempt to wed the Enlightenment's utopianism with Romantic political will, historical struggles and violent conflicts.

Law without the State
and State Law:
from the Middle Ages
to Modernity

Let's go back to the 10th century and the Přemyslid Duke Wenceslas († 935) in Prague. Wenceslas' alliance with the East Frankish King Henry the Fowler in 929, which ensured that Bohemia would be defended against the Magyars and, more significantly, consolidated the Latin Church in the Czech Lands, is regarded as a seminal political move. It provided political stability and established what we might call state sovereignty. Is the British assessment of this historical development similar or is this more of a German take?

The British find it much more interesting that Henry's choice of wife for his son Otto was Eadgyth, half-sister of the English King Athelstan. This act of tribal alliance with the Saxons governing in the territory of Britain bolstered the legitimacy of the Saxon Ottonian dynasty. But you're absolutely right in pointing out the generally accepted view among historians that Duke Wenceslas' diplomatic prowess and his alliance with the East Frankish king stabilised the internal situation, although the notion of sovereignty is out of the question. This is because state sovereignty was unknown in the Middle Ages, only emerging much later with the absolute monarchies of the modern era. Not even *Defensor pacis* ("Defender of the Peace"), the work by the medieval jurist Marsilius of Padua from the first half of the 14th century pitting secular power – whose laws are derived from the will of the people – against religious authority, can be viewed as a treatise on state sovereignty in this sense. This difference serves as a good example that the state and its history need to be distinguished from statehood. The state is a political formation with boundaries and sovereign power, and those living within its borders are subject to its authority. Statehood, on the other hand, also encompasses all the historical events and moral ideals on which the state bases its legitimacy. So it could be argued that, while St Wenceslas' politics are of scant significance to the modern Czech state, they do form an inherent basis for its statehood and legitimacy. Hence our continued sensitivity to the abuse of the tradition of St Wenceslas during the Second Republic and the protectorate. In the story of St Wenceslas, however, we see a very different universal symbol, the symbol of power that does not allow itself to be straitjacketed by any convention and uses strength, as a source unto its own, to fight compromise. Needless to say, I'm thinking about when Boleslav assassinated him in order to usurp power for himself. Subsequently, fratricide, that episode of archetypal violence we find in the dawn of so many civilisations, became a key event spawning a major historical narrative and providing legitimacy both to medieval monarchs and the modern-day rulers of this country. In this context, Wenceslas' hagiography is miles more important than his pact with Henry the Fowler because the oldest Bohemian chronicles mined the legends and these are bound up with the birth of Czech literature. Murder ballads and legends account for the history of Czech statehood as much as any statesmanlike treaties or political and legal decrees.

One thing's for sure: St Wenceslas became a symbol of the Czech Lands and for 400 years – until 1306 – the Přemyslids pursued the duality of political government (a dynamic element, albeit represented by Wenceslas' brother and assassin Boleslav) and broader geopolitical and religious integration (a static element driven by Wenceslas' legacy). Was anything else playing a role here?
The Přemyslids exploited Duke Wenceslas' extraordinary fate. His personal story and accumulated legends were used to manufacture a symbolic constitution for their medieval reign, which was then brought to perfection by Charles IV. Charles IV's imperial reign derived its symbolic legitimacy from two sources: Charlemagne's political project and the ethical role model provided by St Wenceslas. These two figures enabled Charles IV to conflate late medieval secular and spiritual sources of political legitimacy.

In this context we should mention legal sources such as the Břetislav Decrees of 1039.
Law students are taught about this document in the very first semester of their studies as part of their legal history lessons. Note, again, how Cosmas of Prague in his *Chronica Boemorum* lends them symbolic meaning by associating their proclamation with the pillaging of Gniezno by Duke Břetislav in 1038 and the ceremonial transfer of the remains of St Adalbert and his half-brother, St Radim, to Prague. Despite the lack of direct historical evidence, it is likely that the decrees were actually proclaimed right at the start of Břetislav's reign because they were intended to strengthen the rule of dukes, give cultural stability to the still very pagan society, and boost the economy of the early medieval society of the time. Understandably, from a chronicler's perspective it is a lot more appealing to forge links between their proclamation, a military campaign, and adherence to the spiritual legacy of Adalbert, who had advocated many of this legal document's ideas and rules during his own lifetime. Hence we find severe punishment being meted out here for pagan customs, illegitimate marriages, and the failure to sanctify Sundays and holidays. All law students are also familiar with the various penalties, including being sold into slavery and being banished from the country, and the concept of trial by ordeal, where proof depended on how divine providence manifested itself.

Let's return to the Břetislav Decrees, because this is when the first organised system of law started to be applied in this territory.
What is most important about them is the social movement akin to what we witnessed, for example, during Charlemagne's reign, by which I mean the policy of forming a unified Christian people that also dismantles existing customs and hierarchy, replacing them with a much more organised system where the monarch's authority is shaped by spiritual doctrine that views every last person as a morally acting being. The antithesis between the Christian and heathen

world is blurred and the fundamental social paradox of Christianity comes to the fore – it started out by looking for a kingdom from another world (St Adalbert was no exception in this respect) and itself became a vehicle of monumental social and political reform.

The English Magna Carta is from 1215, so we're not that badly off. I think we need to make a distinction here between the historical and symbolic significance of this and, while we're at it, any other document or source of law. If we look at British history, we can see that the monarch tried to scrap the *Magna Carta* as soon as the political crisis with the barons was over. This document's practical impact should not be overemphasised and there is no way it can be regarded as something from which the country's effective political and constitutional continuity has been derived. More interesting, on the other hand, is the continuity of the *Magna Carta*'s symbolic significance. It has always been invoked by rebels, revolutionaries and advocates of the Restoration at times when it has been necessary to renew the social contract and political conciliation in the kingdom. Even the Glorious Revolution and the enthronement of William of Orange as king of England after the civil war was perceived as a renewal of the *Magna Carta*, meaning that essentially it was not a revolution, but a restoration. Consequently, the *Magna Carta* permeates centuries of British history as a document keeping a rein on power and guaranteeing fundamental freedoms and rights, initially for a few privileged noblemen, before being expanded democratically in the modern period to include the entire population. It is also interesting that the United Kingdom does not recognise the term "sovereign people", whose will is at the heart of all power in the state. It is parliament – which represents not the nation, but the commonwealth, i.e. a community of various population groups, including nations and ethnicities – that is sovereign. Conversely, the *Declaration of Independence* and the subsequent *United States Constitution* are both constitutional documents in which the modern notion of a constitutional nation as the sovereign power of democratic people forms the central plank of practical government and political imagination.

We do not have any document like that here, or am I mistaken?
Czechs and other nations do not have a constitutional document safeguarding such strong symbolic continuity of the form of government on the same scale as the *Magna Carta*. Nor is it any coincidence that the *Magna Carta* is also used as a point of reference by modern nations that, in one way or another, have struck out on their own and removed themselves from the British Empire. If Czechs were to leaf through their medieval legal documents, at best they might discover a degree of maturity in the legal and political system of the time that could be compared to other parts of Europe. I hasten to add, though, that basic continuity on the European continent relied on the ability to build on Roman law and leverage its concepts in a new social and cultural situation where, instead of slavery and *paterfamilias* authority, it was the principles of Christian ethics and the independence of social institutions – from religious orders to universities – that became increasingly dominant. Legal sources of Czech medieval society such as the *Břetislav Decrees* are therefore, first and foremost, a mirror reflecting the degree of social and political organisation that had been achieved.

While we're on the subject, how important a document are the Conrad Statutes of 1189? The most significant part of this document was the granting of the right to the hereditary possession of the nascent nobility's property. In point of fact, it created a functioning model of codified relations and orders and tried to accord the state and society clear rules, particularly in relations between the monarch and the nobility. It was not until later, in 1212, that the famous Golden Bull of Sicily was issued. How do you, as a legal philosopher, view these documents?

In the oldest Bohemian legal source, written in Latin, we can see how advanced the Přemyslid governance of the Czech Lands was by that time because this code, like all the codes before and after it, mainly covered existing practices and legal customs. Criminal and, especially, inheritance law, as well as the delicate political compromise reinforcing the monarch's power in the realms of administration and justice, while giving the nobility a greater say in government, all show just how dynamically society was developing. Likewise, the influence of Roman and canon law on the *Conrad Statutes* proves that there was a decent level of legal education at the end of the 12th century, i.e. a time when, in England, the *Magna Carta* we have just discussed did not yet exist. As for the *Golden Bull of Sicily*, issued by the Holy Roman Emperor Frederick II to confirm the royal title of the Přemyslid Ottokar I, the significance of this document is still being debated today precisely because it is of absolutely fundamental importance to the continuity of the Kingdom of Bohemia and Czech statehood *per se*. To quickly recap what happened, Frederick II issued the bull to thank Ottokar I for his support in the battle for the imperial crown. The main privilege it conferred was the Bohemian monarch's hereditary right to the royal title. Duke Vladislaus II had actually already held this privilege back in the mid-12th century, but Ottokar I had to fight very hard for it. The complexity of contemporary internal and external diplomatic relations is also borne out by the Bohemian nobility's right to elect its monarch, which Ottokar I tried in vain to stifle, and the release of the Bohemian monarch from all obligations towards the Holy Roman Empire, with the exception of the requirement to attend certain imperial diets. The bull is also a result of the adroit Přemyslid art of diplomacy, securing internal political independence for the Kingdom of Bohemia and giving Bohemian kings, as imperial dukes, an opportunity to engage in active external politics and consolidate their position in relation to other European monarchs and the domestic nobility. It is also evidence of the influence wielded by Bohemian monarchs in a European context and in conflicts, whether diplomatic or military. Sure, these days we have to be critical about any inflation of the significance of this document and any direct connection with the modern Czech nation's claim to its own statehood, but the fact of the matter remains that even Charles IV, for instance, thought this was a document crucial to foster his own legitimacy and monarchical power. On top of that, we should also perhaps remember that the *Golden Bull of Sicily* actually comprised three documents which, besides the hereditary claim to the royal title, also govern the dedication of estates and goods. They apply not only to Ottokar I, but also to his brother, the margrave Vladislaus Henry. The bull was quickly replaced by other documents which, in those diplomatically and politically tempestuous times, relativised its significance.

Charles IV, the eleventh king of Bohemia, whose mother was the Přemyslid Elizabeth and whose father hailed from the Luxembourg dynasty, was brought up in France by the future pope. As you have said, he exploited the legacy of St Wenceslas to the hilt and turned Prague into the seat of the Holy Roman Emperor. Consequently, 14th-century Prague was the European continent's second main hub, after Paris. Why do we forget these facts despite viewing Charles IV as the greatest Czech?

We need only visit Aachen to grasp that Charles IV was working on two fronts to build up imperial power and legitimacy. First, there was continuity with Charlemagne's project, which, after a lull of centuries, restored the concept of Roman emperorship. This could be achieved only by the continuity of Roman law and municipal governance transferred to church institutions. Parallel to this, he established spiritual continuity between his own reign and the cult of St Wenceslas, and in doing so he was also affirming that the Přemyslid line belonged to the very highest, and deeply historically rooted, European ruling elite. Just look at St Agnes. Her father, Ottokar I, originally promised her in marriage to the son of Emperor Frederick II, the future Henry VII, and she was also betrothed for a while to the English Plantagenet King Henry III, but ultimately she opted for a spiritual life. She started out by setting up the first purely Czech monastic order, before establishing a monastery complex for Franciscan friars and Poor Clare nuns, where she was the first superior. Building on that spiritual inspiration, she attempted to found her own order. It is worth remembering that this was going on at the same time that, in Britain, they were adopting the *Magna Carta*, the validity of which was confirmed by Henry III at the outset of his reign. Then we have Agnes' nephew Ottokar II, who led Crusade expeditions to the then pagan Baltics. There was an economic revolution under Wenceslas II's reign, as evidenced by the codification of mining law, which was to serve as a model for other Central European cities. The Prague groschen, introduced in the Kingdom of Bohemia for Wenceslas II by Florentine bankers, revolutionised monetary policy, the sorts of which in Europe, beyond the Czech Lands, could only be found in Florence and France. So when we assess Charles IV's reign, we also have to take into account this context of the political and spiritual history of the Přemyslids, who played an active part in shaping medieval European society. Charles IV's youth, education, lineage and whole life therefore epitomise, in particular, the role to be played by the king of Bohemia in European and domestic politics, and show the wealth of political and diplomatic experience gained by his Přemyslid forebears that he was able to tap into. Monikers such as *"Pater Patriae"* or even "Greatest Czech" are probably as significant as when British legal theorists and historians, as late as the 19th century, were calling William the Conqueror the "Bastard" in order to cast doubt on the legitimacy of Norman monarchs and emphasise the role of pre-Norman sources of law and political tradition. To be sure, Charles' era is extraordinary in Czech history, but his "Czechness" was something very different from what our Romantic national revivalists dreamed up many centuries later.

Let's not forget that, under Charles IV, the Lands of the Bohemian Crown were established. Besides the Kingdom of Bohemia and the Margraviate of Moravia, they included Silesia, Lusatia and, for a time, Brandenburg. Charles IV was proficient in several languages and, much like St Adalbert, became a symbol of European unity. In this context, we need to stress at all times that medieval politics recognised terms such as "kingdom" and "empire", but not "state", which Niccolò Machiavelli introduced during the High Renaissance. This means that, at first glance, it is impossible to derive the concept of modern Czech statehood, and its geographical scope, from Charles IV's territorial governance. But you are thinking of the general ability of politics to unite diverse territories, their inhabitants, and their various related political interests and cultural or religious traditions. In that respect, you are right, because Charles IV, through his historical efforts and achievements, comes close to Charlemagne's legacy. Indeed, the current project of European integration also derives its legitimacy from Charlemagne's monarchical legacy. The idea of European unity is unquestionably highly stratified. In one of those strata, we would find Charlemagne alongside Charles IV and other monarchs, one of whom that stands out is George of Poděbrady. Parallel to this, we should not forget that the likes of Napoleon and Adolf Hitler were also keen to unify our continent. What's more, we cannot simply transplant medieval political unity into modern Europe with its nations, nationalisms and nation states. Under Charles IV's reign, however, the Lands of the Bohemian Crown were established and organised, thus reinforcing their territorial integrity. In fact, this is also documented by Charles' failed attempt to push through his provincial code, the *Maiestas Carolina*, and the successful attempts to issue his Golden Bull governing, among other things, the election of the emperor and the supreme imperial offices. The founding of the Prague university was then significant for the dissemination of education and the general cultivation of life in the country.

And yet, shortly after Charles IV's death, we see the abrupt radicali-
sation of social and church conflicts. This created schisms throughout the empire, but it was in Bohemia that these conflicts hit with
particular force and were the subject of much discussion at the
university, the royal court, and elsewhere. Another symbolic event
in our national history, the burning of Jan Hus at the stake, also
belongs to this period. It was partly because of this that we were
the first in Europe to engage in reformation, more than a century
before Luther.

Your question is a cocktail of many themes, issues and specific historical situations, but clearly takes aim at a fundamental problem,
namely whether a political community, be it medieval or modern,
can exist without transcendental legitimacy. I would say that, though
the crisis faced by late medieval Czech society is not particularly
relevant to us today, it does offer up rather interesting parallels,
including the fact that radicalism and fanaticism are not so much
a consequence of growing social inequality as they are – on a much
bigger scale – a manifestation of the impotence of those in power
to govern in a way that would iron out the various and frequently
contradictory and conflicting interests of subgroups of the population, and thereby show themselves capable of representing society
at large, which is a primary requirement of legitimate governance.
People are fond of saying that modern democracies are historically
the first societies in which government legitimacy is determined not
by transcendentally established and eternally valid principles, but by
intrinsic rules and standards subject to constant democratic discussion, which may be democratically amended or revoked. And yet see
how those intrinsic rules, which we know in their most precise form
in political constitutions, immediately try to somehow figure out and
finalise principles that would have transcendental validity, such as
"absolute immutability of the democratic nature of the state" or "inalienable human rights". Faith and politics, this is an eternal theme
not only in matters of the legitimacy of power, but, equally, of any

crisis of power or social and cultural decay. This is also why people often turn to history in hopes of finding some higher meaning to their own existence and identifying absolute values for which it is worth living and dying.

Do you think that, in modern history, we might have lost that ability to sacrifice ourselves? And is that loss perhaps what places the existence of our state in gravest peril?
There is a peculiar paradox in the problem you are asking about – there is danger in being unable to withstand danger. Yet we are living in an age where no external force poses an extensional risk to the Czech state or Europe. China's economic boom, Russian attempts to undermine the political stability of the European Union and its individual countries, volatility in the Middle East and Africa and the migration crisis that this has spawned, and many other events and trends in today's global society may be serious political challenges, but they are not imminent threats to our survival. The scale of sacrifice can only be measured against the degree of threat, and that is currently low. For all the manifestations of violence and despite all the social and environmental risks, we are actually living in one of the stablest and safest epochs in European and Czech history.

But sacrifice also carries a figurative meaning that can still apply today, at a time of peace.
Sacrifice has an originally religious function. Sacrificing yourself for the nation means ascribing to the nation something fateful and ethereal, in the face of which an individual's life is of trifling value. A nation really does require sacrifice and, among its members, it elicits this sense of unearthly belonging for which it is worth laying down their lives. In the modern age, this warm feeling is manifested through cold state machinery, hence the nation state – as a social institution – combines the antimony of an ardent national sense of belonging and frigid state power. Friedrich Nietzsche described this

difference in his *Zarathustra*, in which he calls the state a monster, the coldest of all cold monsters, spouting cold lies such as the state is a nation. Calling the state a monster may well be classic, but what is important is the coldness of its body and, in conjunction with that, everything with which modern and alienated individuals typically associate warmness and authenticity, one such example of which, precisely, is the nation. Even that warming sense of national belonging and identity is often, in reality, a fabrication infused in us by the cold machinery of the state. Nietzsche's metaphors capture the essence of the nation state more precisely than any analysis of structural anthropology or sociology. Just a few decades later, Europeans in the trenches of the First World War, whatever side of the front line they were on, were being told to make the ultimate sacrifice in the name of national pride, honour and civilisation. That civilisation's cold steel and military-run wartime administration led them into a bloodbath, the likes of which had never been seen before. We always need to ask, then, in whose name and for what cause we are meant to be sacrificing ourselves. Not even a nation is absolute, so the reasons for warfare and laying down lives for a particular community and its ideals need to be very powerful in democratic societies. Examples would be the threat of invasion and occupation or of a blockade. When Jaroslav Klemeš, who was parachuted into the protectorate during the war, died recently, I noted down his words: "The Germans guillotined my father in Pankrác Prison for helping Jews to flee the protectorate. If I had not done what I did, I would have felt like a coward in the shadow of his sacrifice." Such heroism is rooted in personal and family honour and, besides courage, is driven by a strong sense of justice, without which love for the nation would be reduced to tribalism and the decision to sacrifice one's own life for it would be nothing more than fanaticism. I am unsure whether Czechs or Europeans today would have what it takes to sacrifice themselves in such circumstances because we are not confronted with such a situation, but I hope that, were it to arise, our contemporary democratic and heavily individualised society would be capable of a similar response.

Definitely, but I was thinking of the smaller sacrifices that perhaps, in a way, affect our fate far more than we are able to admit to ourselves. Or, to put it another way, what I had in mind was not just the ultimate sacrifice, but rather whether society today is still a society of erstwhile medieval virtues such as courage, justice, wisdom and temperance.

The medieval or Renaissance society steeped in virtues has obviously been consigned to the past because virtues, in many respects, are antidemocratic. They require constant effort and a desire to become exceptional and better than others, which clashes with the notion of universal human equality. You can always only be virtuous to a certain degree, which differs from one person to another, so by very definition some are more virtuous and others less so. Consequently, virtues do not sit very well with the modern idea of social equality. Potential model virtues are disparaged up front and assailed because democracies, as Alexis de Tocqueville and others knew, have not only this fantastic intensity of freedom, but also a dark side, where, pretending to subscribe to the ideal of equality, they gravitate towards a homogeneous mass of mutually indistinguishable individuals. Critical theory has studied this development in modern society, for example, as the emergence of the "cultural industry", while sociologists have pondered the "lonely crowd" and philosophers have written about the "one-dimensional man". In this sense, we really are living – as claimed, for example, by the philosopher Alasdair MacIntyre – in a society where virtues have crumbled away. We are a society not of virtues, but of morality and its general and universally binding rules. Cultivating and championing "democratic virtues" such as tolerance, candour or temperance and prudence is incredibly difficult and is up against ever increasing social pressure for us to live not as mutually equal and respecting citizens, but as an indistinctive gloop of identical entities. This is also why democratic and egalitarian societies, paradoxically, have this insistent need to moralise everything – including history – instantly. This even goes for medieval history, which modern people view as a linear narrative of development, if not the outright progress of human society. As though we were witnesses to a civilising process in which morals crystallise and coarseness and violence gradually evaporate. The sociologist Norbert Elias demonstrated that this civilising process was possible only because violence is increasingly concentrated in the political organisation of the modern state. Seeing medieval society simply as primitive and coarse, but also as a linear path to modernity, is a prejudice typical of the historical and social sciences. Paradoxically, this prejudice also shows that not even democratic societies can survive without ethics and virtues, and they are transforming into the moralising tyrannies we see all around the world today.

Might the problem be that historians need to speak the language of their age, otherwise they would be unintelligible, as Lucien Febvre said?
Febvre was right, of course, because we cannot engage in history as some sort of exact science entirely detached from the social and cultural context in which it is formed. This is also why it has this constant inner tension between historical facts and how they are judged, accompanied by the temptation to use the past as a vehicle to appraise the present. However, if we stop limiting our search for the meaning of today's Czech statehood in references to medieval power politics or diplomacy, suddenly we can see that the Middle Ages remains inspirational for many other reasons. For one thing, it recognised a highly developed system of law that did not require the politically centralised power of the state. There are certain features of today's global society that are surprisingly similar to those of medieval society, so it is only logical, for example, that the principle

of subsidiarity, the supporting activity of the state, once typical for canon law, is presented as one of the principles of European law nowadays. Likewise, the present-day legal pluralism we see dominating aspects of global society as diverse as trade, human health and criminal law has a lot in common with medieval Europe's legal pluralism. When we consider this, it might be a good idea to break free from those simple notions of linear time and societal development from the Middle Ages to post-modernity and, instead, be a lot more radical in asking ourselves what economic, political, legal or scientific and artistic practices form a bridge between these two eras. If we take the idea of university education as universally shared knowledge, this has not changed since the Middle Ages, but has merely transitioned from confined little islands of society as was into one of the streams of today's flow of globally shared information. The same can be said of art as the fusion of individual genius and an entire school or workshop, which has persisted to this day, even in pop art and the Duchampian tradition of readymades. Rather than temporal and spatial continuity, then, let's work out where different practices and creations connect and overlap. I'm thinking here perhaps of the mining law we have discussed, which went on to serve as a model in other countries on how to legislate this entire branch of industry. In many respects, this transplantation or hybridisation of law is a lot more modern than, say the Crusades, even though history papers are preoccupied much more by the history of military endeavours than by intellectual output or the differences between ethics and morals we have just talked about.

Ultimately this means that medieval society provides us with evidence that law is older than the state...
... in the modern centralised form we know today. Law is able to organise society without state bureaucracy. Likewise, medieval society shows that politics is a more general term than the state because power struggles took place within an entirely different in-

stitutional framework. The main lesson we learn from studying medieval law and politics is that neither the state nor the nation is an axiomatic term describing political or social "naturalness" or "givenness".

And that still holds true in our own era, in which economics and, with it, crime and environmental problems have become globalised. In today's globalised society, we really are witnessing a return to a bolder separation of law from the state, and we can see how entire chunks of commercial, medical and environmental law function independently of nation states. At the same time, law is evidently not a pure structure of logically marshalled norms with a clear hierarchy and straightforward machinery for imposing sanctions. On the contrary, we can see how official law is reliant on unofficial – but for all that more deeply societally entrenched – practices. We can observe how multiple legal regimes exist alongside each other just as, in the Middle Ages, we are aware of pluralism in applicable law. A hundred years ago, most jurists and legal scientists believed that law was either applicable or inapplicable. In reality, it is a lot more complicated than that because the observance and enforcement of legal norms is a matter of scale, so there is a nuanced transition between what is applicable and what is not, as is plain from abundant examples of medieval guild law. And there's one more – perhaps the most important – lesson to be learned from medieval law: the law is not the will of the lawmaker, but the product of many years' experience gained by jurists – the law-educated stratum of society – who practise the law, infuse it with content, and use it to protect clients' interests. This *Juristenrecht*, "juristic law", was always far more important than political will. It is only in the modern age that we have adopted a rationalistic notion prescribing that there must first be a centralised state, in which the political will of either the individual or collective bodies is manifested. This concept dictates that political will leads to the issuance of laws, which judges and other members of the legal system are then simply meant to apply passively so that they do not cause a rift with the legitimate will of the state.

Whereas in Roman law and subsequently, medieval law, we saw the complete opposite...
... yes. The laws adopted by political bodies were primarily intended to govern the public life of the political community, and most of the law was moulded in the search for solutions to specific conflicts on the basis of jurisprudence – the practical knowledge and expert skills wielded by the jurists dealing with those disputes. These days, we would classify the vast majority of both Roman and medieval law as private law, in which statute law has played a secondary role right up to the modern day. Justinian's *Corpus Juris Civilis* from the first half of the sixth century, which had a major influence on the entire Western concept of law, certainly unified the sources of the then Roman law, but this was law which was already in existence, not some absolute and new monarchical will. For that matter, not even the Napoleonic Codes or Austrian Civil Code from the early days of the 19th century were pure manifestations of the legislature's will, but actually a compilation of legal experience gained thus far and an attempt to come up with a coherent interpretation of various branches of law. The main purpose of these codes, which drew on previous knowledge of past decisions and cases, was to cast a critical eye over these precedents in order to introduce a modicum of order and organisation into the ever more chaotic legal swamp. However, thanks to the political situation in post-revolutionary France, where judges were thought to sympathise with the *Ancien Régime*, political will was put ahead of legal rationality, and the judiciary was tasked simply with applying political will that had been shaped within the centralised machinery of the state. It is solely in consequence of this strange political constellation in post-revolutionary France that politicians and even some members of the public suffer from the illusion, to this day, that law is a manifestation of will that takes the

form of a statute. As medieval history shows us, legislation played only a fringe role in the shaping of law right up until the modern age. This is because, until modern times, jurists and laypersons alike subscribed to the notion that law is something that emerges, that is not constructed, and that, as such, is part and parcel of the job description of judges, their secretaries, and magistrates, but not of politicians.

That's a very serious claim flying in the face of prevailing modern notions of law. Can you back it up with any examples?
I can give a very specific example from Czech history just as the Middle Ages were giving way to the modern era. At that time, the famous Bohemian humanist and jurist Viktorin Kornel of Všehrdy (1460-1520) was teaching at the Charles University in Prague, where he went on to become the dean. He subsequently accepted a position as an official responsible for the registers of the estates and worked his way up to become the topmost legal authority on law in the Czech Lands. Consequently, he was elevated to the nobility and effectively took charge of the office of the registers of the estates. This was a very important job at the time because the registers of the estates were not only used to record the nobility's estates and lands, but also included reports from the provincial diets and general legal regulations, making it an antecedent to the modern property register and collection of statutes. Viktorin Kornel, strictly speaking, was an Erasmian humanist and scholar who wrote in Czech, translated from Latin, and professed himself a member of the Unity of the Brethren. All law students today are familiar primarily with his *Nine Books on the Laws, Courts and Registers of the Estates of the Czech Lands*, which he compiled by tapping into his practical knowledge and experience of managing the registers of the estates. And yet this law, expertly and independently found and compiled, was a thorn in the side of the nobility, which wanted the opposite – the scrapping of the registers – and forced King Vladislaus II of Hungary to

remove Kornel from his post. By then, though, Kornel had enough material and knowledge to complete his work and publish it in 1499. Just a year after the publication of Kornel's books, championing the legal claims of the burghers in the battle between the nobility and the towns, the royal *Vladislaus Land Order* was issued, which, by contrast, obliged the nobles' claims. Official responsibility and jurisprudence in one corner and royal will accommodating political demands in the other, these are the two sides of the coin in the development of modern law, and the constant tension between them has continued to this day. Incidentally, Kornel's work exemplified linguistic perfection for the time, so legal education was instrumental in Czech linguistic culture in an age that was still oblivious to the linguistic concept of the nation.

This might be a good time to return some of those general concepts and explain them. How would you define the terms "living law" or "jurisprudence"?
When I said that jurisprudence comprises the practical knowledge and expert skills used by jurists to interpret regulations and address disputes, I was thinking in particular of lawyers' general ability not only to navigate law, but also to apply it correctly and, in keeping with the guiding principles of justice, to resolve "gaps in the law", i.e. situations for which written law has no answer. In this respect, jurisprudence requires a general knowledge not simply of how the law works, but also how it should work in order to meet the widely accepted expectation that, when it is applied, justice can prevail in society. I would like to digress briefly into the philosophy of virtues, if I may. Plato distinguishes between three cardinal virtues that are consistent with the reason, high-spirit and appetite parts of the soul: wisdom (*sophia*), courage (*andreia*) and temperance (*sōphrosynē*). To these, he added a fourth – and principal – virtue, justice (*dikaiosynē*), to indicate proper focus, in our entire being, in what we do and how we live. This basic breakdown was elabo-

rated in detail by Aristotle and then adopted by the Stoics, whose differentiation between the four virtues of wisdom, courage, temperance and justice was embraced, in turn, by medieval philosophy. For law, it is particularly important that it not be overrun by justice alone, with lawyers also expected to be courageous, wise and temperament. And in this sense jurisprudence is closer to practical temperance or circumspection, *prudentia*, even though we tend to associate law instantly with the ideal of justice. This difference is of paramount importance to our concept of law because we often view justice as the intervention of external power in day-to-day lives that are choking with injustice. The sovereign power of the monarch or state organisations are therefore easy to represent as that which protects, enforces and mediates justice. Law is then deemed to constitute a hierarchically ordered system of norms or rules enforced by state power. By contrast, ever since Roman times jurisprudence has shown that law is not political will elevated to a statute or prescriptive system enforced by the state, but a much more subtle web of human skills, knowledge, consciousness, customs and practices, through which people educated in law make it possible for others to resolve their mutual disputes and file justified claims against each other. One of the things jurisprudence teaches us, then, is that law is much older than the state.

And how does this to relate to what you have termed the "living law" or "juristic law"?
"Living law" (*das lebende Recht*) is a much younger and more modern term first introduced into jurisprudence by the Austrian historian and sociologist of law Eugen Ehrlich. He defined living law, in contrast to written law, as something that people truly acknowledge to be the law and that governs their everyday lives. In other words, what matters is not what the state claims to be the law, but what actually guides people and what they themselves deem to be the law. While juristic law shows that it is primarily expert knowledge rath-

er than political will that makes the law the law, living law takes this separation of law from the state and runs much further with it, planting it in the actual life of society. The thing is, Ehrlich lived and worked in the furthest reaches of the Habsburg monarchy, in Chernivtsi, Bukovina...

... the university building of which was originally constructed, incidentally, by the Czech benefactor and architect Josef Hlávka as the residence of Bukovinian Metropolitans.
Ehrlich saw how official regulations proclaimed in the metropolitanate had scant effect on how people of various ethnicities and faiths lived here, in one of Austria-Hungary's culturally most diverse areas. At the time, his theory seemed to verge on the naive and unrealistic, but, in this global day and age, we can actually see how law finds all manner of ways to worm its way into the day-to-day life of globalised societies and how it is apt to do without the interventions of state power entirely.

Are we to assume, then, that today's globalised societies have more in common with the Middle Ages than the modern state?
Categories such as living law and juristic law have been developed by legal history and sociology and are still used to criticise the narrow interpretation of law simply as a manifestation of state or political will. One point they draw attention to is that this will cannot do without legal logic and rationality. In contrast to statute law, juristic law also highlights the paradoxical situation of the modern *Rechtsstaat*, in which it is assumed, on the one hand, entirely in keeping with Aristotle's philosophy, that justice means the rule of law and not of individuals, but, at the same time, certain members of society are authorised to pass off their will as statutes and law binding upon society at large. Consequently, Machiavelli's Prince does not have to employ subterfuge and brutally assert his own will these days because all he has to do is take on the role of a state offi-

cial enforcing applicable law. To be sure, the rule of law protects us from arbitrariness, and yet we increasingly find ourselves exposed to the risk that a statute could morph into tyrannical despotism. Legislation does not just reflect the legitimate political will confirmed in parliaments and other representative bodies of democratic societies. It is also bound up with the technical and rational ability to organise and manage modern society effectively, quickly, predictively, clearly and efficiently. Legality is perceived not as a practical skill, but as the fulfilment of the idea of modern rationality, which is inherently legitimate. As such, statutes are regarded as a technology of power, which goes some way to explaining why today's laws are so wretched that, even as they are being adopted, it is obvious that the legislature will have to amend them if they are to be at all applicable. In any conversation on the legitimacy of power established by general statutes, the discussion automatically turns to the work of the sociologist and economist Max Weber, who genuinely believed that modern legislation was one of the many components characteristic of the general process of rationalisation that gradually seeps into all areas of social life. But, as a sociologist, Weber knew very well that this process of societal modernisation relied not on punishment and browbeating, but on the spontaneous adoption of statutory norms by those who were meant to submit to them. Modern society's general trend of enacting and codifying law therefore, paradoxically, hinges on the extent to which people are willing to accommodate it and accept it as their own – as authentic or living law. We are persuaded both by current sociology of law and medieval legal history that law is predominantly a system that is formed spontaneously, with codification and legislating limited to a secondary role.

How is this "living" or "juristic" law linked to constitutional law? Very closely! Written constitutions are hardly the exclusive consequence of revolutions or coups d'état. Looking at, say, how the American constitution came into being, this is precisely the process we were discussing in connection with the adoption of the Codex Justinianus and the Napoleonic Codes. Despite the revolutionary movement behind it, the constitution of the independent United States of America does not convey a modern political utopia, but musters existing political experience and the rules of the unwritten English constitution and blends them with the democratic aspirations of a fledgling nation that wishes to govern itself while retaining ancient freedoms which, it was convinced, the colonial English powers had breached, thereby forfeiting the legitimacy to continue governing the American people. Within the Habsburg monarchy, we see the gradual adoption of constitutions that are politically quite different and a lot more restrictive and autocratic, yet even these were drawn up in response to real political and social change. In truth, the constitution as a starting point for new ages, that *novus ordo seclorum* of the American founding fathers, is always a mix of continuity and discontinuity in political society and its legal order. No law, including constitutional law, can serve as a mere instrument of social engineering or managerial revolution, whatever many a revolutionary or engineer of human souls may believe. On the contrary, it holds true for constitutional law, too, that this is a much more comprehensive system of norms, practices and conventions aimed at guiding society just as much as protecting it from itself. Aristotle described very accurately the danger and disruption stemming from arbitrary, haphazard and unpredictable ochlocracy, the rule of government by a mob that has demagogues or an erratic tyrant at the helm. Hence it still holds true that the rule of law must be sovereign and must restrict any government by the people. In this respect, Cicero was merely restating Aristotle's truth in his famous dictum *omnes legum servi sumus ut liberi esse possimus* ("we must all obey the law in order that we may free"). However, this ideal of legal certainty, defining the private affairs of the individual and the public world of politics, presupposes that legal argumentation and interpretation will be independent of the will and wishes of the powerful and, at the same time, will not be bent by judges and other legal professions to their own ends and needs. This also happens to be the reason why today's constitutional democracies have judicial checks on constitutionality and why the judges of constitutional courts are typically appointed for a limited period of time.

There is one further question that springs to mind in this context. Can an image of the world, including an image of constitutional law and politics, exist without allusion to the transcendental?
This is a crucial question of legal and political philosophy, by which I mean whether modern society's law and politics can make do with their own images, or whether they need some sort of transcendental basis and have to devise fundamental images that would be a lot closer to theology. Rousseau's general will is a transcendental principle pervading all legislation and the life of the political community in its entirety! It is a derivative of the incontestable authority of God's will. Images of the nation as a constitutional power also come close to the transcendental principle in which national sovereignty has the attributes of a prime mover of the world of politics. But is this deification necessary as a symbolic basis of legitimacy, or is it enough for legality and power to function in systems of positive law and politics? From a sociological perspective, nationalism functioned and, in many cases, continues to function as one of the forms of secular religions. These also include totalitarian ideologies, but, equally so, certain interpretations of modern law and, in particular, human rights as fundamental principles of a modern democratic society. For example, the American legal philosopher Ronald Dworkin discussed the need for "religion without God" in this regard. Nationalism is one such religion, so the big question is whether the legitimacy of modern law and the modern state is always conditional on some such secular religion within which the collective will of the nation could function as a transcendental principle. Notice that this very question contains a paradox: we believe that legitimacy needs

to be established transcendentally and yet, at the same time, we are constantly asking ourselves whether the law works. There is no solution to this disconnect between the symbolic rationality of meaning and the functional rationality of purpose in modern society. Both the history of the nation state and medieval history can offer us plenty of examples of this schism and the paradox of legitimacy, which wishes not only to have merely a functional and immanent basis, but also yearns for a symbolic and transcendental grounding!

Modern Times,
State Sovereignty
and the Nation

Our marker for the start of the modern era is 1492, when Columbus reached America. The main hive of activity swiftly shifted from the heart of the European continent to its coastal fringes, giving rise to two new superpowers: Spain and Portugal. How did these events affect Czech history? More generally, what influence did they have on European society?

We've spent a lot of time dwelling on medieval Czech history and discussing the texts and contexts that are all part of a schoolchild's required knowledge. However, Czech history and the way we teach it reveal a much more general feature of the European relationship with the past that happens to be more complex than the patterns of time we have become accustomed to. Witness, for instance, the dissimilarity between the Middle Ages and the modern period, dated to 1492, and the differences we associate with those two eras, such as the contrast between the Gothic and the Renaissance. And yet if we take a look at the statues of Nicola Pisano and his son Giovanni, or at Giotto's images, it is quite easy to see how every cultural discontinuity still incorporates a whole raft of continuities and references to the past. Everyone who sets off in quest of the very beginnings of the Renaissance consequently ends up at the Pisa Baptistry, where the pulpit is graced with Nicola Pisano's clearly antiquity-inspired mid-13th century reliefs. There is also a political dimension to this aesthetic discontinuity with the Gothic style, which originated in France, and to the rediscovery of antiquity in what were ostensibly the "dark Middle Ages" because of the ideological backing provided by Frederick II, from whom Ottokar I received the *Golden Bull of Sicily*, and who was not only an artful politician and diplomat, but also, for instance, a great champion of science and philosophy, an admirer of Islamic learning, and the founder of the first state university in Naples. The exact same goes for our modern age because the discovery of America was preceded by advances in marine navigation and international trade. The new European society at this time really is taking form as the Age of Exploration progresses, and yet would be inconceivable without the printing press, which was introduced by the goldsmith Gutenberg in around 1448 and which, over time, evolved from this enormous, convoluted piece of machinery into a portable and economically affordable device. On top of that, we need to add the military and industrial use of gunpowder, the invention of the telescope, and the adoption of experimentation as a basic method that modern science could not do without. It is only when we clump together these mutually unrelated transformations of European culture that we arrive at what we have become used to terming a modern society, known for cultivating not only the Renaissance art of perspective, but also science as a system of human knowledge that carries a legitimacy independent of both temporal and spiritual power. At this historical point of intersection, we come across terms such as "fact" or "*lex naturalis*", which have a quite fundamental impact on the modern grasp of law and politics. It is somewhere here that a system of knowledge is born that encompasses very modern social institutions such as the state, and the attendant principle of political sovereignty, as well as natural law. This natural law subsequently forms the basis for the system of international law and modern constitutional law, which in turn guarantees all entities of political power natural rights, including the fundamental right to contribute to the shaping of such power. However, if we are to make sense of these transformations in the 16th and 17th centuries, we must also understand the continuities, including how medieval advancements and culture have been reflected in modern notions of Czech statehood.

This can usually be demonstrated across Europe by looking at buildings.
Definitely. The Middle Ages are unquestionably as much a part of our living history as the Renaissance, the emergence of the Habsburg

Empire, and the modern national revival. On a symbolic level, everyone who visits Prague Castle sees this when they enter St Vitus' Cathedral, where they can admire the 14th-century apse designed by Matthias of Arras and Parler-inspired ribbed vault juxtaposed with the modern stained glass windows of Alphonse Mucha, Karel Svolinský, and Max Švabinský. And, of course, that is even before I mention the fact that this is the resting place of the country's most prominent sovereigns, including Saint Wenceslas and Charles IV, whose reigns have given symbolic legitimacy to the modern Czech statehood and who continue to elicit our allegiance in popular competitions such as "greatest Czechs", even though concepts of Czechness in the 10th, 14th and 21st centuries differ from each other completely in their content and meaning. When it comes to medieval continuities, however, I am thinking not just of the continuity of statehood, or of spiritual and cultural values and artefacts, but also of the purely modern notion of drawing constant inspiration from medieval culture and returning to its roots, whether in the form of Gothic Revival architecture, the Gothic novel or minimalist experiments with choral singing. The Middle Ages are constantly returning to us. We dream about them and measure ourselves against their various versions: the idealisation of chivalry, the cruelty and barbarity portrayed in the films of František Vláčil and Ingmar Bergman, philosophical disputes between nominalism and realism, and a fascination with the occult extending from the Renaissance to the present. Our obsession with the Middle Ages as the period in which modern national identities started to form also belongs here. If it weren't for medieval history, there would have been no 19th-century national revivals, which saw many nations – including the Czechs – invent Romantically idealised periods of national glory and contrast them with their current plight, weighed down by oppression and national subjugation, which they needed to rise up against and fight. From a sociological point of view, then, the Middle Ages means so much more than the Renaissance and early modern period in terms of how our notions of modern national identity – including the idea of statehood and the nation state – have been moulded.

Sociologically, we can see a clear construction of reality here, but does it have any basis in history? What is it invoking?
In terms of legal and political history, the Early Middle Ages were evidently receptive to Roman law and municipal government, which facilitated the basic functioning of society at the time and resulted in the 9th-century Carolingian Renaissance. It is only after this that we see the population rise again in Europe. Highly nutritious leguminous vegetables start to be cultivated and iron is no longer in short supply. This had an even greater impact on agriculture and farming productivity than it did on the art of warfare. Against that background, it is interesting how the Czech sovereigns joined in with this industrial, technical and political revolution. Ottokar I's reign (1192–1230), for example, cannot be judged solely by his diplomatic prowess and the *Golden Bull of Sicily* that we have mentioned, but also, and equally, according to the establishment of towns and the granting of town privileges or borough rights. This process of creating medieval towns in the early 13th century is a truly social revolution, even though just a fraction of the country's entire population lived in them. Naturally, the boom in crafts and industry and the establishment of towns endowed with a high degree of self-government continued under Wenceslas I (1230–1253) and Ottokar II (1253–1278), so in the space of a single century there is this radical economic, political and cultural overhaul of all society. Were it not for this industrial urban revolution, Ottokar II could not have pursued an expansionist policy and tried to subjugate lands both westward (Egerland) and southward (Upper and Lower Austria, Styria, etc.), or even Lithuania and the Baltics, in the process of which he founded Königsberg (now Kaliningrad). Of course, his lust for power was also fuelled by his imperial roots, as his mother was from the House of Hohenstaufen, and driven by

marriage diplomacy, including a failed attempt to have his illegitimate children recognised by Pope Alexander IV and his divorce from Margaret of Austria, but the sheer concentration of power in his hands was without parallel in Europe, which was typically a place of feudal fragmentation at this time. The dozens of newly founded towns that were springing up acted as a counterweight to any attempts by nobles to consolidate their own power. This was also kept in check by the abolition of the nobility's privileges and the enforcement of law of the type up and running in other parts of the empire. This period also saw the establishment of the provincial court – the Bohemian *Landrecht* – and the registers of the estates, which was an act of crucial legal, political and social significance. While, *de jure*, only royal towns and a few minor territories belonged to Ottokar II, with the bulk of the land and estates in the hereditary possession of the nobility, this monarch *de facto* treated the entire kingdom as his own. Although this concentration of power was completely different from that of the 17th century's modern absolutism, Ottokar II's reign is a perfect example of how power is a strong political medium and how politics starts with the concentration of such power. This applies to the medieval empire, of which the Kingdom of Bohemia was the most powerful part, as much as it does to modern states.

Another period we ought to explore if we want to stick with nodal points in history is the development and transformation of the Czech state within the framework of the Habsburg monarchy. I'm thinking here of when the throne passed from the Jagiellonian dynasty to the Habsburgs. Perhaps we should start with Ferdinand I's first declaration of 1526. Or would you single out another date as more important?
These are fundamental dates underpinning the interpretive canon of Czech history. But before we move on from Ottokar II and his medieval expansionist policy to the much more refined diplomacy and

succession policy of the Habsburgs in the 16th century, it's worth recalling that, during this time, society and its political reform, including the organisation of the state, underwent root-and-branch transformation, as documented by *The King's Two Bodies*, a masterpiece by one of the last century's most influential historians, Ernst Kantorowicz. This work was originally published in 1957 and profoundly influenced whole generations of historians, philosophers, and social and political scientists. It was a major inspiration for Michel Foucault in his classic study *Discipline and Punish*, while the Italian philosopher Giorgio Agamben proclaimed it "one of the great texts of our age on the techniques of power". In his book, Kantorowicz discussed the classical theory of the king's two bodies by drawing on his study of legal and theological sources from Elizabethan and Jacobean England, in which the "crown-as-corporation" principle prevailed. This means that, in the person of the king, two bodies are indivisibly united – the physical *body natural*, vulnerable and mortal, and the symbolic *body politic*, which contains the "office, government and majesty royal" and, as such, is mystically eternal and immortal. In this body politic, the monarch and his subjects are also connected, with the king becoming the head and his subjects making up the rest of the body, which is enduring and, unlike the body natural, cannot die. The king's body politic also symbolically cleanses any physical defects of the majesty royal and gives it everlasting duration, so the heirs to the throne simply physically enter the eternal body and fulfil legal doctrine stating that the monarch is a special corporation. In itself, this is nothing new, and all legal historians in Britain are familiar with this doctrine. Kantorowicz, though, proved that this English doctrine of the king's two bodies originated in the medieval jurisprudence of civil and canon law and that, for example, the principle of "the king never dies" evolved from two parallel legal concepts, namely the rules of succession in family dynasties and the immortality of corporations, which is a classic rule of Roman law that also happens to be linked to the principle of the immortality of the erstwhile *populus Romanus*. In this context, it is worth remembering that the book's subtitle is "A Study in Medieval Political Theology" and that Kantorowicz really did show a contemporary connection between theological, legal and political argumentation and symbolism. To this day, there is an entire school of political philosophy contending that modern political terms and symbols have theological provenance. On the other hand, Kantorowicz, cloaked in the completely non-speculative spirit of historical positivism, showed that abbeys – for the sake of example – were treated in medieval papal decrees as corporations offering continuity by adhering to the succession of abbots, who may well die physically, but their dignity remains immortal. Once again, then, we can see legal continuity with the medieval reception of Roman law, a factor that was also reliant on the Aristotelian philosophy of time and nature. What particularly makes the English doctrine of the king's two bodies unique is that the king is regarded as a special corporation because of his immortal dignity and on account of the fact that the body politic is part of the institution of parliament, which means that, ultimately, the organic metaphor of the two bodies encompasses specific legal techniques and arguments guaranteeing the functionality, impersonality and continuity of political institutions.

And how did everything you have described specifically affect the organisation of power in the Czech Lands?
The personification of the state we are familiar with from medieval European and Czech history has increasingly retreated in the modern era, giving way to the functionality of the state instead. Nowadays the device of grand schemes to legitimise Czech statehood through historical speculation, which were typical in the age of national revival, have fallen to the wayside as we grapple, instead, with how general political tendencies, legal arguments, techniques of power and their gradual transformation over time have been manifested in Czech history. In this context, I would also like to

highlight the fact that Kantorowicz actually found fame back in the late 1920s when he published his monograph on the Roman Emperor, German king and close ally of Ottokar I, Frederick II, a figure we have already briefly touched on. This 600-page treatise on a monarch who wielded cruel methods and pursued lofty ambitions to control the whole of Europe, and on the founder of the "First Reich", even served as inspiration for the Nazis as they engineered their perverse plans. So what we saw here was a book by a historian of Jewish origin becoming a bestseller and, paradoxically, progressing in 1936, i.e. at a time when the new economic Nuremberg Laws had been passed, to a fourth edition that Hitler himself was said to be fond of browsing. Another paradox is that whereas *The King's Two Bodies*, which Kantorowicz wrote during his Californian exile at Berkeley, analyses political theology, in his monograph on Frederick II, drawn up three decades earlier in the Weimar Republic, Kantorowicz – influenced by Stefan George and his Romantic admiration for mysticism, strong leaders and historical authorities – actually helped to shape that very same political theology. What this primarily means in the context of our discussion on Czech history is we need to realise that, with each narrative on the historical beginnings of Czech statehood or on those powerful Přemyslid sovereigns and their expansionist policies and concentration of power, we keep running the risk of slipping into political allegory and theology in much the same way as the young Kantorowicz and legions of other historians, social scientists and philosophers did in the last century. Pretensions towards power and the personification of the kingdom as a private possession of Ottokar I and his successors should therefore be viewed against the historical backdrop of medieval law and politics, in which Kantorowicz so lucidly laid bare the general workings of power, including its legal and theological legitimisation through doctrines separating the physical body of a mortal from the symbolic body of an immortal corporation, which could be a church institution just as much as the entire body politic of society. And yet it is not until the modern period that we can talk of society as a single unit. Here, we can see a fundamental about-face, during which the monarch's absolute power starts to serve natural laws and statutes applicable to political society, something that Thomas Hobbes, among others, would term a *commonwealth*. However, the path towards this turning point was long and arduous, and in the Czech Lands was hemmed in by the Habsburgs' ascension to the Bohemian throne, on the one hand, and, on the other, by the Battle of White Mountain and the subsequent absolutist consolidation of power and centralisation of the state. And it was precisely this centralisation of the state and modernising attempts to create a culturally and linguistically homogeneous environment through a policy of "enlightened absolutism", underpinned by Theresian and Josephine reforms in the late 18th century, that, in the end, paradoxically reopened the Czech question, this time as both a constitutional and national question, in which the aim was to preserve the specific culture and language while maintaining political autonomy and a stake in power that was becoming increasingly centralised and bureaucratic.

This was also prompted by the fact that, after 1526, a working personal union came into place, with the Bohemian and Hungarian nobles electing the Austrian Habsburg Duke Ferdinand I as their king. What is your take on this period, particularly in relation to the state?

Let's just return briefly to the ascension of Ferdinand I, a man influenced by the teachings of Desiderius Erasmus in his youth, to the Bohemian throne. The thing is, he is associated with important changes in European developments that went beyond the framework of the Habsburgs' marriage diplomacy and the split of the Habsburg dynasty into a Spanish and Austrian branch. Since, in 1520, Austria was a patchwork of autonomous duchies that did not adhere to the principle of primogeniture, Ferdinand I had to take control of Upper and Lower Austria, Carinthia, Styria and Carniola via the Treaty of Worms. Two years later his brother, the Spanish King Charles, handed him sovereignty over the other Austrian Lands, too. These contractual and royal legal acts unified the governance of Austria and established a monarchy that would last all the way through until 1918. Entirely in keeping with the spirit of the times, he crushed any opposition put up by the estates and towns and strengthened state power through monetary reform and the introduction of a single currency. Under a marriage agreement arranged between Emperor Maximilian I and the Jagiellonian King Vladislaus II of Hungary and Bohemia, Ferdinand was married to Vladislaus' daughter Anne. This was a move that, following the death of Anne's brother, King Louis, King of Bohemia, made the path to the Bohemian and Hungarian throne much smoother, even though – despite stipulations made by the Bohemian estates while Vladislaus was still king – the marriage was never confirmed by the provincial diet. In the wake of failed attempts to gain the Czech Lands in fee or on the strength of an inherited right of succession, Ferdinand I had no choice but to submit to election by the provincial diet. Even so, the Bohemian estates elected him surprisingly quickly, on 23 October 1526, after just a few weeks of negotiation. Their decision was prompted by the Turkish military threat, the near-empty public purse, and Ferdinand's vow to abide by the 1436 Compacts of Basel, respect the freedoms of the estates, and relocate his seat to Prague. Today, of course, we know that most of these promises by Ferdinand I rang hollow, but the need for economic and administrative reform was just as urgent in the Czech Lands as it was in the Austrian Lands and Hungary, where Ferdinand's initial position was nowhere near as stable. In fact, in November 1526 most of the Hungarian estates elected John Zápolya, Voivode of Transylvania, as their king, so the subsequent December election of Ferdinand I in Bratislava and his holding of the title of King of Hungary was restricted to the west of Hungary, Slovakia and Croatia. This remarkable diplomatic strategy continued in 1531, with Ferdinand's election as King of the Romans and coronation in Aachen, and ultimately – in 1556 – when Charles abdicated as Holy Roman Emperor in favour of his brother. During this significant historical process, resulting in the formation of one of the most powerful monarchical dynasties right at the outset of the modern period, Ferdinand I managed to set up central authorities of state power in Vienna, thereby reining in the provincial authorities and curbing the power of the estates, and link up the Habsburg dominions in the Austrian, Czech and Hungarian Lands into a single confederation that, as I have already mentioned, would remain in place for nigh on 400 years, right up to 1918. The original personal union was gradually crafted into a powerful absolutist state which went on to play important international, political, administrative, economic roles, along with other functions that we generally associate with modern state organisation, for many years in Central Europe. While we're on the subject of the formation of a state recognisable to us in its modern form, with centralised power, bureaucratic bodies, a judicial system, and a single economic policy, it is something of a paradox that it arose in the Czech Lands by restricting the autonomy of the estates and removing towns' political rights. Self-government by the nobility gave way to governors, who were placed in charge of provincial government, and alongside them we witnessed the arrival of re-Catholicising spiritual power, symbolised by the Jesuits and the resumption of the office of the Archbishop of Prague. Here, again, Ferdinand I was very diplomatic. At the *Council of Trent* (1545–1563), he sought an exemption for Communion under both kinds in the Czech Lands as a central plank of the *Compacts of Basel* (1436), which, more than a hundred years down the line, were still a guarantee of religious peace here. The significance of the Compacts cannot be stressed enough. Once signed by Pope Eugene IV and Emperor Sigismund, they effectively became a constitutional document guaranteeing fundamental religious freedoms and serving as inspiration for all future Protestant movements, even though the Utraquists considered themselves, if anything, an autonomous part of the Catholic Church. Despite Pius II's refusal of George of Poděbrady's request for the Compacts to be confirmed, this King of Bohemia continued to be known as the "king of two peoples", i.e. those who take Communion under one and both kinds. It was not until 1567 that Emperor Maximilian II repealed the Compacts, paradoxically under pressure from the Bohemian Protestant nobility.

Following the death of Maximilian II (1576), when the Counter-Reformation programme virtually ground to a halt, there was a paradigm shift in the Austrian Lands because Albert V, Duke of Bavaria, was a fervent Catholic and, as Emperor Rudolph had been brought up in Catholic Spain, he obviously benefited from his support.

Developments in the Czech Lands in the 16th century need to be viewed in the context of Europe as a whole. In France, for example, civil war broke out between Protestants and Catholics and prompted the St Bartholomew's Day massacre in 1572. It was not until the *Edict of Nantes* of 1599 that religious peace was restored. Humanist ethics and tolerance preached, among others, by Desiderius Erasmus may well have informed contemporary moral and political philosophy, but at the same time it was clear that only a strong monarch, backed by effective power and state machinery, would be able to guarantee peace between the hostile sides and force them to tolerate each other. It is no coincidence that the completely modern doctrines of constitutional law and sovereignty, familiar to us primarily from the work of the French jurist and philosopher Jean Bodin, came to light in this period. Bodin, though, was an adherent not only of royal authority firmly entrenched in the law, but also of legally regulated free trade and exports of goods. Consequently, modern political science definitively came into being, born of social, religious and political strife. Unlike Machiavelli's older and more classical political theory of power, it is thoroughly entangled with the theory of public law organising life within the state. Bodin's teachings do not dwell on the monarch's physical and symbolic corporeality, but address the entirely abstract creation of the state as a sovereign institution, without which political society could not exist and there would only be universal violence and anarchy.

Jean Bodin is effectively the first sovereign-state theorist. Let's just note that he was born in Angers, France, in 1529 and died in Laon in 1596. He wrote the famous Les Six Livres de la République and "invented" absolutism. Would that be fair to say?

... Well, yes, but he was not alone. Bodin's experience of a civil war of confession was shared by the younger Dutch jurist Hugo Grotius, generally hailed as one of the founders of the modern theory of natural law and, in particular, international law, as well as by the English "Monster of Malmesbury" Thomas Hobbes, whose work and political and legal philosophy we will come back to. However, in this specific context it is important for us to be aware that Czech history is in no way peculiar and does not diverge from the crises plaguing Europe at that time. In fact, if you take the intellectual sources of the Bohemian Revolt (1618–1620), you will find that it was influenced in its ideas by the political and legal theories of federalism and the right to resist a ruler, of the sort we are familiar with from, say, Althusius' work. These were being advocated, for example, in the organisation of the Dutch provinces that, in 1581, had overthrown the Habsburgs and declared the Dutch Republic of Seven United Provinces. The Dutch Republic took the form of a confederation in its state organisation and was effectively a quasi-monarchy in that the general *Stadtholder* was always elected from among the descendants of William I, Prince of Orange. The uprising of the Bohemian estates, then, was not some medieval spat between a monarch and the nobility, but a fully modern conflict in which the form of government took centre stage. The Bohemian estates were pushing for a confederate model of the sort that the Habsburgs, following their experience of Dutch opposition, were particularly wary of. The way the estates saw it, this would place power in their hands and considerably hobble the monarch's room to manoeuvre. On top of that, the estates would be able to exercise the "right of resistance", *jus resistendi*, a classical principle developed by the philosopher and jurist Johannes Althusius at this time. Althusius made the monarch's reign conditional on the approval of the people and on respect for natural human laws and for statutes applicable in the country, otherwise, in Althusius' thinking, the monarch could be deposed. Even more important were his federalist ideas and his principle of subsidiarity, which he developed in his *Politica* at the start of the 17th century. Here, he described a political society as a union of various human groupings – the family, the local community, the province, and the state – that is established by a number of social contracts which, together, result in the formation of a voluntary and federal association in which the individual groupings retain their freedom and independence.

Interestingly, Althusius' legal philosophy, half-forgotten for centuries, was rediscovered in the early 20th century by the German jurist and historian Otto von Gierke...

... who came from Szczecin. And now Althusius' principle of subsidiarity is a common reference point for many experts on European law. Keeping to the point of our discussion, all of this means that the Bohemian Revolt reflected the general *zeitgeist* and the monumental social and political changes that were afoot at the time, offering a foretaste of the modern European identity that was to come. This was far from just a feud between the Habsburgs and the Bohemian nobility on which we could project all other antinomies, among them authoritarianism, freedom, the Holy Roman Empire of the German Nation represented by the House of Habsburg, and the Kingdom of Bohemia represented by the estates. In reality, the dispute between the Emperor and the Bohemian estates on political power, and on the state form it was to take, had escalated and become radicalised, although the estate-organised opposition was still relatively disparate in the early days of the uprising. What's more, the religious conflict over the demolition and closure of Protestant churches was likely a pretext to hold a session of the provincial diet – banned by the emperor – in 1618. Their true aims, then, were probably to give the Bohemian chancellor more power and to introduce censorship. What with the nebulous political concept of the entire rebellion, the lack of external support, notably from the Moravian provincial diet, the fact that directorate members were enriching themselves with Rudolf II's confiscated treasure, and the generally wretched diplomatic inability to negotiate and draw up pacts of allegiance, the Bohemian estates found themselves backed into a corner from the start. Although, in July 1619, the estates' general diet (*Generallandtag*) approved a provincial act of confederation which, following the Dutch example, guaranteed mutual equality for all Lands of the Bohemian Crown and ascribed the elected monarch a representative role with no opportunity to establish dynastic rule, Rudolf II's Letter of Majesty (1609) remained the main formal source of law on religious life in the country, and the protection of the faith was overseen by thirty "defenders", though some offices were reserved solely for Protestants. The Bohemian Confederation required Ferdinand II's unseating from the Bohemian royal throne. However, the estates found themselves unable to group around a clear choice of new king until, ultimately, the Calvinists prevailed over the Lutheran estates in their push for Frederick V of the Palatinate. In the meantime, Emperor Ferdinand II had been consolidating his power and formed an alliance with the leader of the Catholic League, Maximilian I, Elector of Bavaria, whose troops joined forces with the imperial army to march on Prague. On 8 November 1620, they crushed the estates' army at the Battle of White Mountain. The fallout for the Czech Lands was brutal: the scrapping of the Letter of Majesty, the execution of 27 Bohemian lords on 21 June 1621, the uncompromising re-Catholicisation of the country, and the introduction of absolute Habsburg power even while the Thirty Years' War was still raging.

On the upside, Prague still has a memorable Baroque aspect to it, the landscape was cultivated, the school system was redeveloped, the Jesuit college became a university... the list goes on. What makes the development of statehood here different from developments across Western Europe at the time?

Turmoil, violence, war and disruption were rife all over Europe. We could contrast the Habsburgs' recognition of the Dutch Republic as part of the Peace of Westphalia with the resounding defeat and loss of autonomy of the Czech Lands. To this day, the post-White-Mountain period is the subject of historical disputes and ideological clashes. Confiscations and re-Catholicisation repainted contemporary society entirely, subordinating it politically and culturally to the centre of the Habsburgs' absolute power in Vienna. This was a time of widespread decline that was not limited to Czech statehood. Even so, it should be noted that Habsburg absolutism was the logical outcome of the religious disputes, and we would find similar tendencies were we to delve into the English Revolution, although that turned out to be a lot more successful compared to the Habsburg monarchy. The Glorious Revolution and the establishment of the constitutional monarchy of William III, Prince of Orange, in 1688, which explicitly subscribed to the *Magna Carta* and resulted not only in the reinforcement of the rule of law and parliamentary sovereignty, but also – and more importantly – in the laying of foundations for the relatively free society on which, in the 18th century, the British Empire was built, enabling science to flourish while facilitating a competitive political system with a modern cabinet system of government, and even, further down the line, paving the way for the Industrial Revolution and the modernisation of British society. There was none of this in Habsburg-controlled Central Europe. So we have to go all the way back to the 17th century if we want to identify why, for example, so many Enlightenment philosophers – from Voltaire to Rousseau – sought exile in Britain in the following centuries. Voltaire's *Letters on the English* from the 1730s remains the archetypal fusion of respect and admiration for a society that, while European, is different from other European nations in so many respects and, at the same time, serves as a role model and vehicle to criticise the situation at home.

But even England, prior to the 1688 Glorious Revolution, fell prey to a harsh civil war bristling with political hatred and religious fanaticism.
Which gave rise not only to political revolution, but also to Hobbes' *Leviathan*, which stands alongside Machiavelli's *The Prince* as a fundamental work of modern political philosophy that is free of theology and ethics and that views politics as the exercise of sovereign power to the benefit of the entire political community. These days we regard both works as treatises moulding key political themes, schemes, ideas and concepts, which is why people in many quarters may legitimately dismiss them as classically "pure", or "clean", works obscuring the "squalid", or "dirty", reality we discussed at the beginning. However, this backdrop makes us realise that even *Leviathan* was originally written by Hobbes as an immediate response to the religious conflicts of the English Reformation, and to profound political schisms, revolution and civil war. At the time, dignitaries and ideologists believed that these ideas were so incendiary that they branded the author an atheist, an accusation which posed a direct danger to Hobbes' life. In truth, *Leviathan* is also proof of how history purges itself and eventually reshapes originally unacceptable ideas to incorporate them into its own canon. It is important to note that this is not a treatise celebrating the absolute power of a sovereign monarch, but mainly a work in which the sovereign must ensure safety and guarantee political unity through the power of a general statute. It is here that – in response to the conflict between

Catholics and Protestants in England and on the Continent, and re-acting to the associated unconcealed hatred and political violence – the idea of a modern state as a power that must curb ideological wrangling, but remain neutral in doing so, is formed. Legality guarantees the social contract between the sovereign, who is responsible for civil order, and his subjects, who are required to show obedience to him. We should probably emphasise here that, unlike Jean Bodin, who believes that the sovereign is entitled to issue statutes regardless of whether they are endorsed by those who must obey him, Thomas Hobbes bases society and its political order, including sovereign power, on the need for the mutual approval and consensus of those who create it. It is their manifestation of will that forms the social contract, and this provides a basic framework for modern reflections on a free and democratic society. According to Hobbes, our rational capacities are in the service of our passions, so in our natural state we pursue our own interests, thereby endangering one another's lives. Politics is then based on the principle of the mutual coordination of human behaviour, which protects human lives. The purpose of a rationally concluded social contract is to devise a political order that will protect human lives.

How would you then define the "political sovereignty" we often hear cited these days?
First and foremost, political sovereignty is the ability to influence irrational life in society by employing rational reasons, in the same way as individuals use reason in their personal lives to advance their own interests. This is a revolutionary idea because it means that politics is no longer determined by the theology of good nor the cynical imposition of will through brute force or subterfuge, but by a social contract that relies on the power of the persuasiveness of a rational argument, on mutual recognition, and on general consensus. As such, Hobbes' *Leviathan* is not a defence of absolute power in the ilk of Jean Bodin, but the first ever work in which the monarch's sov-

ereign power is shaped by the political order, which is required to serve the entire community, the *civitas*. Anyone looking for the roots of modern civil society will find them in Hobbes. If we are to retrace our steps and see how this brief excursion into the period's political philosophy fits into the historical context of Czech statehood, it must be said that, in the second half of the 17th century, the Austrian Habsburgs drew a lot more inspiration from Bodin than from Hobbes' *Leviathan* and its respect for social interests and the political order of the *civitas*. This explains why the Czech Lands became a country producing exiles rather than a place where, in subsequent centuries, people would seek refuge and safety. As we know, around 1,000 free families and their servants left Bohemia and went into exile following Ferdinand's imposition of the Renewed Constitution (*Verneuerte Landesordnung*) in 1627, which curtailed the estates' rights, introduced absolutism with central power in Vienna, encouraging the growing prevalence of German as the official language, proclaimed the Czech crown hereditary and made Catholicism the only permitted church. Consequently, for example, to this day we can still take ourselves off to England to admire the artwork of the Prague native Wenceslaus Hollar, who – it would be no exaggeration to say – was an extraordinary and exceptional artist of towering influence and European reach within his own lifetime.

He was proud of his origins, signing himself as Wenceslaus Hollar Bohemus.
And then there's the work of Comenius, another example of philosophy and thought in exile, a situation which will be repeated many times yet in modern Europe.

For sure, Czech statehood had been weakened, but do you think we could go so far as to say that this was a "dark age"?
Of course we need to avoid gaudy simplifications claiming that the period after White Mountain was nothing but an age of "darkness"

in the Czech Lands. Nevertheless, the criticism levelled by both Palacký and Masaryk is legitimate when we consider the decline in statehood and the autonomy enjoyed by the then Czech Lands. The thing is, the Renewed Constitution also brought about change, for example, to the effect that provincial officials could only be appointed by the monarch, to whom they were also subordinate. Although the provincial estates could still levy and collect taxes, in the monarchy's economic and legal life there was a gradual transition to centralisation and bureaucratisation. This is evidenced by the fact that the Renewed Constitution replaced oral proceedings with written proceedings, which obviously went a long way to formalising the legal and administrative process. It is also worth remembering that the "darkness" cannot be trivialised from a revivalist perspective, as borne out by the personal story and work of one of the foremost 17th-century Czech thinkers, the "Jesuit" and "patriot" Bohuslav Balbín. Furthermore, as you pointed out, a quick glance at the Baroque architecture, art and Bohemian landscape reveals that, even in the Czech Lands, modern industry was shaped and culture flourished in the 18th century to such an extent that, to this day, other Europeans come to the Czech Lands to drink it in. Without it, Prague would lose its "magic". What would Czech painting look like had there been no Škréta or Brandl, or sculptures and carvings had there been no Brokoffs? And the architecture of Lurago and Santini also represents the pinnacle of European Baroque art. For that matter, the national revival would be inconceivable without Balbín's defence of the Czech language and Czech erudition! As Zdeněk Kalista pointed out, were it not for Baroque poetry, the work of Karel Hynek Mácha would be unthinkable. In this context, I think it is great how the churches, for example, recently approached this period of history. In response to Cardinal Duka's original thoughts about the possibility of re-erecting the Marian column on the Old Town Square, representatives of the Protestant churches were dismissive, but also took the opportunity to suggest that they work together to explore the theme of the entire 17th century, i.e. the post-White-Mountain period, which is when the original version of this monument – destroyed during the "building of the state" in 1918 – was created.

I would just chime in here to draw attention to a contradiction. Despite what they say, the Marian column did not just symbolise Catholicism and the Blessed Virgin Mary, to whom people would turn in times of peril and war. Ferdinand III erected it in 1650 in thanks for the defence of Prague against the Swedes and to commemorate the end of the Thirty Years' War. Isn't that a paradox?
It is, but everyone realised that there needed to be an end to entrenched stereotypes about the age of "darkness", which continues to aggravate social and political discourse today. In this respect, Czech Catholics and Protestants are paradoxically keen to demythologise historical debate about this period of religious wars, violence, confiscation and exile, which often elicits bitter reactions and passions in secularised Czech society even now. They can rely on the support of historians who are averse to all of those contemporary myths that refused to die, such as the myth about the last Moravian, which made its way into a song by Karel Kryl and tells the story of the gallant members of a Moravian regiment who fought and fell to the last man at the Hvězda summer palace. The plain truth of the matter is that these were mercenaries from every corner of Europe, so we can be sure that they did not all sacrifice their lives in battle. In fact, their commander, Heinrich von Schlick, switched sides once the battle was lost and carved out a great career for himself in the service of the emperor. We need to disabuse ourselves for good of those revivalist stereotypes and myths claiming that the Battle of White Mountain tarnished the Czech political lustre, and that the Czech nation and its language were subsequently suppressed when German supremacy took hold. Václav Beneš Třebízský wrote about this. Similarly, Alois Jirásek described a period of "darkness". And it is truly intriguing that this black-and-white view of the Battle of

White Mountain and the events that followed have stuck in the nation's collective memory right up to the present. Incidentally, that ecumenical commission for 17th-century history in the Czech Lands could draw on experience gained in the past by a similar commission on the work, figure and legacy of Jan Hus, which was set up in the first half of the 1990s by Cardinal Miloslav Vlk on a recommendation from Pope John Paul II. People called that commission a "laboratory of ecumenism", but it was by no means limited to the relationship between the different churches in Czech society. It went a long way to changing our view of Jan Hus without anyone casting doubt on this figure's central significance to our history. A recent television programme on the life of Jan Hus to commemorate the 600th anniversary of his burning at the stake was also consistent with that general social and cultural transformation and, in its civility, it was a radical departure from the bellicose and marshalling Hus invented by the film director Otakar Vávra and the novelist Alois Jirásek. I am confident that a discussion on the "dark age" could be just as liberating for our modern national myths and the black-and-white view of our own history.

Let's revisit that term "statehood", around which our dialogue is constantly revolving, and try to define it. According to Otto's Encyclopaedia, the state is a permanent (organic) union of people dwelling in a particular territory with one will and one power. And that will is effectively statehood. Today's encyclopaedias tell us that it is a complex of institutions, ideas, and values holding sway in a defined territory. Isaac Deutscher, for his part, said that statehood was the gravitation of citizens to the state as to their own. If my memory serves me right, you define statehood differently.

In the first place, I refuse to view society, the political community or the nation as an "organism". You see, the biological metaphors that were so popular in the 19th century among the Romantics and, later, among sociologists, political scientists and anthropologists, not only resulted in lots of misconceptions, but also spawned no end of evil, including notions of racial supremacy or the individual as a tiny part of the total social organism, in which he simply plays a predetermined role. Furthermore, organic metaphors give this misguided impression that society behaves like a biological formation whose primary endeavour is to preserve its own existence and growth in the face of opposition from other "organisms", i.e. nations and states. As we now know, neither the state nor the nation is anything "natural" or" organic", carving out a place for itself in the world according to biological laws. Rather, these are artificially created formations with a historical origin, symbolic logic and pragmatic purpose, as we can see, for instance, in the political philosophy Hobbes formulated in the second half of the 17th century. Nevertheless, what is interesting about the definitions you have provided is that they actually describe what Jean Bodin was contending all those years ago, i.e. that the state is formed where the population in a certain territory is subject to a single sovereign power. That definition of the state kept going right up to the 20th century, when the sociologist Max Weber, in his famous lecture *Politics as a Vocation*, delivered in that watershed year of 1918, defined the state as a human community that (successfully) claims a monopoly over the legitimate use of force in a given territory. So this is one of numerous forms of social power that is taking root in political institutions and, in order to be treated as legitimate, is grounded in their functionality and core values. Statehood is inconceivable without legitimacy. That, paradoxically, lies in effectiveness, which can be measured or even quantified, and in values, which are absolute, and hence cannot be relativised, but only prioritised or – conversely – inhibited. There is a profound truth to Masaryk's sentence that states keep to the ideals from which they were born. On the other hand, the state does not stand and fall solely with ideals. It relies primarily on the ability to organise the political life of the population in a specific territory into a single community so that the people will trust its institutions and accept its decisions.

On the other hand, trust and the recognition of a particular power are never unconditional, unlike the claims of a state's sovereign power to its own monopoly. In this respect, looking beyond political organisation and the general governance of society, statehood also encompasses much more complex problems of citizens' allegiance to their state and, ultimately, whether citizens identify themselves with their own state, which is an unqualified condition for the legitimacy of any democratic state. One of the essential characteristics of modern society is the nation's ability to forge this strong bond with the state organisation. As such, the modern state has unquestionably always had a propensity to be constituted as a nation state.

Perhaps we ought to touch on Czech Statehood Day, which is held on 28 September, the day on which Boleslav slew his brother Wenceslas in 935. Czechs have been celebrating this date since the 13th century. What makes this celebration paradoxical is that St Wenceslas didn't want the state, hence he had to be assassinated so that the state could come into being.

That is precisely what I am thinking of: from the perspective of structural anthropology, the beginnings of the state are the same as the first steps of a religion, including fratricide, or a law that is fundamentally steeped in crime and guilt, or order established by those who triggered the anarchy in the first place. In this context, Wenceslas' story takes on a hue that is nothing short of mythological, and the contradiction of politics and religion is this dramatic Old Testament story in which the people of Israel call on Samuel to anoint a king rather than appoint the traditional judges because they want to be like all the other nations and have worldly power over them to judge their disputes and guarantee their safety. The Lord responds with those famous words – recorded in the *First Book of Samuel* – complaining to Samuel about the Israelites: "Hearken unto the voice of the people in all that they say unto thee: for they have not rejected thee, but they have rejected me, that I should not reign over them. According to all the works which they have done since the day that I brought them up out of Egypt even unto this day, wherewith they have forsaken me, and served other gods, so do they also unto thee. Now therefore hearken unto their voice: howbeit yet protest solemnly unto them, and shew them the manner of the king that shall reign over them." These are fantastic verses in which God bemoans the fact that those of little faith have abandoned Him, so, rather than making a very specific pact with them, He chooses to follow a path common among other nations, i.e. to organise His own community within a framework of temporal power and that worldly power's laws. Sociologically speaking, this is an example of the functional differentiation between politics and theology, to which more and more nations and generations subsequently aspired in many different ways that encompassed diplomacy, peace talks, bloodshed and fratricide. This included Boleslav's fratricide and Wenceslas' canonisation. There is also a story from the Talmud that documents this split between divine and human law. The rabbis were locked in dispute and were unable to reach agreement, so Rabbi Eliezer, whose finely and elegantly argued and substantiated legal opinion had been rejected by most of the other rabbis, proclaimed that, if he was right, a tree in the garden would move by a yard or two in proof. Though the tree really did move, the other rabbis did not find this convincing in the slightest. Eliezer then said that the river would flow backwards and the walls of the synagogue would bend. But not even these miracles were enough to persuade the rabbis. Finally, Eliezer turned to the heavens for confirmation that his arguments were correct and, indeed, a heavenly voice declared this. The other rabbis, however, simply shook their heads in disagreement and said: "We take no notice of heavenly voices, since You have already, at Sinai, written in the Torah to follow the majority." And according to this Talmudic story, God started laughing and, amused, kept repeating: "My children have triumphed over Me, my children have triumphed over Me." I would say that the most important part of this whole story is the divine laughter because, among other things, it conveys the ridiculousness of all human attempts to divinise any worldly power and to create a cult out of the state, a nation or any other human product. However, it is also notable how the rabbis are unshakeable in clinging to the belief that worldly matters must be resolved with worldly power, and not by alluding to divine power and will. If national communities, too, have some sort of underlying existential condition, it must be the same sort of light and unrestrained laughter, rather than deathly gravity associated with destiny and bonds forged in fratricide and other crimes.

The Nation,
Culture and History

At the end of the last chapter, you touched on laughter in human culture and religion. This is also a core theme, for example, in the thinking of Milan Kundera, who, in his famous speech in Jerusalem in 1985, said: "No peace is possible between the novelist and the agélaste. Never having heard God's laughter, the agélastes are convinced that the truth is obvious, that all men necessarily think the same thing, and that they themselves are exactly what they think they are. But it is precisely in losing the certainty of truth and the unanimous agreement of others that man becomes an individual..."

Kundera showed that philosophising with literature packs a much bigger wallop than philosophising with a hammer. Unlike many philosophers, he captured precisely the essence of Nietzsche's philosophy and what remains of it in a time when the written culture of the shared word is retreating increasingly and ever faster in the face of the narcissistic culture of digital imagery, symbolised by the selfie, where the main moral mandate has become such a need for permanent exposure and publicity that nothing is kept secret from anyone. Orwell's Big Brother is redundant when we can get the job done ourselves as ever-present little brothers. Kundera picked up on this ubiquitous totalitarianism in modern culture perfectly without describing it in ideological or political schemes. Where the internet and visual media accelerate and inflict ideas alone, literature can slow us down and keep our thinking afloat. In the slow-motion pace of the novel, a world reliant on the constantly spiralling consumption of instant ideas is shown to be an absurdity that takes itself deadly seriously. Kundera preserved the novel as a purely modern literary form, developing in it the original philosophy of comicality as the baseline of a world that imputes to itself absolute seriousness. This is why, even more than allusions to the philosophy espoused by Epicurus or Nietzsche, I prefer Kundera's interpretations of Rabelais, Cervantes and Stern as authors who give full rein to this novelistic function of interpreting the comicality of the world and human existence. We want to bring order and organisation into everything and yet are deaf to God's laughter reminding us that the playful sentence written on the postcard in *The Joke* can have tragically serious consequences, and that deadly serious ideas and ideals may result in the grotesque demise of those who fight for them. This applies to any ideal, principle or value, whether national or cosmopolitan. In this respect, there is another important characteristic that links Kundera to Nietzsche: resistance to any culture of deification. Nietzsche originally tried to fight off cults of deification by insisting on the antinomy between the Apollonian and Dionysian principle, before ultimately arriving at the literary character of Zarathustra, who finds every exercise in deification nothing short of ludicrous. A century later, Kundera drew on Nietzsche's observations about the weight and lightness of being to write a novel that, in form and substance, points out the absurdity of all definitive answers to questions of human existence.

That is Kundera's big theme not only in *The Unbearable Lightness of Being*, but also – and mainly – in his most recent novel, *The Festival of Insignificance*. Indeed, in his *Immortality*, too, we can read that: "the border between the important and the unimportant ... has become unrecognisable... If all of time turns into child's play, one day the world will die to the sound of all our childish prattle and laughter."

Kundera picks up on Nietzsche's loathing of all the "isms" which consume the modern age and which it harnesses in its efforts to lend itself gravitas, historical uniqueness and civilisational exclusivity. Without contrasting particularly national and universally human culture or sinking into other contradictions of modernity, he reminds us that this modernity always relies on overlaps and lies in the ability of general cultural forms and literary genres to transform themselves, historically and locally, and to bedeck themselves in all sorts of ideas and inspiration in precisely the way this has been demonstrated by the history of the novel. What makes Kundera's novels so self-referential is the way they deal with their own form and history, while acting as metaphors of modernity itself. In this sense, Kundera's work is completely original, and therefore it is hardly surprising that, for example, the American philosopher Richard Rorty interpreted his novels as distinctive philosophical texts, in which the logos lay in ironic judgement and the ethos in favouring literature, with its inwardly free expression, over philosophy, with its need to create external rules of human behaviour. I would say that, though this interpretation is misguided because irony in Kundera's work is much more about how to survive our existence than a philosophical sort of judgement, this does nothing to alter the fact that Milan Kundera's work is neither the product of a purely national culture, nor part of any universal cultural canon. Since it can make do quite happily without any these simplifying and despoiling categories of the modern age, I wouldn't hesitate to describe it, in the truest sense, as post-modern and post-national. It is a distinct literary form of thought, reason and culture at a time when quite a few people are casting doubt even on these core categories of our modern heritage.

Kundera's underlying cultural message could also be articulated as this: when the significant sinks into insignificance, we must stay cheerful.

But, I would note, no society can exist without culture. No matter whether we're talking about national or any other societies. Culture can get by without nations, but a nation cannot exist without culture. Likewise, if there is no culture, there can be no nation state. I am not thinking so much of the anthropological rule saying that culture unifies and creates the homogeneous landscape of modern society, as the philosophical tension between culture, which is always concrete, and the organisation of the modern world and society, which is general and simplified and belongs to a system where we apply rules of conduct. Here, Kundera agrees with Philip Roth, who places the words "literature disturbs the organisation" in the mouth of one of the characters in his novel *I Married a Communist*.

Certainly, Kundera demonstrated this vividly at the turn of the 1960s, when he wrote his short story *I, Mournful God*, the play *The Owner of the Keys* and the essay *The Art of the Novel*. For me, Kundera was something of a revelation. He was absolutely gutsy, completely different from the others. He lectured on more offbeat authors and he would come up with this entirely fresh context. He was simply exceptional. As his wife Věra says, he grew up "under two pianos". This cultural family environment, as well as his inclination towards French literature, Diderot and the Enlightenment, structured his personality in such a way that, in his literature, he defied the Czech narrative tradition and created his own poetics based on the roman à thèse.

Literature is always specific, which means the testimony it provides us with cannot be simplified or adapted to the rules of generalisation that govern how ideologies work. Literature is culture's revolt against sociology, the uprising of personal experience against impersonal data. Ideologists love heavy books and light solutions. Culture, on the other hand, exists where the complexity of the world becomes bearable thanks to the lightness of the word, image or melody. This contradiction of culture as a shared sense of specific experiences and society as an organisation revolving around general rules is something that, in itself, is a peculiarity of the modern world, inhabited as it is both by individuals laying claim to personal autonomy and by nations asserting political self-determination. I like the observation by the writer GK Chesterton, a devout Christian, that the world is full of Christian virtues gone mad. The same can be said of the national revival and emancipation. The modern world is full of these ideas of national liberation and self-determination that are going mad day in, day out. Culture is both a defensive and an offensive weapon because it can be brandished to inflict ethnic cleansing and yet also serve as the last resort in staving off such purges. Culture, as we know from anthropology, structures our collective understanding and related experience of the world. Whilst sociology all too often reduces social problems to inequalities in income, power and knowledge, anthropology reminds us of the cultural dimension of these issues and the prejudices with which modern humankind approaches them. It escapes sociology that social reality is conditioned by the non-contemporaneity of contemporaries, and that its presence is determined by what the sociologist and phenomenologist Alfred Schutz once called the "world of predecessors" and the "world of successors". Ultimately, then, culture is a sense of this temporal continuity in society, and such awareness confers the ontological status of inevitability, constancy and naturalness on the arbitrary.

Okay, let's turn our attention to this sense of temporal continuity. In the 19th century, when the modern Czech nation was forming, we developed from what was originally an agrarian and plebeian community into a relatively self-confident society in the space of just under a hundred years. As early as 1882, the university split into Czech and German branches, in 1883 the first Czech scientific journal, Athenaeum, was founded, we gained a majority in the Czech parliament, the Czech language was accorded rights equal to those enjoyed by German, and so on. But this concentration on language also poses certain dangers. How would you define them? The national programme, as a programme encompassing language and literature, and the struggle to rescue the language and defend it against the trend of central denationalisation and the centrifugal tendency towards the fragmentation of dialects are strategies rife in Romantic Europe. Grammar becomes the first political weapon! Obviously, this concept is dangerous because it singles out all those who do not speak the language as "back-stabbers" and "foreigners" whom we cannot understand or simply refuse to understand. Instead of Enlightenment understanding, we risk being plunged into darkness by the Romantic obsession with languages, customs, traditions and historical myths or legends. Of course, with the hindsight of two centuries and all of the Czech nation's historical experience garnered in that time, Kollár's Slavic messianism is now objectionable. Which makes Palacký's elaboration of the national question, in which he also defined it as a constitutional and territorial matter, all the more important. Palacký's concept of national history was also a concept of the Czech nation's historical place in universal human history. The Czech question was a social and humanitarian issue long before Masaryk. There were historical and social reasons for the emphasis on the defence and purity of the language because, unlike the Poles or the Hungarians, the Czechs did not have an extensive bourgeoisie or higher and lower nobility. Consequently, all learning stood or fell on the ability to keep the tongue going and to build it from below through literature – mostly poetry, theatre, music, and Czech-written scientific treatises.

So we could say that the cultural and linguistic concept of the Czech nation was part of the intellectual climate of Romantic nationalism as it evolved in Europe during the 19th century. At the same time, it was a consequence of the rapid industrial advancement that prompted swathes of the population to migrate from the countryside to the city. All that these people possessed, and all that they brought with them from their rural communities to the often German-speaking towns, was their Czech language.

Nationalism is a purely modern societal phenomenon where a group which has been labelled and which designates itself as a nation seeks various forms of social and political self-determination. That is why national identity is automatically associated with the state, which in the modern era becomes the nation state we saw Italians and Greeks clamouring for just as much as the Germans and Czechs. And let's not forget that, by this time, powerful imperial states – the likes of France, Spain, and Great Britain – had existed on the European continent for centuries. Then, all of a sudden, you get these national movements beginning to form in that same space, and not only do they aspire to create their own state, but they are also bent on playing a role that, in its importance, places them on a par with the imperial powers. German nationalism is a classic case. It was the German nationalist historian Friedrich Meinecke who, at the beginning of the 20th century, came up with the division into cultural and political nations that you mentioned. It's worth recalling that Meinecke seems to embody the paradoxes and tragedies of modern German history. On the one hand, he's this nationalist, anti-Semitic critic of liberalism, but on the other he lambastes the Nazi government and views Nazism as a foreign regime "occupying Germany". After the war, he helped to found the Free University in West Berlin and was a prominent academic figure behind the renewal of German society. Even before the First World War, Meinecke divided nations into those whose identity was dictated primarily by cultural heritage, encompassing language, literature, cultural traditions and religion, and those whose common identity was defined by political history and constitutional architecture. Today, we tend to talk about the difference between *ethnos* and *demos*, i.e. the ethnic and political concept of the nation, and yet we can see how the two categories complement each other and overlap. Take Switzerland, for instance, a country in which diverse and deep-rooted cultural identities create an equally deep-seated concept of a political nation. By contrast, the sharing of a common cultural heritage is no barrier to the emergence of different political nations – witness the historical example of the American War of Independence and, closer to home, today's clear distinction between Austrian and German political identity, even though, as recently as the 1930s, it was the absence of political national identity which resulted in that Austrian political tragedy where millions of people welcomed Hitler as a liberator who would annexe the Austrian Lands to the greater Third Reich.

But the state is older than the nation, so in the UK, for example, there is not much to distinguish nationality in the sense of ethnicity from nationality in the sense of citizenship.

Yes, the state is older than the nation, as we can see from European history, but it is interesting that, even in those countries where – unlike France – there was no revolution to shape a new political nation, let's say the United Kingdom, a political culture was gradually moulded in which the increasingly democratised society began, over time, to view itself as a political people, as a peculiar national form known as the "British people", despite their many cultural, linguistic and religious differences. Not a people with a capital P, but people creating a political community, that "commonwealth" embracing all sorts of culturally diverse nations – the English, the Scots, the Welsh, and those once ruled by the British Empire. In this respect, nations can just as equally be split into "old" and "young", by which I mean some are born out of revolution and political resistance, while others have fostered their modern identity through long years of political history and shared experience, until they reach a point where they start to refer to and see themselves as a single national unit. What makes the case of the UK interesting, however, is how multivalent that word "nation" is. It defines much more than a cultural or political grouping. Since the beginning of the modern age, it has related to economic and class divisions, too. For example, Disraeli, an eccentric man who would go on to become prime minister, was rightly incensed by the fact that there were actually two nations inhabiting Britain at that time: the poor and the rich. We must never lose sight of the ambiguity of the term "nation" when we talk about national identity, the nation state or nationalism as a modern political movement.

A moment ago, you said that no community can exist without culture. But what is this "culture" actually? How would you define it?
It would be unable to exist, as borne out by the history of the nations we refer to as political. If a certain community of people lives in a shared territory where it is subordinate to a sovereign power, it will necessarily form, over time, its own patterns of behaviour, system of morals, customs, skills and general practices that we could collectively call "culture". I like the definition of culture as all those things we don't even know that we know. Culture is everything that we perceive to be natural even though we must have learnt it from someone, somewhere, at some stage, and that we share both with our contemporaries and our predecessors. If we look at that "old" English nation, it may well have been formed earlier than many other nations, but this was a gradual process that encountered important political and cultural events and the conflicts of the Elizabethan age. The cultural roots of present-day English identity can be traced back to two decisive acts from the early 17th century, namely the publication of the King James – or Authorised – Version of the Bible in 1611, and the First Folio of Shakespeare's plays from 1623. The English Reformation stands and falls by this translation of the Bible, while Shakespeare's plays are one of the central planks of the Elizabethan Renaissance. At the same time, they established standardised English, and a standardised language is a prerequisite for the functioning of any nation state. All national societies need a smidgen of linguistic and cultural homogeneity. The Britain we know today, then, has cultural roots in a four-hundred-year-old era and society that people in the present would not understand and in which they would feel absolutely alienated.

And could we say that culture is what establishes nations and their states?
I dare say that politics nurtures culture just as much as politics is swayed by culture. Montesquieu, in his magnum opus *The Spirit of*

the Laws, described how government and laws are always influenced by culture, the climate and other externalities, so they cannot be examined in isolation. In other words, anyone who wants to make sense of politics must also understand the general morals and culture of the nation in question. That is not to say that government or laws, and politics in general, are merely a plaything of the prevailing cultural stereotypes and prejudices. The relationship between culture and politics is not a relationship of inferiority and supremacy, as the Romantics believed when they placed the heroism of the spirit above everyday political and civic activity. This is a complementary relationship, as illustrated by the post-war division of both Germany and Korea. If you divide a single cultural nation politically for several decades, you will arrive at a point where, despite the shared history and language, two culturally diverse societies have effectively emerged. And it is fascinating, three decades after the fall of the Berlin Wall, to see that there are still differences between the inhabitants of the former East and West Germanies! It is evident in election results and in the way people dress or talk to each other on the street.

But, in our civilisation, we always imagine a state in modern times to be a democratic state, or am I mistaken?
Definitely. And that's also why nationalism, in addition to the categories of nation and state, always accepted democracy, one way or another, as the prevailing form of governance in the 19th century and was originally coloured by strong elements of individual and collective liberalism, according to which a nation is free only when it governs itself. That is why the French historian Ernest Renan's definition of a nation, according to which "the existence of a nation is a daily referendum", still holds true. But let's return to the division of nations into cultural and political, because it is here that we can trace the causes of the political tragedy plaguing all modern nationalisms. The cultural definition of a nation presupposes a common

heritage, which is also typically the legacy of *Blut und Boden*, blood and soil. The metaphor of the "national spirit" can then be seen as something that not only connects the nation, but also panders to a *raison d'être* involving some sort of unique historical or civilising mission. Besides the notion of state, the nation therefore requires "higher" metaphysical justification...

... and so, in modern history, we bear witness to the most diverse philosophies of nation and national history.
... in which the unique spirit of a particular nation, the bearer of ideas and ideals, preferably of all humanity, is supposedly observed. With German nationalism, this was literally an obsession. German nationalists were often also supporters of cosmopolitanism and humanism, but this did not prevent them from viewing other nations belligerently, if not downright disparagingly, as "inferior breeds". An eloquent example of this is Hegel's philosophy of history, according to which the universal spirit – politically embodied by the state – is actualised in national history. The specific will of political leaders and national history thus contribute, together, to rationality in their own history, culminating in the creation of an organised state. Hegel claims that this is always more civilised than civil society or a common market. This explains why German intellectuals cultivated their nationalism in opposition to all the "low" manifestations of the human spirit, such as trade or the capitalist mode of production, and admired "high" cultural ideals and the sacrifices that humankind is able to make as offerings to them. It is no coincidence that one of German nationalism's main treatises from the beginning of the First World War is called *Merchants and Heroes*, subtitled *Patriotic Reflections*. The author, the famous German sociologist and economist Werner Sombart, contrasts the English mercantile spirit with German heroism and national spirit, which does not content itself with low "civilisation" because it has the historic task of winning the world war – a cultural war between the cap-

italist *Weltanschauung* of the English and the heroic struggle of the German nation, which embodies the higher culture of authentic humanity and humanism. For Sombart and others, the First World War was a collision of world views and a reincarnation of the religious wars, since it ostensibly pitted against each other two different sets of beliefs and persuasions about the meaning of human existence. The German nation's historic task in this military conflict was to promote a culture of heroism, which was meant to crush the lowly culture of Anglo-Saxon capitalism, rife with hedonism, bean counting and decadence. It is interesting how, today, this fraught cultural chauvinism is drifting towards multinational clusters, so quite a few people, say, view the European Union as an organisation designed to protect the more advanced Europeans against primitive American capitalism or against hordes of immigrants from lower civilisations.

Even Putin's Russia portrays itself as the last state to defend traditional Christian values in the face of Western decadence. How old is this figure of speech?
Terms such as "culture war" or "clash of civilisations" are inextricably linked to modern nationalism and the formation of nation states. Sombart simply exploited this label, which is historically bound up primarily with the modern relationship between France and Germany and all the cultural ties, intellectual tensions and devastating wars between these two countries in modern European history. German history, as the influential German sociologist Wolf Lepenies notes, is the history of the transformation of a cultural nation into Bismarck's cultural state, inhabited not by individual active citizens, but by culturally close vassals of an authoritarian state. According to Lepenies, the Germans like to talk about higher culture and contrast it with lesser "civilisation", considering themselves a cultural people, *Kulturvolk*, whose special path, the *Sonderweg*, is to cultivate other nations and all of humankind. That is why German identity is said to include the paradox that "simply being German is

not German enough" because it is the Germans' historical destiny to cultivate other nations in the name of universal humanity, the standard-bearer of which is Germanness. In the wars with France, a fledgling German state was formed in which the political leaders and mere mortals alike viewed culture as an absolute value brooking no compromise. Cultural unity replaced democratic politics built on public debate and social conflict because cultural ideals and absolutes cannot be put to the vote! The German spirit is intolerant of both the liberal values rooted in English civil society and the bureaucratic mindset of the French state. Not to mention the culturally "foreign" Jewish element that was trying to assimilate socially and culturally. In fact, it is somewhere hereabouts that we need to be digging for the root causes of German anti-Semitism! In modern Germany, it is culture that dictates to the market and the state how they ought to function and what they need to conform to. For the French, the Germans were nothing more than romantic dreamers, while the Germans saw the French just as state bureaucrats. In this context, Julien Benda once remarked that the Prussian struggle against Napoleon's army was the first in a series of "culture wars". We could add that engaging in mobilisation through culture remains a major political risk today, despite the terrifying experiences of the last century, when culture became just another word for genocide and Nazi officers' fingers would glide over the piano keys as they played Beethoven before gripping and twisting the gas cock in Auschwitz. National mobilisation in the name of cultural ideals that have been elevated above the mediocrity of political reality is thus one of the most grievous consequences of nationalism, which was transformed from an originally liberal and democratising political movement in many countries into a fortress in which prejudices about cultural, if not racial, supremacy prevailed.

But in each country these prejudices are different due to the divergent ways in which history has developed. How does this cultural *Sonderweg* relate to politics in, say, the UK, Germany and here in the Czech Republic?

In Czech, this difference is not as glaring as in English, where "civilisation", so despised by German philosophers, is clearly linked to citizenship and civil society. When English speakers hear words such as "citizen", "civil society", "civility" and "civilisation", which, needless to say, originated in Latin and in Roman law, what instantly springs to mind is the political structuring of society, from sovereign power to local authority and the various ways in which people regulate and organise their communal lives, whether by virtue of or in the absence of such authority. This is a political form of life in the true sense of the word. On the other hand, "culture", in English, only means a set of certain morals, skills or practical activities that we cannot live without but that are of no political significance. This is why, for instance, British society, for good or bad, has always been multicultural. Contrasting with this, there has always been a strong prejudice in German society that politics is just a culturally inferior form of social life, and that culture in the true sense of the word is an anti-political higher form of the authentic being of the individual and of the nation as a whole. As Lepenies observes, German history is a history of the overestimation of culture at the expense of politics, particularly parliamentary and democratic politics. Interestingly, these misgivings about democratic culture based on the open debate of mutually equal citizens were shared by figures as politically diverse as Theodor Adorno and Arnold Gehlen. In German intellectual history, this inveterate prejudice remained intact until Jürgen Habermas came along with his philosophy of communicative rationality, which was a genuine attempt at reconciling the political with the search for the meaning of human existence in the authentic lifeworld, the *Lebenswelt*. Paradoxically, however, the spectre of German idealism still haunts Habermas's work, despite all efforts to develop concepts and arguments of analytical political and legal philosophy.

Is this supremacy of culture over politics, which we have lifted from the Germans, a topical Czech issue, too? I mean, we also continue to view culture as something loftier than politics, which we despise.

Exactly! Although the modern Czech national revival was formed to oppose Germanisation and to confront Germanness, we have fully adopted this same cultural stereotype and anti-political concept of culture as something elevated, above "dirty politics". It is as though we, too, would prefer to see ourselves as a country and nation of poets, writers and thinkers, for whom political conflicts are alien, and who are contemptuous of politics as a dull job for windbags and demagogues.

This is evidently why today's populists are confident enough to employ this language when they speak in public, and to talk about parliament as a "house of blather".

From this perspective, Masaryk achieved something that is still quite unique and almost unbelievable when, in the face of this ingrained prejudice of the politics-scorning cultural nation, he managed to sell the idea of national identity not as some special path, the *Sonderweg*, but as part of a global democratic revolution and the universal movement of modern humankind. Masaryk's change of tack was a swing away from German idealism towards the American philosophy of radical democracy espoused by John Dewey. Although Masaryk repeatedly criticised pragmatism as a philosophical trend particularly evident in the work of William James, his notions of a democratic society, his political work and his personal life resembled Dewey's concept of democracy, education and the role of intellectuals in society quite remarkably in many ways. Masaryk's revolution remains a work in progress. Its essence lies in rejecting the idea of the chosen nation and the *Sonderweg*. Set at odds with these is the understanding of democracy as modern humankind's ultimate cultural mission, where freedom and equality do not stand in opposition to the spiritual existence of the individual and the nation. Masaryk was able to assert the idea that national identity is steeped as much in cultural heritage as it is in Renan's daily referendum. This means, above all, that national identity can never be drawn solely from cultural history, but must also be built on common political will. We are connected not only by history but also – and in particular – by choice. It is fascinating how notions, illusions and phantasmata about the special designation and exclusivity of a particular nation are instantly appended to the nation, the nation state and national identity as though we were pursuing some big plan of history and our task, as Czechs, is to find our place in that plan. Nowadays, we are not just wise to where extreme interpretations of these typically Romantic ideas could lead, but we also know that national liberation and self-determination make sense only if they suppress collective exclusivity and accept a universal framework of values and culture. Of course, that framework can never be fully implemented. We know this, for example, from American history, in which the universal notion of freedom and equality spent many decades unable to effectively prevent the particular slave economy and segregation policy here. So national identity is not a given, but always and above all a struggle. Masaryk's ethic of getting small jobs done every day is also very inspirational today because it emphasises a pragmatic side not only to politics, but to culture in general. And I think, in this context, it is worth mentioning what Tocqueville took away from his stay in America: democratic societies tend to gradually reduce freedom in favour of egalitarianism. In other words, although democracy offers people the opportunity to excel and develop their individual talents, they are increasingly pressured to become the same as everyone else.

In Czech, too, we use the Germanism *Gleichschaltung* for this process.

I would say that, for today's Czech society inhabiting a democratic landscape, this *Gleichschaltung* is one of the main cultural risks that we need to stifle individually and collectively. Sometimes we hear people say that virtues have evaporated completely from present-day democratic societies. That is not entirely true. Virtues in the sense of medieval or Renaissance ethics really have disappeared from public life. However, democratic societies are pushing back against this pressure to exorcise anything different and exceptional by creating and striving to promote their own virtues, because without them they would sooner or later turn into tyrannically-controlled masses. For example, the Canadian philosopher and politician Michael Ignatieff discusses "ordinary virtues", which in his thinking are tolerance, forgiveness, trust and resilience. In his view, the members of various ethnic or religious groups need to be able to reach agreement and it is essential for them to be able to live in a single political community. Interestingly, Ignatieff grasps these virtues as specific human skills and describes them as the antithesis of the universal and abstract nature of human rights. While human rights create a general system of rules and aim to deliver justice, ordinary democratic virtues are much more fundamental because it is impossible to survive without them. This contradiction between human rights and virtues is another reason why I would formulate the rather more sanguine proposition that virtues have not completely disappeared in democracies, but, on the contrary, they have become a matter for all citizens as members of a democratic nation and individuals with inalienable rights and freedoms. When all is said and done, the very honour of democratic politics depends on this policy of civic virtues. The duty of respect for dead generations and for those who have yet to be born belongs here. What else is national identity if not this policy of virtue and respect?

How would you say that nations have changed in the 21st century, and what changes are taking place as regards nation states and their role in the newly organised Europe, where the population is becoming more and more multicultural?

It is interesting how similar all the lauding and execration of national history is to the praise and contempt of the nation state and its role in modern political history. We should avoid both extremes. However, as we know, modern-day totalitarianism originated not from the nation state, but from its failure and collapse, as eloquently illustrated by the fate of the Weimar Republic. Likewise, we must not water down our reflections on genocide and its link to state violence. *The Crisis of Genocide*, a fantastic recently published study by the historian Mark Levene, draws on the work of the Polish-British sociologist Zygmunt Bauman to analyse the nation state as a potentially dangerous force, given its constant efforts to rationalise and transform society into an increasingly homogeneous and more integrated entity, thereby also – metaphorically speaking – removing all the "scum". Unlike Bauman, though, Levene does not explain genocide and the Holocaust through this internal development of the state, where a higher degree of civilisational pressure spells greater violence and barbaric extermination. For Levene, genocide is the result of a struggle for survival and prosperity within the cruel arena of international politics.

So what is the internal mechanism of genocide?

According to Levene, it is a paradox where a sacrificial group that is completely defenceless is also considered to be powerful and dangerous by those who would destroy it. Genocide cannot therefore be explained merely as failure by the state in the face of ethnic nationalism and violence, but as a much more complex consequence of mutual relations between states and the aftermath of international conflicts. Let's not forget that the pre-war empires – and it doesn't matter whether we're talking about the Habsburg monarchy, tsarist Russia or the Ottoman Empire – found themselves having to withstand not only internal nationalist pressures, but also external pressures exerted by other imperial powers on the global political stage at that time, such as France and the UK. Genocide and ethnic cleansing took place during the Balkan Wars and the First World War within these empires, which later gave rise to states such as Turkey, the Soviet Union and even Nazi Germany. This means that the Communists and the Nazis have much more in common with imperial politics of the past than would appear at first glance. We cannot associate ethnic violence solely with the emergence of new nation states, but also with the erstwhile imperial policy and the inability to create a nation state as a democratic state. Timothy Snyder's monograph *Bloodlands* actually says outright that the policy of terror pursued by Stalin and Hitler was a consequence of the failure of the modern state, and that these forms of violence are not entirely new, but have a broader historical and cultural-political context that is by no means limited to modern nationalism. The modern nation state, then, can be neither mythicised, as nationalists are still wont to do, or demonised, as their critics often do. I think historical studies that open our eyes when we turn not only to the past, but also to the present and the future, with all the attendant intellectual and moral challenges and risks, prove that history still exists as a science but, at the same time, also holds existential significance and importance for us.

The National Revival and the Right to Self-determination

National identity cannot be extracted from cultural history, you say, but it has been that way in our country since time immemorial. The campaign for the Czech language even had two predecessors back in the Baroque, whose personalities were as bold as they were contradictory: the exiled Comenius (1592–1670) and the Jesuit Bohuslav Balbín (1621–1688).

If we want to understand the national revival, we need to grasp two different problems. The first is the metaphorical wording used when we say "revival" or "reawakening". This is premised on the mistaken – but all the more strongly entrenched – belief that nations are natural and ancient communities that can be awakened from their historical sleep like some Sleeping Beauty. Love for the nation is reckoned to have the strength of a kiss that will bring it back to life in the modern era. The second – very different – problem is about understanding the complex and mercurial loop that sees a people become a nation and a nation become a people. The cultural community formed by language and a shared past is transformed into a sovereign political power, and yet this power cannot be enforced other than as a cultural community of all the citizenry. Democracy as a form of government and the power-based vertical structuring of society presupposes a horizontal bond and emotional attachment among all the members of a nation. The distinction between *ethnos* and *demos*, i.e. between the ethnic and political concept of the nation, is just an artificial typological difference. Against that backdrop, we can see how the two categories are permeable and mutually complementary.

This is the dialectic of nationalism as a "reawakening", which, by celebrating the past, edges towards a clear agenda for the future, as we have already discussed. Let's try to deal with the revival in more detail, because sometimes I get the impression that we are

behaving in the same way as at the beginning of the national revival, by which I mean we are turning away from today's Europe rather than integrating into it. Why is that?

We live in a society that earns legitimacy by promising steady growth, rising standards of living, and better chances for all its members to improve and enhance their living conditions in the near future. In this sense, the political left and right are two sides of the same cultural coin pledging that the government of man-made political society will phase out what people have so far called "the force of destiny" by unlocking achievements and cultivating resources. Destiny is us! The motto of any democratic nation could sound something like that. Modern humankind has rallied Romantically against an unjust world and vowed to build a happy community on earth where liberty and equality are wed to fraternity. Suddenly, however, it is becoming obvious that, as the power of humankind grows, the environment we have been used to for millennia and we have Romantically admired and celebrated is evaporating. As Hannah Arendt observed, the time has come to be grateful for what is here without having been manufactured and is not a product of human will. In today's society, individuals are creatures increasingly deprived of their environment and everything that comes with it, from the landscape to cultural identity. At the same time, doctrinaires and ideologists, even here in our country, are enjoining the individual to be brotherly in the name of the nation, general humanity or a communist or any other utopia, without considering that the essence of fraternity lies in the fact that it cannot be enforced and dictated. The history of the national revival has clearly illustrated how Romantic efforts to create a community of brothers and sisters sharing a common culture, language and history have also shaped a political agenda in which the powers that be are tasked with protecting and promoting a particular culture. The Czech-English anthropologist and philosopher Ernest Gellner, in his fêted *Nations and Nationalism*, very ironically and rightly derides the notion of a "national revivalist" whose task is to awaken and give new life to a nation as dormant as the Sleeping Beauty we have mentioned. Although nationalism makes a point of presenting itself as the historical awakening of an ancient and natural collective power, in reality its emergence is a symptom, rather than the cause, of societal modernisation. Nationalism defines itself as a movement which is intended to restore natural and universally valid forms of collective life, yet ethnic and linguistic differences mean that such forms, paradoxically, can always only ever inhabit the realm of the particular. It is generally maintained that, in the modern age, national cultures become stronger and stronger to the extent that they ultimately result in the formation of a nation state. In fact, it is the other way around. National culture and identity are so muted that the only way they can assert themselves and keep afloat is to harness political power, preferably in the form of a sovereign state. Many cultures that could potentially become national cultures enter the modern age, but only some of them actually succeed; others are gradually dissolved in the broader culture of some other nation state. We need only remember the cultural and linguistic differences within Germany or Italy, or think of the Silesians and Kashubians from Gdańsk Pomerania, or the Sorbs. And if we return to that sentence by Masaryk in *The Czech Question*, that the world expects our fresh-awakened nation to deliver the "redemptive word", it is also worth quoting the sentence that follows: "If we do not voice that redemptive word to the world, it will turn away from us and we will become the bedrock of other nations." In other words, Masaryk is confirming Gellner's contention that national identities are actually weak and need political institutions and ideals if they are to persevere. It is the nations that have roused themselves – not nations that have slept through their historic wake-up call – that carve out a niche for themselves.

That includes us, the awakened awakeners of the "national revival", which in the Czech Lands roughly dates back to the last third of the 18th century. This is usually associated solely with the revival of the Czech language. In point of fact, in this context we could discuss it as the very important transformation of the feudal community into a civil society fashioning its own culture.

The "awakening" metaphor is based on the ontology of the nation as a given of societal life in which, ultimately, all matters are determined by power and vitality in the performance of historical tasks. If we detach ourselves from this nationalist historicism, we can see that nationalism is not the main driving force of modernisation, which sweeps away everything that stands in its way and enforces homogeneous culture and similitude wherever cultural heterogeneity and pluralism have previously been prevalent. According to stereotypical criticism of nationalism, this ideology is inherently a form of ethnic cleansing in a given nation state because it remoulds the former principle of the confessional state into a form of *cuius regio, eius lingua* for the given territory, the given religion, and thus foists a nationalist principle on the entire population, requiring of it not only the payment of taxes and obedience to the law, but also the cultural transformation of minds and souls. However, as Gellner very accurately explained, this argument is totally wrong-headed because nationalism does not impose homogeneity out of an arbitrary need for power. On the contrary, it is the universal modern need for cultural homogeneity that we see mirrored in particular nationalisms. Gellner thus completely overturned the interpretation of nationalism prevailing in the mid-20th century, according to which nationalism exerted pressure on modern society to homogenise. Countering this theory, espoused by the likes of Elie Kedourie, Gellner put forward the idea that, in fact, it is the general homogenising pressure of modern industrial society that ultimately leads to the emergence of nationalism. If you want to build an industrial society and a modern state, you need a population that is not only mobile and educated, but that also behaves according to certain clearly defined cultural standards. Modernity fosters a new culture based on uniform education that allows for widespread communication and mobility. So it is not nationalism that subdues the state, but the modern political organisation that adapts earlier cultures and shapes them into a new, unified and higher national culture, which it protects because, in return, that culture ensures its functionality and development. In pre-modern societies, culture legitimised political power. In the modern era, however, the opposite is true: power creates its own culture, which can permeate all of society and become universal. Gellner compares this distinction to the difference between wild and garden cultures and concludes his whole treatise on nationalism as a symptom, rather than a cause, of cultural homogenisation by commenting on an important and, from our perspective, crucial paradox of modern economics, politics and culture: "Internationalism was often predicted by the prophets and commentators of the industrial age, both on the left and the right, but the very opposite came to pass: the age of nationalism."

What is the relationship between the modern state, nationalism and political self-determination?
In modern times, the state as a political institution embodies the Enlightenment imperative of a single logical space where all those who accept its rational rules and principles can understand one other and bond. All citizens are capable of understanding one another, reaching a consensus, and installing a legitimate government, but they must accept the general rules of mutual coexistence, including rules on the establishment of this government. The emergence and functioning of such a state requires considerable cultural effort. This includes the creation of equal political and social conditions, as well as administrative centralisation and cultural education. If you're codifying the law, you also need to codify the language! The people who shape modern society are teachers and professors, not judges and police officers. In that society, social norms and education prevail over

legal norms and brute force. Nationalism does not seek to strengthen one local culture at the expense of another, but to suppress local cultures in the name of a single homogenised and highly standardised national culture. In other words, the traditional domination of dialects ends and a new era of codified language beckons. Nationalism exemplifies to us, among other things, that the political ideal of equality doubles up as an opportunity for individuals to adapt to ever more rapidly changing modern society and help themselves to better chances in life. Questions of nationality and the right of individual nations to self-determination need not always develop into the establishment of an independent state, but always involve the organisation of power within the state, whether in the form of federalisation, the introduction of local autonomy, the securing of specific cultural and linguistic rights, and what have you. The right to self-determination is thus a political consequence of the cultural self-confidence of a nation calling for the international or constitutional standardisation of its own culture. At the same time, its various forms within multinational states show that even the historically phenomenal ability of state power to make and enforce a policy of cultural homogenisation has its limits. For instance, the recognition of minority rights or political autonomy is effectively a recognition of these limits. On the other hand, there are strings attached: an expectation and promise of political loyalty and integration. That state entities and their law cannot exist without culture was accurately described as far back as Montesquieu in his *The Spirit of the Laws*. However, he was thinking not of various ethnicities' pre-political culture, but various political societies' morals and customs that precede each and every law and condition its validity. That is why Montesquieu's "spirit of the laws" is a far cry from the later Romantic concept of the "national spirit", which is completely in thrall to German Romantic idealism and the notion that one or another nation is chosen to engage in historical tasks in the name of humankind, but mainly, alas, against peoples and nations that, for some reason, are not chosen.

It could even be said that, in his 1748 *The Spirit of the Laws*, Montesquieu was both a philosophical rationalist and social anthropologist in that, besides probing the division of power, he also examined the influence of climate and culture on the laws of various countries. That was groundbreaking, wasn't it?

Montesquieu reminds us that laws cannot exist without culture. We could add that, by contrast, culture without laws is the bedrock from which tyranny is hewn and which spawns the demons of a modern nationalism that has declared the will and spirit of the nation to be a fundamental law which can be brandished to justify all sorts of things. The problem with the right to self-determination is that, one way or another, every nation gravitates towards political independence, the culmination of which is state sovereignty. For nationalist separatists, all other forms within a multinational state – whether a constitutional monarchy, a federal republic or a confederation – are merely a precursor and makeshift solution on the path to full sovereignty. Paradoxically, these are precursors to the formation of their own homogeneous culture via the laws of the country from which the separatists want to secede anyway in order, legally or illegally, to establish their own state.

These days, nationalism is often thought to be a reaction to the increasingly unifying and integrating European Union, which supposedly forces member countries into policies that are alien to their national cultures. At the same time, we even see nationalisms in the member states that routinely declare themselves to be pro-European political movements. What do these centrifugal tendencies mean in present-day Europe, which can only succeed in a globalised world as a single political and economic unit?

The borders between modern nations are frequently soaked in blood because the territorial boundaries of a state do not coincide with the ethnic composition of the population. This is why modern democrats rely on the more general mechanism of political integration, encompassing democratic negotiation, consensus and compromise, and the closely associated values of republicanism. The idea that nations, if they govern themselves democratically, will not fight one another, but will cooperate and inch towards a cosmopolitan republic is deeply rooted in both the Enlightenment and Romanticism. This forms the premise, for example, of the entire Kantian tradition of political philosophy, in which liberty comprises the Enlightenment duty of reason and, equally, Romantic freedom and the effective fulfilment of human existence. Nevertheless, it is clear from modern history that nationalism has many political levels: aggression, desire for conquest, encroachment, self-defence and federalist consensus. Nationalism fights over political boundaries and the form of government, but, interestingly, it never challenges the state as a political institution or its sovereign power. Modern nationalism carries around with it this emancipatory story about a historical drive for democracy and constitutional freedoms, but it also has the baggage of a pugnacious and venomous ideology that has prompted many wars, genocides, ethnic cleansing, and other historical crimes and injustices. To this day, we can still see bloody struggles for independence, waged in the name of this or that nation and its "natural" and "historical" right to self-determination, in many places across the planet. The states that these nations want to break away from oppose that right more or less with a show of strength or even with naked violence. Consequently, we are witnessing political violence and confrontation, for example, in the Kurdish parts of Iraq, Syria and Turkey, in South Sudan, and in many other countries, including the Russian Federation, China, and the Philippines. Even in today's rich and democratic European society, we still have diverse forms of post-modern nationalism, such as Scottish, Flemish, Basque and Catalan nationalism. Typically, these pursue a policy of both economic and state sovereignty.

Let's stop and consider, for a moment, the manifestations of nationalism in Europe's present-day post-modern and post-industrial society.

The economic argument is based on what we might call the parsimony of a richer nation that is loath to pick up the tab for other parts of the same political unit. The increasingly wealthy Flemish are reluctant to help mitigate the fallout of the industrial crisis in the Walloon region, the Basques and Catalans refuse to subsidise impoverished regions in the south of Spain, and the Scots entertain this belief that they could be richer than the English if only they could harness their natural capital and accrue all profits made from oil extraction in the North Sea shelf. This argument is also familiar to us from the history of the Czechoslovak federation, in which both nations harboured a feeling that it was somehow stumping up cash for the other and that this was an injustice that needed to be stopped. This argument tends to resonate, even though any economist will tell you that having a common market and economic policy is always more advantageous than any form of isolationism, even within a single state unit. Just as paradoxical is the argument raised by nationalists who want to become independent and secede from existing state units, and yet define themselves as pro-European political movements keen to anchor their state, once independent, in the structures of the transnational and post-sovereign European Union.

Is it at all right, then, for decisions on such fundamental issues to be taken in referendums, where emotions quickly run high and prevail over rational reflection?

First and foremost, it must be said that, unlike authoritarian or totalitarian regimes, democracy has a great advantage when it comes to dealing with national and nationalist issues: even in fraught times, there are usually no explosions of organised political violence or acts of terrorism. The handful of broken shop windows and noses in Quebec following the referendum in 1995 are the exception confirming the general rule that democracies strengthen national identity while weakening its violent manifestations. Even where there have recently been terrorist attacks, such as in Northern Ireland and the Basque Country, this violence has either been completely eliminated or at least contained.

Why?

Because democracy is a general form of government that can be practised within a nation state and, equally, at local, regional, transnational or global levels. The elasticity and flexibility of democratic decision-making, in which power always hangs by a thread and relies on majority will and public opinion, leads to a greater desire for self-determination, but also to greater responsibility for all action taken in connection with the struggle to break part of the country away and for the ramifications this has for the political future of the new entity. This was particularly pronounced in the fight spearheaded by the Scottish nationalists and their campaign during the referendum in 2014. The Scottish National Party conveyed itself as a progressive pro-European force which cares deeply about prosperity and trade cooperation with the rest of the UK and the European Union. The Scottish nationalists were so prudent that, though they were demanding independence and sovereignty, their fear of losing the votes of conservative and pragmatic voters prompted them to claim that, even after declaring independence, Scotland would retain its constitutional allegiance to the British royal crown and its economic affiliation to the pound.

I think I am right in saying that Vladimír Mečiar and his HZDS offered the same in their political manifesto in 1992. Mečiar was also demanding a common currency and army, but a separate economic and foreign policy.
Yes, that is correct. These were the internal paradoxes of the Scottish referendum. On top of that, you have to add the external paradox

of fundamental political efforts to establish a sovereign nation state openly subscribing to the post-sovereign and transnational project of European integration, yet wishing to be a member country of the European Union created as a result of secession from a place that was an EU member state in the first place. This was also why, following the referendum in which, less than two years later, UK citizens voted to leave the EU, Scottish nationalism was revised and forged an even closer link between the national question and the European question. Scottish nationalists insisted on a new independence referendum, a stance that heavily diluted their performance in the 2017 general election because as far as most Scottish voters were concerned the issue of Scottish independence – despite Brexit – had been resolved for the time being. After the Velvet Revolution, we in Czechoslovakia also found ourselves in a constitutionally and politically unique situation in the early 1990s. With the collapse of the Soviet Bloc, our state sovereignty had been restored, only for it to have to be transferred – following the break-up of the Czechoslovak federation – to the small state unit that was the Czech Republic. While this baton was being handed down, all the constitutional institutions of this sovereign country were hard at work on the fundamental task of gaining accession to the European Union. This is an entirely different situation from that faced by the Scots and Catalans, who were living in a democracy, because European integration becomes both a parallel process and a safeguard that a democratic and constitutional state can be built up. When we talk about nationalism in Western Europe today, we can see totally different dynamics and links between national sovereignty, the possibility of secession within the framework of an EU member state's constitutional order, and EU membership itself. I will leave to one side the possibility that secession, even if carried out fully on the basis of democratic will and in keeping with constitutional and international law, could foment such political indignation in the original country that its representatives would block the new country's EU membership application. In my view, there is another much more important question in this context that all Europeans, whatever their political beliefs and ideologies, need to ask themselves: How does any newly created, independent and sovereign state hope to build a common and democratic European society if it was formed on the strength of its population's refusal to remain united with a democratic country that is also an EU member state? I think this is a very legitimate question to which today's stingy nationalists from rich areas of Europe are unable to provide a potent and persuasive answer. In a democratic and transnationally unified Europe, the nationalist programme of state sovereignty and political independence comes across as a paradox that usually leads to a constitutionally and politically overcomplicated or make-do solution, the likes of which we have seen in Belgium's permanent constitutional crisis and the occasional power paralysis, and in the further shifting of authority to Scottish institutions dubbed "devo-max", i.e. the maximum extent to which power can be devolved while still maintaining a common state.

How do you view Spain, which has a very young constitution, adopted in 1978, and Catalan attempts at sovereignty?
Catalonia is a completely different kettle of fish and we should avoid a simplified comparison with, say, Scotland, but also with the Quebec independence referendum, which I will come to. As you observed, the Spanish constitution is very young – like the Czech constitution – and holds symbolic value as the underlying document guaranteeing democracy and freedom in post-Franco Spain. In addition, it also guarantees the autonomy of the individual historical lands, including Catalonia, and the considerable decentralisation of the power and administration of the Spanish constitutional monarchy. This asymmetric decentralisation of power is common to both the United Kingdom and its historical rival Spain. It should be emphasised that such asymmetries are easier to establish for a constitutional monarchy than a republic, where constitutions tend towards symmetric

solutions acceptable to the people, i.e. the political nation, mainly in the form of federalisation or a confederation. The United States and Switzerland are typical examples. As in Scotland, so too in Catalonia have separatist efforts gained political traction as a result of the economic crisis at the turn of the second decade of this century. A crucial difference is that the British constitution, because it is unwritten and archaic, is much more responsive to political and any other crises, whereas the Spanish constitution, as a symbolic text, invites ungainly legalistic solutions that can descend into the trench warfare we are now witnessing between Catalan nationalist politicians and the central Spanish government. Of course, the central government could insist that the Spanish constitution does not recognise the existence of the Catalan nation, nor the possibility for the Catalan parliament to hold a referendum on the independence of Catalonia. Naturally, the central government could deploy police to patrol Catalan streets and authorities. Huge fines could be imposed on the Catalan separatists who organised the referendum, or they could even be sent to prison. However, there is nothing the Catalan nationalists could wish for more than the "legal manufacture" of martyrs who, in their eyes, would sacrifice their own freedom for the freedom of the nation. So the Spanish government can defeat the Catalan autonomous nationalist government in a fight over the letter of the constitution, but it is losing the symbolic struggle for the hearts and minds of the people of Catalonia. In this context of making martyrs, I am always reminded of the Boston Massacre in 1770, which Americans still commemorate as a milestone in their historic struggle for independence. This incident was precipitated by a petty quarrel about whether it was beneath the dignity of an English soldier, when looking for odd jobs to earn extra money, to take up an American colonist's offer for him to empty a public toilet. A crowd gathered round and confronted his majesty's troops. The frightened soldiers, confused in the mayhem and fearing for their lives, shot dead five American colonists. That was all it took for what was initially a trivial altercation to enter the modern mythology of the American democratic nation liberating itself from unjust British domination. When the American colonists adopted the *Declaration of Independence* in 1776, they joined other nations and political powers as a politically sovereign nation people. According to the *Declaration*, the right to self-determination was natural and based on the "self-evident truths" that people are created equal and are endowed with inalienable rights.

To what extent can state violence be used in a democracy?
Democratic societies are very sensitive to all manifestations, no matter how small, of state violence. And here we find another common characteristic of today's European nationalism: it paradoxically benefits from the peace that has prevailed in Western Europe since the end of the Second World War. It is barely conceivable that English soldiers or the Spanish guard would deal with national revolts in the once time-honoured fashion of bloody suppression. This is illustrated, for example, by Bloody Sunday in January 1972, at the time of the biggest troubles in Northern Ireland, during which a unit of British paratroopers took action against a Catholic rally and shot dead thirteen people. Nearly four decades and several inquiries later, Lord Saville's report concluded that these killings were "unjustified" and "unjustifiable". This incident remains one of the darkest moments of the entire conflict, like the Irish nationalists' terrorist attack in Omagh in 1998, which claimed twenty-nine lives, including children, at the tail end of a long streak of violence. In other words, a democracy – unlike a dictatorship – is required to justify violence not only legally, but also, and especially, to the public. In nationalist conflicts, this is doubly true, so restraint, negotiating skills, compromise and temperance are a lot more important than coercive means, even if these are justified by law and under the constitution. Going back to the referendum, the secession of an autonomous region cannot simply be dismissed out of hand as unconstitutional, making any attempt

illegal and subject to heavy-handed suppression. Political will can never be fully expressed in the prescriptive language of a valid constitution, as lawyers and politicians are wont to believe, and the right to self-determination is the most striking example of this. However, political will can definitely be guided by constitutional procedures in order to minimise political risks posed by the possible collapse of a country or open conflict between its inhabitants, as cruelly experienced by Spanish society during the civil war in the last century.

But it would be preferable for nationalists' political will to respect laws defining the boundaries of their constitutional autonomy even when the circumstances are emotionally charged. Is that even possible?

We could come up with a basic axiom concerning the right to self-determination here: a nation's right to self-determination, where this targets independence and the establishment of an autonomous state, typically combines legal and illegal means. The ratio of such means plays a crucial role in predetermining the form and future development of the new state. If we want an example, we can look again to the *Declaration of Independence* and the American struggle for independence from the British Empire at the end of the 18th century, which in these parts we have come to call the American Revolution. In the early days of the independent US constitution, there is thus an "illegal" rebellion against the laws of the Westminster Parliament and against British colonial administration. The American Revolution was a peculiar combination of democratic mobilisation and the restrictive rule of law based on a written constitution. If the Catalans chose to fight openly for independence, and in doing so availed themselves of political violence, the role played by the illegality and unconstitutionality of the Catalan referendum would not, from their point of view, be any different from the role of a heroic struggle in which "founding fathers" wish to enter the history books and school readers as warriors battling for historical justice against a usurping enemy power. I don't want to sound like a political cynic, but I feel a need to show how important the synchronisation and interplay of political will and constitutional norms are in any constitutional democracy. In the 2017 Catalan referendum, for instance, the most glaring defect was not so much its unconstitutionality as the very way in which the Catalan parliament adopted the referendum law, as well as what it contained and what conditions it laid down. Nationalists, holding the slimmest of majorities in parliament, passed the law during a single session in early September 2017 instead of following the ordinary legislative process. In doing so, they set the very lowest thresholds for the validity of the referendum, i.e. it was to be decided by a simple majority vote of those participating in the referendum, and the referendum outcome was to be valid regardless of turnout. However, by following this tack the nationalists themselves undermined not only their democratic intentions, but also the mandate for any potential future negotiations on the independence of Catalonia, which, as a result of the adoption of the law, was starkly divided into two irreconcilable camps. The opposition parties called for a boycott of the referendum. More importantly, this law was not only unconstitutional according to the Spanish constitution, but was also unlawful in Catalonia itself, where a change of statute requires a two-thirds majority in the Catalan parliament. This meant that it was more than just a conflict with the Spanish central government and the constitutional court, which responded instantly by suspending the force of the referendum law. Nor was it a conflict just between the Spanish constitution, which does not allow votes on the independence of the individual Spanish regions, and the right of the Catalans to self-determination, which the Catalan nationalist government claims to be defending. At issue here was an act that, even under Catalan autonomous law, was unlawful. Furthermore, it exploited societal divisions and attempted to turn, through electoral counts, what was effectively the minority will into nationwide will supporting the independence and sovereignty of Catalonia.

But such shifts always occur whenever emotions trump rational facts, and this – as we have already discussed – happens whenever secession is at stake in a referendum...

Yes, but not to be too legalistically hard on the Catalan separatists and the central Spanish government, we would do well to remember that these elements of legality and illegality and the minority will of the elite masked as the general will of the people accompany almost every referendum on a nation's right to self-determination. In Canada, for example, the only one of the ten provinces not to approve the 1982 constitution was francophone Quebec. Subsequent negotiations between the federal government and provincial government premiers led to the acceptance of a number of amendments guaranteeing the greater decentralisation of power for Quebec and recognising it as a "distinct society". Note that there is no mention of nation here, yet everyone was thinking of cultural and linguistic identity, as well as the tradition of written and codified law, which is lacking in the English-speaking part of Canada. However, these amendments from the late 1980s, known as the Meech Lake Accord, were never ratified. In the meantime, Quebec nationalism had grown into a powerful separatist movement headed by the new Bloc Québécois, so Quebec premier Bourassa promised that a referendum would be held shortly, in 1992. This empty promise, though, was not as important as the federal elections held in 1993, in which the Bloc Québécois won in its home province and finished second federally. This handed it the constitutional role of the official opposition and the opportunity for the party's leader, Lucien Bouchard, to lambaste the federal government's policies every day in parliamentary debate. At the time, the separatists enjoyed the backing of half of Quebec society, as ultimately evidenced by the outcome of the referendum in October 1995. The result was a razor-thin one per cent victory for supporters of the Canadian federation, who had fought the Quebec separatists tooth and nail politically. Their actions included, of course, a challenge to the referendum, which was heard by the Superior Court of Quebec. Unlike the Spanish constitutional court, however, Quebec's supreme court did not scrap the referendum, though the justices did declare that the lawful secession of the province would have to proceed in accordance with the Canadian constitution and that, were the referendum to return a yes-vote, any unilateral declaration of independence by the Quebec politicians would be overtly unconstitutional. The Quebec separatists denounced the court's ruling as "undemocratic", and in doing so paradoxically invoked international rules rather than domestic constitutional law. Like the Scottish separatists, the Quebec nationalists wanted political sovereignty while maintaining economic cooperation and partnership with the rest of Canada. So they were calling for partnership yet refusing to discuss a constitutional arrangement with a federal government representing Canada's interests. This is another general feature of the amphibiously legal and illegal right of self-determination. Eventually, the federalists won. The separatists, frustrated by the close result, smashed a few shop windows and broke the odd nose or two, but in the end no one could question the legitimacy of the decision. Quebec nationalism had made its mark on the constitutional architecture, thereby blunting its political edge. In this respect, I am afraid that in Spain the knives are being sharpened, nationalism is on the rise, and society is fundamentally split. Come the next economic crisis, this could have incalculable political consequences.

But in Canada the matter appears to have been resolved by the court.
In the Canadian context, the Supreme Court of the country settled the matter by upholding the Quebec supreme court's position that the unilateral secession of Quebec would be openly unconstitutional. However, if a majority of Quebec citizens voted clearly and categor-

ically for independence in a referendum, the other provinces should enter into political negotiations on this secession. This is an example of judges clearly ruling on questions of law and constitutionality, while at the same time setting limits that cannot be exceeded by law and that require political will and negotiating strategies rather than legal norms.

And that brings us to the crucial question of the conflict between will and reason, that is, between political power and the law. What is behind this conflict between legitimacy and legality?
The gap between political power and the law can never be completely bridged by any constitutional document or absolute dictatorial will, but we have clearly seen recently how this tension between will and reason rises. The current manifestations of nationalist separatism within the EU and elsewhere are reviving a typically modern problem: the tension and conflict between legitimacy and legality. Formal legalism can never fully constrain political will, but unbridled will is destructive for any political order, with calls for legitimacy morphing into tyrannical despotism. The notion that if, in a multi-national state, you do not incorporate the right to self-determination in the form of an independence referendum into the constitution, no one can ever demand such a referendum, under the threat of criminal sanctions or naked violence, is self-destructive, as we have witnessed, for example, in present-day Spain. That is why the Canadian way is much more practical. It clearly rejects unilateral secession as unconstitutional, but then again there is the Clarity Act, providing that, if there is a "clear majority" on a "clear question" in a Quebec independence referendum, the federal government and the other provinces are required to begin secession negotiations with Quebec, as we have discussed. This is one of the possible ways in which the law can react more flexibly to political change, i.e. how legality can implement procedures to rationalise the legitimate manifestations of democratically formed political will.

Why is it that politics and constitutional law are often unable to solve problems and conflicts that, although nationalist in form, are actually linked to more general social and cultural changes?

The current growth of nationalism, for example, is directly related to globalisation. Quite a few people view the nation state as a last chance to save themselves from "global evils", whether fabricated or real, be these capitalists, immigrants, terrorists and other fanatics, or organised crime. Global heterogeneity is pitted against national homogeneity here, and political sovereignty is considered to be a temple of legitimate government and a stronghold of cultural defence. National populism is growing out of this social and cultural tension. The traditional disconnect between the nation as a race and the political people is re-emerging. Yet as we know, this schism cannot simply be resolved with a clean slate and the division of *ethnos* and *demos*, even though political scientists and moralists often gravitate towards this. Rather, we need to constantly remind ourselves that ethnic demons slumber even in all political concepts of a democratic people, and, by contrast, the political ideals of freedom, democracy and republicanism are present in ethnic national identities. Only a nation viewing its own history and its present as such a schism and a constant cross-over between *ethnos* and *demos*, with all the attendant risks, is a nation that is truly awakened and emancipated. The right to self-determination can only be held by a nation that also perceives this right as an obligation to defend itself and as a wake-up call so that it does not slide into dreams that gradually lapse into nightmares.

Cultural Idealism
and Political Realism

Let's return to our national revival. The work of Bohuslav Balbín, a Jesuit who wrote *Dissertatio apologetica pro lingua Slavonica, praecipue Bohemic*a in 1672 and 1673, can be regarded as the very first starting point in the revival of Czech as a language able to stand on its own two feet. How does the Czech national revival and its interpretation differ from similar tendencies in the Europe of that time?

If we are to discuss the Czech national revival, we must bear in mind the general social and cultural dynamics that went into the formation of modern nations and nation states. We must refocus on what is common to the Czech national revival and other national-awakening movements in modern Europe and elsewhere in the world. We cannot simply repeat, parrot-fashion, pedagogical paradigms or, even worse, political science's rhetoric on Czech history, abounding with searches for a "basic formula for Czech history", "the historical contribution of Czech politics" and its "historical flashpoints". Such endlessly rehashed banalities, typically accompanied by allusions to the "European dimension" or "Czech crisis", only confirm the poverty of Czech political science. Instead, let's try to understand the Czech national revival as one of many historical streams of modern society's general penchant for creating a highly standardised and homogeneous culture, in which successful efforts to save and codify Czech as a self-standing language eventually – courtesy of historical and political circumstances – resulted in the emergence of an independent state.

The initial period of the national revival is usually taken to mean the years from 1770 to 1805. This is the time of Kramerius and his periodicals *Krameriovy císařsko-královské vlastenecké noviny* and *Pražské noviny*, as well as the emergence of Czech theatre, which started out at the Kotzen Theatre in 1781, with the Estates Thea-

tre subsequently performing in Czech from 1783. How would you characterise this period?

As a situation that is similar in many respects to the Early Renaissance in Elizabethan England, even though that was two centuries prior. Society is a communication system capable of describing itself, and of shaping and developing itself according to that description. This applies as much to the creation of national Czech society as it does to any other society, so the establishment of individual means of communication, such as newspapers, literature and theatre, as well as music and the visual arts, played an absolutely crucial role at that time. Just as the modern English nation could not have come into being without an official translation of the Bible – the King James Version – and Shakespeare's plays in the first half of the 17th century, as we have already discussed, the same can be said for the genesis and formation of the Czech nation because, were it not for the *de facto* constitution of its language and high literary culture, the nurturing of a homogeneous national culture and the identity this engendered would not have been possible. Interestingly, speaking of translations of the Bible, the first translation into English was penned by John Wycliffe in the second half of the 14th century. When Jan Hus found inspiration in Wycliffe's work, this emphasis on the ability to share the word of God in the living language of believers was strongly present in his mind. However, this medieval "national revival" has little in common with modern national history because a modern nation can only arise with the help of a highly organised society, bureaucratic administration and, above all, means of communication capable of interlinking the social hubs and the fringes. In this context, it was important for the formation of the modern English nation that, contrary to Wycliffe's times, the early-17th-century King James Version was prepared by a whole team of translators with the clear assignment to produce a translation sensitive to the linguistic culture of their society while also politically legitimising James's rule and ousting the Puritan translation, passages of which could be interpreted as justifying a rebellion against the king. The new translation thus had the advantage of being authorised by the power of the absolutist state and, at the same time, the printing press meant it could quickly be disseminated among the more affluent strata of the then English society. The book as a medium was no longer limited to a very narrow group of medieval scholars, as had been the case in Wycliffe's or Hus's time. Instead, it spread through society horizontally, mirroring how production was becoming cheaper and English society was growing richer.

Let's go back to the media, which was established here a hundred years later than in neighbouring Germany. There, the first newspaper, *Aviso*, was started in 1605, whereas here we had to wait until 1719 for *Pražské poštovské noviny*, which was followed in 1789 by Kramerius's *Krameriovy císařsko-královské vlastenecké noviny*. This was at a time when *Zürcher Zeitung*, structured much like present-day newspapers, had already been in publication in Switzerland since 1780. Kramerius's newspaper, though, played a completely different role: it was a vehicle teaching people to read, acquainting them with the rudiments of hygiene, the basics of well-functioning agriculture, and so on. This newspaper was pursuing an educational, socialising mission. How did this difference affect the way our countries developed?

The media's influence on the formation of national society and its democratisation is crucial. In England, these changes took place much earlier. Here, the first European constitutional monarchy was created at the end of the 17th century, in the wake of bloody revolutionary events. The policy of official licensing to publish books and other printed matter was effectively abandoned in England when parliament let the Licensing Act lapse in 1695. This ushered in post-censorship, which was much milder than censorship interventions anywhere else in Europe. Half a century after John Milton's passionate defence of the freedom of speech and criticism of censorship in his famous polemic *Areopagitica*, addressed to the English parliament, we really do see the emergence a society whose political freedoms and parliamentary rule were rightly contrasted by Voltaire, Montesquieu and other Enlightenment philosophers with the then absolutist governments in France and elsewhere in Europe.

By the second half of the 18th century, autonomous Czech political life is languishing and historical consciousness is puttering out in the Czech Lands. It seems to have been revived when Hájek's *Bohemian Chronicle* was criticised by Gelasius Dobner, the founder of modern Czech historiography. What does this tell us about the situation in the Czech Lands at that time?

Understandably, the situation in the Czech Lands was very different in terms of political culture and economy. In the eighteenth century, France – a state then and subsequently dominating European politics – found itself lagging economically and politically ever further behind England. The same applies to the Habsburg monarchy and the economically distressed and politically fragmented Germany. At the end of the 18th century, the Josephine reforms invigorate the rational organisation of the state, but this political centralisation also comes at the cost of cultural centralisation. In particular, this upped the pressure on those cultures and ethnic groups that did not speak German. Against this backdrop, there is no way that Kramerius's efforts are merely an undertaking designed to awaken culture. Their clear political goal is to defend a language and a specific culture from the homogenising cultural pressure provoked by the political centralisation and administrative rationalisation of the state. As the central power and bureaucratic organisation of the monarchy grows, and with it the role of German as an official and commercial language, historical consciousness is weakened and Czech identity shrivels. In this culturally and politically precarious situation, Dobner's criticism is a reminder that modern critical history may well be important for national identity and culture, but fanciful stories are no good to it. This is effectively the first modern endeavour to make the science of history independent of some fabulous national past and the attendant political urges.

Does Dobner illustrate, up to a point, that our idea of the Czech national revival is imprecise? Was this not originally a movement that promoted cultural awareness but whose political contours were fuzzy?

From day one, the Czech national revival was a political movement, regardless of the fact that it was manifested by the publication of newspapers, the collecting of folk tales and legends, and the writing of poetry. In this context, it is very important not only that the national revival was being moulded by national zeal and an interest in the "roots" of popular culture and language, but also that modern and ethnographic sciences, employing methods independent of national myths, were taking shape at the same time. Here, Dobner's criticism and its inner ethos of science as a vocation detached from politics foreshadows subsequent disputes about the authenticity of manuscripts and even about the very role of history in documenting the national past, i.e. the "meaning of Czech history" that we have already mentioned. However, the definition of what constitutes a political exercise differs considerably from one European society to the next in those times. The end of the 18th century is a period when political nations are coming to life. France, by dint of its revolution, transforms from a feudal system into a nation state based on the sovereignty of the French people. At the same time Václav Matěj Kramerius started publishing his patriotic newspaper, i.e. July 1789, the French Revolution erupted with a vengeance. And before that, in 1776, the independent American nation was established. So this period can rightly be described as the "Age of Revolution", when new nations are born in defiance of empires. This even includes the

Haitian Revolution, where the social and political conditions were completely different because it began as a slave insurrection against French colonial rule and led to the establishment of the sovereign republic of Haiti in 1804. And if we cast our eye over other parts of the world, we see the Irish Rebellion of 1798, aided by French troops. While this republican revolt was unsuccessful, it did prompt the British parliament to pass, in 1800 and 1801, a number of laws establishing the United Kingdom, including the Union with Ireland Act 1801, which incorporated the island of Ireland into the system of British parliamentarism. While this is going on, new societies in Latin America are starting to revolt against Spanish and Portuguese colonial rule. These revolutions also result in the emergence of independent republics. By the time of the Serbian and Greek struggles for independence from the Ottoman Empire in the first few decades of the 19th century, the Enlightenment's political ideals are fully entangled with the Romantic fight for national self-determination and independence.

At that time, sometimes referred to as the second period of the national revival, dating from 1805 to 1830, the Czech Lands are beginning to publish dictionaries and theoretical treatises in Czech, debate abounds, and criticism is surfacing. Was European Pre-Romanticism a role model for the Czechs?

Most definitely. Sometimes there are misconceptions that Czech revivalists cooked up the nation in the yards of our farms and on the porches of our cottages, self-absorbed as they were with the Czech landscape. The truth of the matter is that they were scholars fully abreast of everything that was happening in Europe at the time, and their activities were an organic part of general cultural, social and political developments on the continent. For example, one of the first works by the young František Palacký was a translation of the Gaelic poetry *Poems of Ossian*, which were purported to have originated in the 3rd century but were actually forged by their "translator", James Macpherson, a Scottish poet from the second half of the 18th century who later went into politics and ended up as a British MP. As we can see, Václav Hanka and Josef Linda were hardly original or alone in their "manuscripting", because countless similar ancient texts were being "discovered" throughout Europe at that time. The Welsh people, for example, have Edward Williams, who went by the bardic name of Iolo Morganwg. At the turn of the 19th century, he devised an "ancient" druid language and traditions that had supposedly survived the country's Roman incursions, Christianisation and Norman Conquest. Despite their proven fiction, they are paradoxically still preserved in the country's most important cultural holiday, the *Eisteddfod*. To this day, speakers of Welsh are more familiar with the Celtic verses of this "bard" than with authentic medieval Welsh poetry. The period we are talking about was a time when the new scientific fields of ethnography, anthropology, sociology and comparative linguistics were forming. It was also an age in which national literature and history were flourishing. In hindsight, the falsification of literary and general history, its "discovery" and its invention are understandable when we consider that the humanities and modern literature were taking shape in parallel. Hanka, for instance, was not just any old forger, but also a very good linguist and the author of an important language reform that made changes still in effect today. As you can see, the boundary between fiction and fact was very porous at that time.

The second period of the national revival is strongly associated with Josef Jungmann, one of the first teachers of Czech in the Kingdom of Bohemia. This primacy aside, what else would you pick out from his work?

Jungmann built on the Romantic concept of language as a fundamental source of national identity. This is why his scientific work in the linguistic and literary fields also created a canon that had at least the same political weight as historical constitutional arguments. His organisation of Czech science around the *Krok* periodical resulted in the formation of the first group of Czech scientists, including František Palacký, Jan Evangelista Purkyně, František Ladislav Čelakovský and other key figures of the then-awakening national life. His contribution to the development of Czech as a fully-fledged language goes far beyond his *Czech-German Dictionary*. For example, in his translations he coined new words that would be both accessible and usable in everyday speech. Together with Josef Dobrovský, he also created the modern canon of Czech literary history, an act that was as important as Palacký's subsequent establishment of the momentous canon of Czech national history, which has survived and is surprisingly topical to this day. Turning to criticism of Jungmann's linguistic concept of national identity, it certainly polarised relations between the Czech- and German-speaking populations and undermined the idea of provincial constitutional patriotism, but let's not forget that this was a time when the Czech-speaking population was having to come to terms not only with the linguistic Germanising pressure exerted by political and administrative changes in the then-monarchy, but also with pan-German Romanticism, which posed a much more fundamental threat to the collective identity of Czech-speaking inhabitants. Jungmann's work, then, is a reminder that the codification of language is just as important to a nation state as the codification of laws.

František Palacký, whom you have already mentioned, led the way in the next period of the national revival. *The New Czech Chronicle* is published, in 1882 the university is divided into German and Czech parts, etc. How come Palacký's influence was so powerful that he was dubbed "Father of the Nation" in his own lifetime?
So much has been said about Palacký, his concept of Czech history and his political and cultural activity, and his soubriquet is so distinctive that anything we say about him will immediately touch on central symbols of our collective memory. If we were to look for an

angle from which we could still talk about Palacký today without parroting common knowledge or banalities, I think we could plump for the year 1848. This is when the first part of the Czech translation – factually supplemented and extended – of his *History of the Czech Nation in Bohemia and Moravia* was published. At this time, there is an important revolution playing out in the Habsburg monarchy and elsewhere in Europe which, despite temporary defeat, has dismantled the political *status quo* that had been maintained on the continent since the Congress of Vienna in 1814-1815. It "awakened" European nations from Sicily to Kraków, hastened industrial modernisation, and eventually led to constitutional guarantees of rapidly democratising citizenry even in autocratic regimes. Palacký was intimately familiar with political and scientific life elsewhere in Europe, where he was a seasoned traveller, so his contribution to Czech scientific life in general and historiography in particular was truly exceptional as early as the 1840s.

Why was he so exceptional and what made him so?
Because what we're talking about here is not just the Enlightenment's schematic historiography, but a comprehensive philosophy of history. Palacký was inspired by some of Hegel's thoughts and, in particular, described historical events – from a more general standpoint – as a logical and continuous sequence of battles between the Slavic and the Germanic. He viewed the Czech nation as a historically and essentially independent nation defining itself in contrast to the history of Germanic nations. This goes hand in hand with the way in which Palacký ascribes fraternal peaceableness and democracy to the Slavic nations, but warlike aggression and authoritarianism to the Germanic peoples. In this typology, one of the Slavs' negative traits was a tendency to anarchy; conversely, Palacký lauded Germanic organisation and entrepreneurship. In this regard, Palacký did not consider one historical strength to be positive and another to be negative. Instead, in the spirit of Hegelian philosophy, his prem-

ise was that the polarity and the constant conflicts and influences between the Slavic and the Germanic were productive in history and often led to historical progress, new ideas, and the synthesis of values and culture. Add the fact that the peaks of national history were associated with a Protestant line that took in Hus, Chelčický and Comenius to the concept of history as the logically organised development and clash of various collective forces, and you get not only Palacký's, but also Tomáš Garrigue Masaryk's, philosophy of history. This continuity from Palacký to Masaryk, which has historiographical, political and generally cultural links, is precisely why Palacký can never be ignored in any narrative about Czech history. What's more, he successfully combined political and constitutional history with the more general history of society, culture, science and art.

In this context, we really ought to mention Palacký's 1848 *Letter to Frankfurt*, in which he defended the existence of the Austrian state, but called for it to switch from centralism and absolutism to the principles of federation and democratisation. Vienna was unable to do that and Europe at large didn't really understand what he was getting at. Palacký remained alone. Did we bring it on ourselves, or was the situation in Europe at the time also to blame?

Let's stick a while longer with Palacký's concept of national history as a constant confrontation between the Czech and German elements, because Palacký's constitutional thinking is also directly related to this. In Palacký's philosophy of history, Czech statehood functioned as a pivotal commitment worn on the sleeves of various generations of the Czech nation in disputes and clashes with German political interests and expansion, which also explains why, in this history, Hussitism – as both a religious and a political rebellion – represented the absolute apogee of national history and the axis around which modern Czech collective memory and its derived national identity were formed. But you are right that the whole of this philosophical concept of history would pack much less of a punch today if it were not simultaneously bound up with Palacký's monumental, resolute and long-term political engagement. Interestingly, at the beginning of that revolutionary year of 1848, Palacký responded to the turmoil in France by saying that the Czech nation should remain, politically, within the bounds of the law. That's why his relationship with the radical St Wenceslas Committee was underwhelming and, instead, he joined the gubernatorial commission appointed by Count Stadion. Palacký had two reasons for this moderate reformist stance: the mitigation of potentially violent conflict between the Czechs and the Germans that could explode at any time from the revolutionary tinderbox, and his own programme of liberal constitutionalism, for which he was seeking to win over the Czech estates and which he was advocating in the aforementioned commission. It was not until 11 April that he wrote the *Letter to Frankfurt*. This was an open letter addressed to the preparatory committee of the Frankfurt Parliament as the future Greater German Assembly. This letter, as we all know, was officially entitled the *On the Relationship of Bohemia and Austria to the German Empire*, and it was not so much Palacký's personal rejection of an invitation to become a member of the preparatory committee as a manifesto of the Czech political nation and Palacký's Austro-Slavism, which he subsequently set out in detail in eight newspaper articles published as *Idea of the Austrian State*. This context is essential in understanding the importance Palacký attached to the constitution and state organisation in order for nations to exist together and alongside one another and to develop politically and culturally. Palacký quite insightfully thought that a constitutionally reformed and federalised Austria would be a surer way of securing the existence of the Czech political nation than a Germany unified on linguistic and cultural principles. Concerns about German expansionism subsequently proved well founded by the tide of events and wars in Central Europe in the second half of the 19th century, which led to the unification of Germany and, at the same time, to its militarisation and the expansionist policy that ultimately culminated in the First World War.

Let's go back to the revolutionary year of 1848. Palacký, as you mentioned, was a member of Stadion's reform commission and of the provisional provincial government, but he did not last long here.

When the Reform Commission and the more radical St Wenceslas Committee merged to form the National Committee, Palacký became a member of that organisation and briefly accepted Count Thun's offer of a post in the provisional provincial government. After it transpired that this was an attempt, under the guise of autonomist politics, to create a counter-revolutionary counterweight to the revolutionary Viennese government, he immediately stepped down from the provincial government. Palacký also failed in his attempts, subsequently, to champion the idea of Austro-Slavism at the Slavic Congress because, for example, the Russian anarchist Bakunin and delegates representing Polish emigrants gave such ideas short shrift. However, on 12 June, the Congress was cut short by the revolutionary uprising in Prague, during which Palacký acted primarily as a negotiator between the opposing parties and as a politician seeking a compromise. For example, after the students had taken Thun hostage, he made them release him. Having then been elected to the constituent assembly, by early August he had drafted an Austrian constitution based on the principles of Austro-Slavism and a balance between the central power of the monarchy and the federalist form of government. He continued to press for this even after further unrest broke out in Vienna and the constituent assembly moved to Kroměříž. Palacký was under the political misapprehension that the failure of the revolution in the German lands and in Vienna meant there was an opportunity to push through federalist and Austro-Slavist proposals, but ultimately this did not happen. The assembly was dissolved and, instead of a vote, the March Constitution, or Stadion Constitution, was imposed in March 1849. In place of federalist constitutional reform, there was repression, and Palacký was not spared. This political and constitutional failure, combined with police pressure, saw him retire from politics completely for a while. His public authority was so strong, however, that in 1861 Franz Joseph I named him a life member of the House of Lords, the first Czech of non-aristocratic origin to be so appointed. Palacký didn't last very long at all here because, apart from proselytising autonomy in the spirit of Austro-Slavism, he also criticised the February Patent, or Schmerling Constitution, which was adopted in the same year and effectively introduced a system of constitutional monarchy with a bicameral imperial council, as the legislative body, and provincial diets. Because Palacký's criticism that these constitutional changes were inadequate went unheeded, in September 1861 he declared passive resistance and never again returned to the House of Lords. He concentrated on his work as a deputy of the Czech provincial diet, where he mainly promoted electoral reform, again without success. Though his political career was not particularly auspicious and he gradually lost his authority among the liberals from the emerging faction of Young Czechs, Palacký remained an icon of public cultural life until his death.

I would like us to return, for a moment, to Austro-Slavism as a constitutional idea. How does it manifest the difference between constitutional law and a nation's right to self-determination?
When, in April and May 1865, Palacký wrote the series of eight newspaper articles we mentioned, now known collectively as *Idea of the Austrian State*, the situation in the monarchy had become politically uncertain again. There was increasing talk about a dualistic form of monarchy and the emperor was gradually straying from the liberal politicians surrounding minister-president Schmerling. In fact, in July the emperor replaced Schmerling with the conservative Belcredi, who suspended the February Patent. In this atmosphere, Palacký

writes that if Austria is to continue to exist, it must rely on the state idea, but can no longer be based on the mystical origins of the sovereign line and the negative reasons for its own existence as an empire defending Christian Europe against Turkish invasions and internally protecting the Catholic faith against reformist pressures. The basic thrust cloaked by this historical message is that, in modern times, it is not possible to pit freedom and government against each other, and therefore Austria, just like the United States and other countries, should build constitutional architecture in which freedom and power are not contradictory. Palacký even revisits the revolutionary years of 1848 and 1849, claiming that, despite Bach's short period of neo-absolutism, this general move towards freedom has prevailed and it is therefore time, in addition to civil freedom and equality, to enforce the principle of the constitutional equality of peoples living in the then Austria, not just the dualistic division of power between the Austrian and Hungarian parts of the monarchy. It's probably a good idea, at this point, to put Palacký's well-known remark "We were here before Austria and we shall be here after she is gone!" into the broader context (by the way, this is just a variation of his words in *Letter to Frankfurt* that "… if the Austria state did not exist, we would have to endeavour to create it as soon as possible for the sake of Europe and, indeed, humanity itself"). This sentence is preceded by Palacký's warning of the emergence of nationalism and the inter-nation conflict that would occur in the event of dualistic constitutional reform. He writes: "The day on which dualism is proclaimed shall also, by the irresistible force of nature, be the day on which pan-Slavism is born in its least desirable form, and its godparents will be the parents of dualism. What will follow can be deduced by each reader himself. We Slavs shall look on with true pain, but without fear. We were here before Austria and we shall be here after she is gone!" As the Czech philosopher Karel Kosík once noted, Palacký's idea of the Austrian state is actually the idea of Central Europe, which also presupposes a concept of humankind and the world. That world, I would add, cannot be dualistic, only pluralistic. And how to harmonise these pluralities is an endless task for present-day and future Europeans who want to eschew nationalist and other madness.

Your observation on context is important because the slogan "We were here before Austria and we shall be here after she is gone!" is often ascribed a meaning opposite to that originally intended.
Palacký clearly stands out as an advocate of a multinational Austrian (or any other) state that can reform itself according to the modern constitutional principles of general equality and the democratic right of nations to autonomous political organisation within a unified federal whole. It is intriguing that his idea again lost out when Prussia's defeat of Austria in the Battle of Königgrätz in 1866 triggered other political shocks that resulted in the introduction of dualism in the following year, accompanied by the adoption of the December Constitution on 21 December 1867, which consisted of seven acts, including a catalogue of fundamental rights and the Compensation Act, and killed off the idea of Austro-Slavism for good. Despite this political loss, Palacký's idea was very important because it was an exhaustive effort to merge two seemingly incompatible constitutional principles, namely a constitutional monarchy with a federal government. Even today, we can see how difficult this is when we look at the constitutional crises in Spain and the United Kingdom, and also in Belgium, which – unlike the first two countries, where the individual regions have varying degrees of autonomy – has adopted federalism as a constitutional principle. And one last observation to round off our discussion on Palacký: the constitutional idea of federalised autonomy primarily defines the nation not as a culturally ethnic, but as a politically territorial, entity. In spite of all the friction over culture and language, this is mainly about the right to political, rather than cultural, self-determination. In order to exist politically, *ethnos* must behave like *demos*. This is an impor-

tant principle of liberal constitutionalism that still holds true today. Otherwise, we would be stuck at race, and a modern state aspiring to democratic openness would turn into the tyranny of the master race, as witnessed, for example, in the modern development of the German nation up to 1945.

But aren't the cultural existence and political existence of a nation intertwined issues?
Certainly. And Palacký's concept of national history is a shining example of this. This is how Josef Pekař described Palacký: " he simply wanted to emphasise the historical merits and cultural sacrifices of his tribe, to purge its memory of spiteful interpretations and actions, and legitimate its claim to equality and freedom from oppression." Today, we can also highlight the fact that a constitutional idea is important because it is in that idea that the political definition of the nation precedes, but does not deny, the cultural definition. So even if a linguistically-conceived cultural nation becomes lost among others, its historical constitutional claims single it out and ascribe to it the right to self-determination in its present existence. The line plotted by the Czech nation's constitutional history was also an important defence of cultural life, because Czech cultural identity was weaker than the Greater German identity at that time. The legitimisation of the general constitutional idea, which was confirmed and came to fruition in the historical development of the Czech nation, directly opened up space for the cultural and social advancement of national life. In Palacký's philosophy of history, which manufactures a history for the Czech nation, there is also a political realism that wants to prescribe the future direction and development of this history. I admire Palacký's sentence "Freedom without a moral base, without law and justice, is nothing more than a predator's instinct; it is the caprice and tyranny of the despot." It sounds exactly like something that Alexis de Tocqueville – another great politician, philosopher, historian and writer of Palacký's time, and a dyed-in-the-

wool liberal with faith in the law and justice – would write. And that is a statement we can still subscribe to today!

After Palacký, Tomáš Garrigue Masaryk comes on to the scene. Born in 1850, the founder of Czechoslovakia is said to have had three role models: Hus, who fascinated him with his ethics of truth; Comenius, whom he held in great esteem for his concept of education; and Havlíček, for his ideal of freedom. Masaryk's Realist Programme also takes its cue from Havlíček, who in 1849 wrote: "Only a nation that is in fine fettle and educated can enjoy freedom and the attendant good governance; in particular, we must always be mindful of this truth, taught to us by the experience of history. An uneducated nation, if bled out by revolution upon revolution, will not attain freedom and law, but will always be swindled again before long and pushed back into despotism. A morally bankrupt nation, though it be educated, always makes, by its debasement, the rod of absolutism for its own back...".

We should probably start by mentioning the Czech political parties and groupings of that time, because in the revolutionary year of 1848 the National Party was formed. However, if anything it was an interest grouping that these days we are more likely to classify among the activities of civil society than among conventional parties. Though it was only after the downfall of Bach's regime that this grouping started to become more politically engaged, as early as the early 1860s there were schisms and criticism of the social authorities that the likes of Palacký and Rieger belonged to. When National Party MPs declared passive resistance in response to the Austro-Hungarian Compromise, this was exploited by the "Young Czechs" to make a stand against the "Old Czechs" once and for all in 1874, when seven of their MPs attended a session of the Imperial Council in Vienna, thereby ending passive resistance. The "Young Czechs" formed the National Liberal Party and subscribed to Havlíček's political legacy. Thus, from the 1870s, we could say that competition between the political parties hotted up, with the more conservative "Old Czechs" on one side and, on the other, the liberal "Young Czechs" who, besides wanting to rein in the influence of the Catholic Church and the historical nobility, were demanding universal suffrage for men and other constitutional freedoms of the individual. However, it was not until 1892, in the wake of election victories as the 1880s gave way to the 1890s, that a comprehensive *Manifesto of the Young Czech Party* was published, i.e. at a time when social democracy was already up and running in the Czech Lands. There was no truly pluralistic party democracy to speak of in the Czech Lands until the formation of the Social Democrats in 1878. Yet even the Czech Social Democrats were initially organised within the framework of the All-Austrian Social Democratic Party (*Gesamtpartei*). Only in 1893, for tactical reasons, did they become organisationally independent and form the Czecho-Slav Social Democratic Workers Party. For the best part of the 19th century, Czech political life cannot be described as party politics, but rather as civic activity carried out by societies to raise political and cultural awareness. These societies were fraught with various tensions, and they would split and form splinter groups. This could never be a substitute for political competition, in which decisions would be taken on political agendas and the ideologies of various parties, let alone on who would be in government and who would be in opposition. Radical democrats, such as Karel Sabina and Josef V.Frič, were exceptions for their time. As Palacký's political fortunes show, the revolutionary year of 1848, which completely transformed politics in many European countries, had little effect on Czech political culture and life. So when we picture political realism, we have to remember that originally it comprised not a specific political programme, but the broadest of intellectual and morally free preconditions for political activity and engagement. The condition of education and moral integrity, which legitimises the opportunity for good governance, constantly recurs here.

Let's return to Masaryk, who founded the Realist Party on 1 April 1890 and published the "Realist Programme" on 1 November of the same year, when he was teaching in the Czech part of Charles University. We should bear in mind that Masaryk studied in Vienna between 1872 and 1876, and in 1878 he did his habilitation thesis there. He was appointed as an associate professor of philosophy in Prague four years later, and it took another fifteen years before he was promoted to a professorship. They could not forgive him for his stance on the forged manuscripts and his ideas, which were revolutionary at the time. What made his "Realist Programme" so important to us? Could this be one of the key nodal points in our history that you have been mentioning?

Masaryk had been working on his programme of political realism for a long time beforehand. For example, even his later writings on Havlíček, from 1896, are not just following in the footsteps of the Young Czechs as a subscription to a generally recognised authority. Rather, they are a comprehensive rendering of the history of the national revival from 1848 to the present. In this respect, the role of the predecessor of political realism attributed by Masaryk to Havlíček had two functions as, besides legitimising Masaryk's political agenda, it also served as a prescriptive interpretation of the entire political evolution of Czech society from 1848, and of the very meaning of the right to national self-determination. Havlíček, then, is lined up directly alongside Palacký, even though the work and the ideas of the two men differed in numerous respects. Masaryk certainly felt a close affinity to Havlíček's democratic ethos and absolute emphasis on education, as well as his resistance to Slavophilia and political messianism. He also grasped the tension between the natural-law and legal-history justification of the Czech nation's right to self-determination, which was typical of Palacký's philosophy of history and cloaked the utilitarian argument that state organisation benefited the free development of individuals and nations. Masaryk described Havlíček's realism as though it were an almost Aristotelian virtue of temperance, with the ability to find a middle way between the extremes of the passivity of reaction and the grandiose slogans of radicalism. Yet, at the same time, Havlíček's realism is associated primarily with constant critical discussion and public awareness and educational activities. While, from the point of view of the form to be taken by the state, Havlíček contrasted absolutism and constitutionalism, we are compelled to note here that, in his work, the condition of free public discussion is clearly formulated in Czech political history as a basic prerequisite for a legitimate constitutional government. If I were to go overboard with my comparisons and reach into current political and legal philosophy, Masaryk viewed Havlíček's realism in the sense of Jürgen Habermas's philosophy of communicative rationality and discourse ethics, according to which politics becomes more legitimate the more people engage in public discourse that is not disrupted by the influence of power, where the debate is governed solely by the rational persuasiveness of individual arguments, and that also has an important civilising effect on society *per se*. Similarly, Havlíček believed that freedom of the press was an important means of policing both the legislature and state administration, which is no less important than judicial independence but which, at the same time, leads to a higher political culture and strengthens the moral cohesion of society. Political realism for Masaryk and other politicians of this time primarily meant critical debate by free citizens that was based on and governed by reason, on the basis of which, channelling Havlíček, a political community in which freedom and power would not contradict each other could be formed.

Over time, Austria-Hungary changed, working towards limited liberal, though not democratic, constitutionality. How would you define the contours of our Czech path in this context?
The Austro-Hungarian Compromise, which introduced constitutional dualism into state organisation, did also contain other forms of

provincial and historical "settlement", but killed off the idea that the monarchy could be reformed according to democratic and federal principles. This alienated Czech politics, which had to find new directions and impetus for itself.

In 1879, we entered into active Austro-Hungarian politics, but lost hope of constitutional goals. According to František Ladislav Rieger, this was called "crumbs-under-the-table politics"…

What's more, social democracy is just establishing itself at this time, and with it we see this whole new political problem, accurately rendered and described by Masaryk as the "social question", opening up in Czech politics, albeit – paradoxically – in the Austro-Slavist spirit and under the wings of the *Gesamtpartei*. Instead of the step-by-step gains being made in the political environment, an entirely new political concept of social rights and justice is also annexed to the right of nations to self-determination. But there is a political struggle extending beyond the national framework, aimed at changing not just the constitutional regime, but also, and directly, economic and social conditions. In place of political or constitutional changes, there are demands to proceed immediately to the transformation of society at large. Masaryk understood this movement very well. His political success lay not only in the continuation of the revivalist program, with its legitimising story about education and moral integrity in politics, but above all in the ability to link the Czech question and the social question and, over time, to connect all this with a vision of "world revolution". Reading Masaryk's later reflections on a "new Europe", we are still surprised by the peculiar combination of utopian visionariness and political realism that we would search for in vain elsewhere in 19th-century Czech revivalist politics, but without which the emergence of an independent Czechoslovakia and its legitimacy as a democratic, republican, civil, culturally open and educated state would be inconceivable. Czechoslovakia was thus paradoxically created by the continuity of revivalist ideals and the discontinuity of the political Romanticism associated with them, and its replacement with realism. No state can get by without realism, just as it cannot do without the Romantic ideals that established it.

The Republic
of Educated Citizens,
or Masaryk's Attempt
at a Central European Utopia

After 1918, Tomáš Garrigue Masaryk began to build a republic, in part, by establishing a Czechoslovak nation, and the Slovaks never came to terms with this. The first time they wanted to secede was only four years or so after the founding of the republic, which was plainly of no help in furthering the new understanding of statehood. Where did we go wrong with the Slovaks?

We cannot simply say that the political Czechoslovak nation did not exist as a sovereign people. *Res publica* means the possibility of governing in a public space, and this in turn presupposes at least the linguistic ability to negotiate and share one polity. In this respect, the construction of a Czechoslovak nation as a state-forming force and constituent power made sense, even if it turned out that the cultural and political differences had been underestimated. It was not aligned with the aspirations and ambitions of the Slovaks, who had been literally fighting for their bare survival in the Hungarian part of the monarchy prior to 1914, but over the next two decades they managed to emancipate themselves and become a self-confident nation in the new conditions of the Czechoslovak Republic.

It's not just a question of language. A common state also needs some common history. A recent survey has shown that most Czechs consider the best period in modern history to be the First Republic, whereas the Slovaks plumped for the years from 1948 to 1989 and then the wartime Slovak State. In the absence of a common view of history, the closeness of languages solves nothing.

This is true. The relationship between Czechs and Slovaks goes to show how even nations that are very similar and don't harbour a mutual hatred so fierce it spills over into war or other conflict can sometimes misunderstand each other or be unable to reach a political consensus because of their different historical, cultural and economic development. Note, though, that every attempt at democratisation since 1918, from the Martin Declaration to the Velvet Revolution in 1989, when the talk was about an authentic federation, has involved the question of nationality. This is the kernel of the problem when it comes to democratic government. Left unresolved, a republican Czechoslovakia would find it difficult to function, something the founders of the common state were aware of.

So why didn't they address this matter more thoroughly from the beginning? After all, there was the so-called Pittsburgh Agreement of May 1918, in which we promised the Slovaks that they would have their own administration, their own assembly and their own courts. That agreement was signed by American Czechs and American Slovaks alike.

Let's not forget that Masaryk was a „deviant" in Czech political culture, by which I mean he was very detached from mainstream opinions, prejudices and political practices. When he rewrote Czech history as a historical struggle for humanism, democracy and a republican government that was to become a part of the "world revolution", he was swimming upstream against a nation that was forming itself linguistically and culturally and was keen on shrouding itself in its own myths. Masaryk's battle for a Czech identity steeped in an open and democratic nation ran counter to the vast majority of what was dominating politics at the time. Consequently, the only way he was going to become president was by some remarkable concurrence of international circumstances and in the wake of a very extraordinary event, such as the First World War. It was only by adopting the idea of national self-determination and autonomy as part of the global struggle for universal values that he was able to convince allies of the meaningfulness and viability of an independent Czechoslovak state. Any claim that it would be an artificial state unviable as soon as it came into being is a false premise. This is a conservative argument raised by monarchists and ethnonationalists. They entertain the delusion that, as only nations are natural, only nation states built on purely ethnic and cultural foundations can function politically and constitutionally. Of course, they are mistaken, because a nation is just as artificial a construct as a state. And Masaryk's legitimation of the Czechoslovak state by successfully imposing a state with clearly universalistic foundations on a nation defining itself culturally and linguistically is proof of this. In retrospect, it looks like this was a matter of course, but the democratism and liberal openness of First-Republic society was not natural, nor a given. It had to be fought for, and Masaryk held his ground so admirably that today we can create myths about what we call the First Republic and – contrasted with other historical periods – idealise it. However, if we are to approach these myths critically, we should first factor out the contradictory and very dangerous myth that the Czechs had always lived merely as an ethnic group that had never matured into an adult political nation, meaning they were unable to defend the existence of an independent Czechoslovak state. As though there were a schism here between the Czech nation and statehood, with the nation being unable to defend statehood in critical moments, even if this will cost it its life. That's a profound mistake because the Czechoslovak state, despite all the difficulties and conflicts, functioned right up until the political and international order buckled in Europe and across the world.

Yes, but the First Republic failed even to heed the peace treaty of Saint-Germain, in which we promised autonomy to Carpathian Ruthenia.
The Czechoslovak Republic was created amid the drama at the end of the First World War, and by the 1920 elections the nature of the regime had yet to be decided. No one knew whether it would be socialist or constitutionally democratic and liberal. The birth of the republic, then, was hardly dictated exclusively by ethnic conflicts, as some critics of Czechoslovakia would still have us believe. Instead, it was determined by the more general ideological and po-

litical conflicts shattering the world at the time. Despite the initial opposition of ethnic Germans and Hungarians, it is worth pointing out that their minority political parties participated in the first parliamentary elections in 1920, and the Social Democrats' split from the nationalist blocs was not only a great help for political and social differentiation within the fledgling republic, but also created an opportunity to moderate ethnic conflicts and shape political cooperation and coalitions. Let's not forget that, in 1920, the Social Democrats emerged triumphant among everyone – the Czechs, Slovaks and Germans. Masaryk left his clear mark on the programme pursued by contemporary Social Democrats, showing that the philosopher's "social question" had a very specific political dimension. Masaryk's *Social Question* is just as crucial to understanding his philosophical and political thinking as the *Czech Question*. These two questions go hand in glove and cannot be probed and judged separately. If we sit down and think about the endlessly repeated mantra that, during the national revival, the Czech nation couldn't depend on the traditional nobility and its high culture, so it set out its stall as a plebeian nation and still clings to that plebeian identity, we realise that the Czech question was always also a social question about the identity of the rural and urban strata that were being marginalised by the modernisation process. There has always been a political plane to the Czech question that encompasses the democratic and republican form of government on the one hand and social justice on the other. In this respect, the sharing of language and culture prevented social marginalisation and consolidated the sense of reciprocity and togetherness in a society whose economic, political and administrative institutions were exerting ever more pressure on cultural homogeneity and a preference for one language at the expense of others spoken together and between one other by the nations of the multi-ethnic Habsburg monarchy. Obviously, once the monarchy disintegrated, this problem and all the risks attached to it were inherited by the republican and democratic Czechoslovakia.

When and why did ethnic problems in Czechoslovakia become unsolvable?

When they couldn't be resolved by European diplomacy. The expectations everyone had of the whole twenty-year period between the world wars were of such magnitude and diversity as to be impossible to satisfy. The Czechoslovak tragedy in 1938 closes this period while raising the curtain on the utter destruction that would be wrought by the coming war.

Why didn't the Czechoslovak project succeed further down the line either?

After the Velvet Revolution in the early 1990s, Czechoslovakism was virtually a dirty word, just another name for Czech chauvinism suppressing Slovak political ambitions. In reality, the Czechoslovakism project was an attempt to create a constitutional nation that would remain both open and inclusive, and capable of forming a democratic republic along with all other nationalities living in the territory of Czechoslovakia. As we know from the sociology of nations, there is no nation state without ethnic minorities, which can be very diverse and have different political aspirations and needs. Consequently, the nation state must devise various national policies while at the same time rigorously separating the notion of a political nation of people from the cultural and ethnic concept of nations and nationalities. Spain is one example today, but in the past the Czechoslovakism project was part of this more general effort to separate democratic politics from purely ethnic identities and use them to build an inclusive republican and democratic society in the spirit of the Masarykian ethos, according to which education and nurture are essential if democracy is to grow. Since we've started discussing the Slovak issue, besides touching on the resumption, in 1919, of the *Matica slovenská*'s cultural activity after more than forty years of Magyarisation policy in Slovakia, we should also mention the fact that the education process and politics in First-Republic Slovakia were governed, for the most part, by Slovak politicians and supporters of Czechoslovakism, such as the Social Democrat Ivan Dérer. The Agrarian Party leader Milan Hodža was also education minister in his time. To this day, it is admirable how the Slovak nation managed to emancipate itself not only politically, but also scientifically, in the space of two decades. In 1937, for example, *Vedecká syntéza* – a very broad-based association inspired by Viennese logical positivism – was formed.

And yet those attempts to break away existed from the very dawn of the republic, as I have already mentioned. There is even a drawing by Adolf Hoffmeister from, I think, 1922, in which the Slovaks are depicted as burying Czechoslovakia. Do you think the Slovaks always wanted independence?
Today, even Slovak historians – I'm thinking, for instance, of Dušan Kováč – write that Slovak politicians accepted First-Republic state centralism as a necessary stepping stone to Slovakia's extrication from Hungarian influence. However, this centralism was viewed as a temporary policy, not as a permanent constitutional solution to the Czecho-Slovak question. Support for science and education, nevertheless, was hardly limited to the Czechs and Slovaks, as we can see from constitutionally guaranteed rights, the specific national policies pursued by individual governments, and, for example, Masaryk's personal million-crown donation towards the establishment of the *Hungarian Scientific, Literary and Artistic Society in Czechoslovakia*. Naturally, we must not forget the important role played by Russian exiles, without whom it is difficult to imagine how the famous – and still internationally acclaimed – Prague Linguistic Circle would have functioned. As for the German minority, its gifted members had the advantage of being able to study at the more prestigious universities in Austria and Germany, but there were also two polytechnics closer to home: the Czech Technical University in Prague and the Brno University of Technology, each linguistically split into Czech and German parts. Similarly, Charles University

was divided into German and Czech sections in 1882. Education policy and scientific life in Czechoslovakia's First Republic are hardly stellar, but it is remarkable how, in this multiethnic landscape, education was given free rein while hatred and political dictatorship were raging in neighbouring countries. What's more, First-Republic Czechoslovakia provided sanctuary and an escape route for Europe's greatest philosophers, scientists and writers, such as Edmund Husserl, Hans Kelsen, and Heinrich and Thomas Mann, to whom the small rural town of Proseč granted right of residence as the first step on the way to Czechoslovak citizenship, which subsequently enabled their families to emigrate to the United States.

And, as officially communicated to me in the Bundestag, it was thanks to our generosity towards the Germans after 1933 that the favour was reciprocated in the 1980s, when, having been stripped of Czechoslovak citizenship, I was granted German citizenship... And as one of our classic playwrights turned president Václav Havel would have it: "Them's the paradoxes, right?" That's why citizenship is always so much more than nationality. It is a political ethos shared across states and history! Nationality is a technical legal term that applies to both natural and legal persons. Citizenship, on the other hand, is a concept that encompasses not only the mutual relationship between the state and its citizens, but also inter-citizen relations as percolators of political and moral ideals. Nor is citizenship ethnicity. As a matter of fact, citizenship liberates us from ethnicity by reaching beyond it. Asylum law is a good example of how even vulnerable people with no home – the stateless – can become citizens enjoying full rights and freedoms. And how free and democratic states can give legal protection and social security to those who have had to flee their own homes. The First-Republic history of science and education shows how society and the whole country can thrive by opening up to external influences and seeking out what they are lacking or what is beyond their reach. This cultural and political openness,

195

a policy to nurture the republican spirit of Czechoslovakia's citizens, continues to remind us that democracy is conceivable only as a project of political, cultural and intellectual openness.

In fact, TG Masaryk only engaged in activity he associated with democracy, namely human progress. And Dušan Třeštík added: "Not everyone wanted this, especially those left lagging behind in southern Moravia and in southern and eastern Bohemia. They remembered the good old days of peace and quiet, and none of this present progress, when the Viennese throne and altar held sway. Masaryk's revolution of progress and democracy was spurred on, in particular, by an army of teachers and junior civil servants."

It is interesting and paradoxical how Masaryk criticised "schoolmaster politics", which was steeped in pontification and treated ordinary citizens as needy beings who were required, first and foremost, to be deferential and blindly parrot authoritative opinions. Masaryk believed that education and politics inhabited almost identical areas of human life, relying on mutual recognition, collaboration and cognition. In this sense, the building of the first Czechoslovak Republic was a typical 19th-century project that could not take place until the 20th century. Masaryk identified the national revolution and the emergence of the Czechoslovak state with progress and the global revolution that was refashioning modern people's minds and hearts. Channelling the spirit of Palacký's concept of history, Masaryk dismissed monarchies as authoritarian and inherently violent and mechanically structured political units that once ruled half of Europe but, because they pursued repressive policies, lacked legitimacy. According to Masaryk, national and ethnic conflicts and tensions could be defused not by sovereign power and its coercive machinery, but only by democracy and freedom. The Allies, spearheaded by President Wilson, campaigned for these ideals – together with the principle that small nations should have an equal seat at the table – in the post-war peace treaties, and as far as Masaryk was concerned they were essential for peace in Europe and for addressing the conflicts between the nations living there. In his *Making of a State*, he even hypothesised that the lessons learnt from the war would guide Europe to unification and gradual federalisation: the continent would no longer be controlled by one or several superpowers; instead, security and cooperation would be legally and politically guaranteed for everyone, including the smallest nations. In his eyes, the Great War was simply the culmination of the liberation movement, which saw the existing autocratic monarchies of Austria-Hungary, Prussia and Russia defeated and paved the way for "the possibility of a democratic Europe, and thus of freedom and independence for all nations". For Masaryk, the principles of federalisation and autonomy were at the core of democracy as a political order and form of modern life.

This was probably why, as his friend Ivan Hálka wrote, he agreed in his dealings with the German deputies that our national anthem should have a German stanza. This idea, however, triggered a monumental backlash from patriots. "Go to hell, you loathsome traitor," screamed the newspaper *Národní listy*. Is this proof that he was a steadfast champion of democratism, which he believed to be on a higher plane than the particularistic Slavophilia and Pan-Germanism?

Masaryk's Europeanism, or "Europeism" as he was wont to call it, was rooted in the conviction that democracy was also a project that was geared towards the education of citizens and entire nations while seeking to further their mutual cultural understanding. He contrasted this Europeanism with Slavophilia, which he found too limited and negatively inclined towards non-Slavic – especially Germanic – peoples. Europeanism was thus antithetical not only to Kollárian Pan-Slavic messianism, but also to all other forms of nationalist messianism, including Pan-Germanism. Europeanism went beyond the restrictive categories of Slavism and Germanism, and even of East and West, as recognised by the political romanticism of the

19th and early 20th century. Masaryk was also a critic of all philosophies espousing cultural regression, such as Spengler's *The Decline of the West*, because, the way he saw it, the beacon of democracy had not been lit in either the East or the West. Rather, he believed in a truly planetary movement of all modern humanity. In the postwar era, Masaryk opined, "democracy has yet to be consistently implemented anywhere; all democratic states so far are nothing but an attempt at democracy". Democratic states, then, are states of the future that have yet to be created and developed on the basis of the ideals of freedom, equality and fraternity. What is interesting in this context is not so much that Masaryk contrasted democracy and its popular sovereignty with the monarchy and its aristocratic power based on divine will and grace; much more important is the fact that Masaryk, like many other sociologists and philosophers of his time, surmised that democracy would spell the end of monarchic rule and mark the arrival of new politics underpinned by governance and self-government, thereby harmonising the assorted social and constituent powers and forces. He thought that, in a democracy, bureaucracy is transformed into power that is placed at the service of the popular administration in the name of humanity, which, like society at large, is based on rationality and education. Here, expertise meets general democratic proselytism. Masaryk clearly found inspiration for this concept not only in Bolzano's utopian *On the Best State* of 1831, but also – and even more so – in Dewey and other philosophers of American Pragmatism, although otherwise he was generally critical of pragmatism.

Masaryk had a vision or, as you say, he was a utopian, but he was also an educated realist. And Václav Havel tried to build on that legacy.
I think that every great statesman or stateswoman is both a utopian and a sceptic. If they are to establish and build a state or change society, they need a vision that is different from the world in which

they live and which they want to change. Utopia is an early modern genre in which rationality and education always took centre stage. At the same time, however, we must not forget that Thomas More intended his famous work to be an ironic commentary on, and criticism of, the contemporary political and social situation. Without this irony, utopia ceases to be a literary genre and becomes a political plan to build a despotic society. Irony is a manifestation of scepticism about the possibility of establishing utopia as a real political society, but simultaneously urges all readers or listeners not to resign themselves to the status quo and to work on changing the situation. Irony, then, is a particular form of human judgement and a critical spirit that, while not giving up on the possibility of redress and change, remains sceptical of all policies promising to "fulfil ideals" of any kind. In this sense, the attempt to create the Czechoslovak state as a state of educated and self-assured citizens who, by harnessing rationality, come to recognise that democracies and the ideals of humanity are universally valid, really is a type of utopia. This has left a profound imprint on modern Czech culture, for better or worse. We quite rightly realise that democracy must also include education policy, but we also oftentimes pretend that politics is just an inferior activity in the service of education, culture and great thoughts untainted by quotidian political bickering and clashes. Yet politics and education are interdependent, albeit without scholars being able to dictate to politicians how to make decisions, or politicians dictating to scholars how to think. However, any rational democrat should support education as it creates conditions for informed and civilised debate.

This brings us to the most important thing that Masaryk came up with: he believed that Europe's fresh start lay in higher learning. Today, paradoxically, we do not invest enough money in education. We don't even have university postgraduate studies for state offi-

cials and politicians in the vein of France's École nationale d'administration. Why is that?

Democracy cannot function where ignorance prevails. We are as keenly aware of this today as politicians and philosophers were a hundred years ago. Masaryk, in his utopian way, went so far as to declare that a democratic republic required a new person, a modern Adam, denuded of old habits and able to adopt new ones built on humanity, which is just another way of saying democracy. In this context, he also spoke of "exact inventiveness", or imagination based on precise thinking. It is this that brings us to cunning strategies capable of casting aside the politics of messianism and anthropomorphism and teaching citizens to behave as sovereign individuals engaging in debate and action in public without resorting to backstage tricks and crooked deceit against those with whom they form a single political people. Democracy is inconceivable without this underlying imagination that allows people to govern as free and equal individuals. That is precisely how we should be viewing Masaryk's observation that democracy is not just a form of government or administration, but an opinion on life and the world.

What it boils down to, then, is that a democratic republic is a kind of social contract – one that needs to be respected by citizens.

Exactly! Masaryk even criticises Rousseau's concept of the social contract. He turned the entire fiction upside down and said that this contract doesn't come until later down the line, at a certain stage of human progress brought about by the advancement of learning. The social contract marks not the beginning, but the culmination, of civilisation! Justice is the mainstay of the state, and the natural law of democracy is the equality that forms its ethical basis. In this context, it is also interesting how Masaryk criticised the scholars of jurisprudence and legal theorists who had rejected the ethical basis underpinning the existence of the state and its laws, and how he saw, in this juristic abstraction dictating that the state justifies itself by its very existence and its law by its normativity, an example of the erstwhile scholasticism which democratic political science and legal theory needed to shed. For Masaryk, natural law that is formulated ethically, rather than religiously, serves as a baseline standard for any state and any legal system.

This would explain the fundamental effort to form a more universal natural law that runs through all of his work.

The way Masaryk sees it, in a democracy citizens double up as *poiétai*, i.e. the poets and creators of life who, through the exact imagination we have mentioned and the wisdom that is borne of education, can correctly determine what is right and good for them. In this sense, democratic republics really were a new era of humankind, and all Masaryk actually did was globalise Palacký's national philosophy of history by enshrining it in a world movement and in the organisation of humanity into a modern global civilisation. According to Masaryk, humanity relentlessly spreads around the world, and the renewal of national autonomy and state sovereignty is part of this universal movement and the struggle for the birth of a new humankind.

Had any solution actually been possible, considering that Hitler came to power in Germany and, in the twenty years of the Czechoslovak Republic's existence, the Germans had not felt like equal citizens?

Masaryk knew full well that, in the absence of a solution to the nationalist matter of the ethnic Germans, it would be impossible to establish a stable Czechoslovak democracy. With this in mind, in the same breath he would stress that their minority right to self-determination was not a right to secession, but was necessary to impart a new, democratic form to the centuries-old relations between the Czech and German ethnicities in the Czech Lands. As the question of democracy is also a question of nurture and education, for

Masaryk minority rights meant, above all, the opportunity for minorities to be educated in their mother tongue, to be free to develop their own culture, and to have access to the authorities in an "official language". Unlike the Romantics, Masaryk was a political and cultural realist who knew very well that national life was not dictated exclusively by language, so a nation state that was ethnically and nationalistically heterogeneous could not have a single official language. A democratic state must communicate with all of its citizens because it is, after all, their creation. Therein lies the spirit and purpose of "minority official languages".

I would go back to why we failed to resolve the German question.
Here I think we should return once more to the "Czech question" we discussed at the beginning. Jan Patočka criticised Masaryk for not seeing the analogy between the Czech and German questions as, in his opinion, they addressed the same problem, namely the issue of marginal existence and cultural and political backwardness compared to other European nations. According to Patočka, the Czech question provides a philosophical timetable and solution to the German question because German history was an important part of European cultural entity in the Middle Ages, but in the modern age it has suffered cultural and political decline. This decline stands it apart from Czech history because it was amplified and complicated by modernisation in the form of Prussian militarism, authoritarianism and the belligerent state. Consequently, the ideals of humanity moulded by Lessing, Kant, Goethe and Schiller were gradually supplanted in 19th-century Germany by new materialism and the might-is-right theory. Systematic will, rational organisation, the power of technology, and energy mobilisation were typical for this entire epoch, which witnessed the growth of the Prussian imperial state – aptly described by Patočka as "the first technocratic state in Europe". Patočka claims that Masaryk's interpretation of the German question as the historical onset of Prussian militarism, which,

after 1866, takes over the imperial idea and leadership from Austria, was flimsy and misguided. Not because the Prussian solution to the German question was essentially flawed, but because of his inability to see this process as part of the much more general philosophical problem of the materialisation of reality and politics, which, in Patočka's words, "hands the state mechanism ever more control over all of life and engineers the belief that reality is a planned and thoroughly organised force that operates with purposeful, unscrupulous certainty".

Does this philosophical speculation cloud political reality and the needs of everyday political work?
You are right that the Czech question's political context and the tasks it faced were different and that, for example, it did not have to take a critical view of the modern policy of state raids and militaristic organisations. Patočka, however, left these glaring political differences or cultural similarities to one side and focused instead on a philosophical re-evaluation of Masaryk's thinking and the context of his philosophical concept. He wanted to understand Masaryk as a philosopher grappling with the modern world and society as a *crisis* of humankind for which there was an ethical solution and a religious purpose. Although Patočka had analysed, for instance, how Masaryk's thinking was influenced by Brentano's philosophy or, generally, positivism, and had criticised some of his views on German idealism, he did emphasise the importance of Masaryk's concept of religion as a morals-based, scientifically justified and politically consensual religion of individual responsibility. According to Patočka, Masaryk's positivism paradoxically insisted that all reality had a metaphysical moral basis. An analysis of this apparent paradox and the contradiction between positivism and Platonism in Masaryk's work opens up completely new possibilities to ponder and discuss it, for example, in direct connection with Dostoyevsky's and, especially, Nietzsche's philosophy. In *An attempt at Czech national philosophy*

and its failure, a treatise from the 1970s, Patočka criticised Masaryk for being unable to see that the modern age of the 20th century was not a time in which there had been a single war unleashing a world revolution of democracy against authoritarianism, but that this era was one long period of warfare and revolt, and, as both Nietzsche and Dostoyevsky would have said, a period of growing nihilism, in which liberty and personal freedom simultaneously commanded and lost all subjectivity. Patočka is certainly very harsh about the internal contradiction between Masaryk's positivism and his suspicion of idealism and metaphysics as a "lack of courage to engage in actual philosophising", but he also acknowledges that Masaryk was able to fundamentally question the crisis and decline of humankind, for which – like Nietzsche and Dostoyevsky – he finds positivist proof, namely the self-alienation of modern humankind and a loss of faith that leads to killing, including suicide. As such, Patočka's criticism of Masaryk is not political, but primarily philosophical, and dwells on Masaryk's unwillingness to single out philosophy as an autonomous activity of the spirit that is independent of positive science, morality and religion. In the treatise we have mentioned, Patočka actually draws support from Heidegger's famous statement that "only a god can save us", and speculates that Masaryk would probably have subscribed to it, even though he was not a patient philosopher and only instinctively sensed how deep the philosophical problems of metaphysics were. I would say, however, that Patočka's philosophising on politics as an active intervention of the spirit and a search for the meaning of existence is no less problematic. The fact that, in our thinking, we could look at the depth and meaning of our existence and, on that basis, navigate our way round the chaos of the present day and plot the path of a free life therein, is in itself empirically readily rebuttable because human history is illustrated – literally – with many images of the alliance between philosophy and dictatorship. The classic notion that philosophy liberates or even saves the world is a dangerous preconception since history teaches us that, for every Socratic free spirit, there are several philosophers preoccupied with the Platonic desire for a political service given over to ideas. I contend that the greatest liberation, on the contrary, comes in discovering that no philosophy can legitimise today's politics or culturally or intellectually unite today's complex society. To paraphrase: thank goodness no philosophers nor anyone else can save us today! Only we can save ourselves. And I think Masaryk's philosophy is relevant precisely to this democratic ethos, which holds true regardless of any search for or inkling of the metaphysical depths of humankind's existence and crisis.

Why do we so easily lose sight of this democratic ethos, despite bandying Masaryk's name about so often?
For Masaryk, democracy is never just a constitutional form, a government regime, or a technique of power, but also a form of life and, above all, a moral task that has a salutary purpose and hence a religious essence. In this sense, Masaryk's concept of world revolution is a particular example of political theology and eschatology. However, seeing as democracy and the republic are a positive task for him, besides political theology we must also analyse world revolution as a specific form of political realism. Masaryk was a political realist, as corroborated by the name of the party he founded and evidenced by his wider perception. Nevertheless, today's society, including politics, economics, law, and international relations, is much more complex and its problems cannot be fixed with the simple ethical or political solutions Masaryk had envisaged at the time. In this regard, it is paradoxical that this great figure of 19th-century philosophy and politics continues to serve as a frame of reference for today's Czech politics. In fact, the situation we find ourselves in today is the completely opposite of Masaryk's. While he and his generation were building a state in the hope that they could use it as a vehicle to create a democratic society and a political nation, we are faced with the challenge of defending and asserting our democratic identity and

republican values against those who abhor them and yet are making their home in the state we are forming. In this sense, a struggle is still being waged for a republic of educated citizens, which in Central Europe remains a utopian dream interspersed by the nightmares of modern nationalism and racism that we thought had been flushed out, along with its history of extreme violence, long ago. It is as though, for some strange reason, the surface skin of learning and civility, under which the irrational forces and destructive instincts that Sigmund Freud wrote about in his day are constantly gurgling, were thinner and more prone to rupture in Central Europe.

Intellectuals and Politics

French philosopher Julien Benda's *La Trahison des Clercs* was published in 1927 and has been translated into many languages – into English, incidentally, as *The Treason of the Intellectuals*. His work has been revisited recently, for example, by the political scientist Jan-Werner Müller in order to contrast Benda's call for "anti-passionate" thinking, wherein the only passion ought to be a passion for rationality, with the current wave of populism. Benda was critical of the betrayal of the universalist position by intellectuals, who, by interpreting their role as they did, had forsaken equality and democracy. As far as he was concerned, it was this betrayal that had led them down the path of class struggle, nationalism, and racism. Interesting times...

... definitely, because coincidentally 1927 was when Czechoslovakia's First Republic peaked politically, culturally and intellectually. While Benda was accusing contemporary intellectuals of betraying universal reason and ideas by subscribing to nationalism and other cultural prejudices, our young Central European state was successfully combining the building of this nation state with the universalist ideals of democracy and republicanism.

Is this a paradox?
Far from it. Benda was simply coming from a typically French cultural tradition where anything that is not universal initially draws suspicion. By the way, this tradition still remains firmly entrenched in France. What makes it interesting is that it shows how even universalism can easily slide into cultural prejudice.

But if we are to address the alleged betrayal of scholars or intellectuals, we should first clarify who these intellectuals are...
... and what their job in society is and whether there is a place and a role for them in politics. And I also think we should do away with

harsh judgements, whether by Benda or anyone else, summarily accusing other intellectuals of treason when, in fact, they are often only taking a different view of what philosophy or learning is and what its role in modern society should be. Masaryk's concept of democracy as something that steadfastly guides us towards, and instils in us, humanity belongs to the philosophical and sociological register of the 19th century. For him, democracy was an intellectual and moral task, and therefore the scholar and teacher automatically constituted both a cultural and political elite shouldered with enormous social responsibility. Long-running opinion polls show that, to this day, Czech society ascribes lots of prestige to learning. Acutely aware of the responsibility of intellectuals and scholars, it sometimes has unrealistic expectations of them. But let's put the specific situation in Czech society to one side for the time being. In the 20th century, this whole sociological discipline emerged that was preoccupied with intellectuals as a particular social group with its own special role in modern society. Whereas Benda was demanding that intellectuals remain true to universalism and fight nationalism and all cultural particularisms, the sociologist Karl Mannheim regarded intellectuals as people who, courtesy of their learning and knowledge, were the only group that could achieve the rational and value-based unification of fragmented modern society. As Mannheim's intellectuals were supposedly free of social prejudices due to their rational knowledge, they were also able to unify complex, contradictory and functionally differentiated modern society, both rationally and in its values.

But Mannheim faced opposition from Frankfurt School sympathisers. How do you view that school's representatives today?
Representatives of Frankfurt critical theory, with Max Horkheimer at the helm, lambasted Mannheim's sociology of knowledge. By grasping truth and knowledge as part of a socially constructed and bounded reality, Mannheim questioned the Marxist concept

of truth as an objective philosophical category. At the turn of the 1930s, Mannheim was a professor of sociology at the University of Frankfurt. One of his pupils was Norbert Elias, later a famous sociologist himself. However, throughout Mannheim's time here there was a lot of tension between him and the people from Horkheimer's critical Institute for Social Research. These philosophical and sociological conflicts came to an end when the Nazis staged their coup and Mannheim fled to London, where he began teaching at the London School of Economics, while Horkheimer and others transferred the Institute's activities briefly to Geneva and then, in 1935, to New York, where critical theory – albeit in much different forms – continues to be cultivated at the New School for Social Research. This episode of intellectual history from the last century is itself an example of the expectations, disappointments and, most of all, transformations of a social group we have become accustomed to calling "public intellectuals". Though the term "public intellectual" carries no sociological or political meaning, it does concentrate the ethical expectation that intellectuals, rather than leading society full on with their rationality, will be the voice of its conscience, if not the conscience of humankind. This is why the group is such a loose patchwork of opinions and includes the likes of Jean-Paul Sartre, Simone Weil, Albert Camus, Raymond Aron, Michel Foucault, Karl Jaspers, Hannah Arendt, Jürgen Habermas, Bertrand Russell, Raymond Williams, Isaiah Berlin, Karl Popper, José Ortega y Gasset, Umberto Eco, Germaine Greer, and many other publicly active intellectuals, thinkers and philosophers following – one way or another – the tradition of the Enlightenment scholar, the *homme de lettres*. Nevertheless, the modern expectations associated with intellectuals, scholars and philosophers had a spanner thrown in the works by Edmund Husserl, who, in his 1935 lecture on *The Crisis of European Humanity and Philosophy*, went beyond universal practical activity, such as policy serving the common good of a particular nation or political society, to define the particular function of "free and universal theoretical reflection", which encompasses all ideals and is able to describe the "universe of all norms". This supreme function, Husserl claims, is reserved for philosophy, so philosophers become functionaries of all humankind and therefore have the never-ending, but unbending, task of contributing to a universal, ideal-oriented society.

Václav Bělohradský challenges Husserl's definition, arguing that functionaries of humankind are always functionaries of empire.
Václav Bělohradský is a close friend of mine and yours, and I, for example, still regard *Myslet zeleň světa* [Thinking the Greening of the World], the book of your interviews together, as one of the most important Czech philosophical publications of the last half-century. I would say that Bělohradský is one of the most important figures in Czech intellectual life at the turn of the 21st century. He is an extraordinarily inspiring and original thinker, but must not be taken literally. Although he thinks as a philosopher, he expresses himself as a writer, and this is a problem for anyone who wants to argue or debate with him. Just as Bohumil Hrabal managed to imbue his writings with all the beauty of philosophical thoughts, Václav Bělohradský composes philosophical and political essays with the flourish of a wordsmith unfettered by patterns of reasoning or rules of logic. Sometimes I wonder how much richer Czech literature would have been had he decided to become a writer instead of plotting the path of a philosopher and public intellectual confronted by all the wriggling and writhing bound up with this peculiar and fast disappearing calling. But back to Bělohradský's criticism of Husserl's philosophers as functionaries of humankind, which he discussed in his 1989 essay *Příchod doby cikánské aneb Evropou se jen potulovat* [The Advent of the Gypsy Age, or Wandering Aimlessly around Europe]. Bělohradský looks at these philosophers and their – figuratively speaking – "empire", and counters them with the "gypsies" kicked out by European civilisation as an unseemly

and maladjusted ethnic group. For Husserl, gypsies don't belong to Europe because they are "constantly roaming" and therefore cannot understand the continent's universalist foundations. Bělohradský, on the other hand, believes that it is the philosopher's job not to be a functionary, but a gypsy, of humankind and to explore ways out of all metaphysics and history with their grand narratives and objective laws. Besides this original metaphor, Bělohradský's criticism also echoes the important – and at the time philosophically very popular – call for a hermeneutic revolution in Western culture, seeking the abandonment of objective truths and ideas and the adoption of the "new idea" that truth is always shared among people and is therefore inherent in speech itself, which is not an object and belongs to no one – not the Leader, the Party, the Philosopher, nor anyone else.

But Bělohradský has taken that from postmodern philosophy. Lyotard, Vattimo, Eco, Foucault and Derrida were espousing similar ideas...

It goes without saying that Bělohradský is directly picking up on what contemporary philosophy refers to as the linguistic and postmodern turn and connects it with the Central European philosophical tradition. His concept of hermeneutics ultimately leads to the basic notion, first developed by Karl Mannheim, that philosophical ideas must be interpreted sociologically and politically. Tellingly, Bělohradský's samizdat volume of essays published in 1984 by Václav Havel's Edice Expedice was entitled *Přirozený svět jako politický problém* [The Life-World as a Political Problem]. Not, note, the "philosophical problem" Bělohradský's teacher Jan Patočka had been wrestling with half a century earlier, but a "political problem". Although Bělohradský was heavily influenced by Patočka, he remoulded and rewrote his teacher's philosophy to make it his own. Working our way down from Husserl via Patočka, then, we arrive at Bělohradský and see this view that philosophical problems and themes such as authenticity, laws, subjects, objects, language, techniques, polemics, truth and rationality cannot be separated from the life and experience shared by those who belong to a certain political community. Here, Bělohradský is following a specific development in 20th-century thought that gradually transformed philosophical phenomenology into sociological hermeneutics. I like the part of the preface that Václav Bělohradský added to the original volume's extended version in readiness for the first official edition published by Český spisovatel in 1991: "In the first texts, I am still in thrall to the idea that the philosopher must seek out an authentic version of the world and see to its purity. By the final texts, I had come to believe that the philosopher should be doing something else entirely: systematically criticising the claims of various versions of the world to be an authentic version of the world." These sentences are nothing less than a declaration of war on his own thinking because, for Bělohradský, authenticity has always been a central philosophical theme. The search for and defence of everything authentic, but at the same time opposition to every authentic version of the world! Another reason I feel such close affinity with this normative paradox is that it has all sorts of things in common with the theory of social systems, according to which claims to validity can never be universal in modern society, but are always limited and bounded, for example, by economic, political, legal, educational, religious or scientific systems. I know that Bělohradský would probably object because for him, as for the French philosopher Jean-François Lyotard, "system" is just another way of saying totalitarianism. In reality, however, even today's systems theory demands that every version of the world be rigorously examined to determine whether it is claiming to be authentic. Those claims always presuppose universal understanding, objective validity and an understanding of society and humanity in its totality, which is precluded by the complex nature of today's society and its functional differentiation. That's why I prefer the texts in which Bělohradský declares war on himself and on all total thought patterns.

Bělohradský may have rejected the role of the functionary, but by recently making an appearance at one of Andrej Babiš's populist movement ANO conferences he joined the "functionaries of empire". Would you say there's any truth in that?

I think one of the philosophers to whom Václav Bělohradský is closest is Richard Rorty, with whom he shares the belief that democracy takes precedence over philosophy, and literature over logos. For him, democracy is just another name for heterogeneous situations and value pluralism, so I regarded this specific appearance not as a ticket to join the political movement or an attempt to become a functionary furthering its manifesto, but as a stab at reaching out to this area of our inconsistent political present. In other respects, obviously, Václav Bělohradský and I often lock horns. In fact, some of our public exchanges have filled whole books, such as the recently published *Lidská práva: (ne)smysl české politiky?* [Human Rights: A (Non)sense of Czech Politics?], a collection of essays that was given a very spirited reception and elicited lively reaction from philosophers, lawyers, political scientists and others. Even so, I don't think we can simply dismiss Václav Bělohradský's political engagement here with shallow judgements asserting that this is the action of a self-contradictory opportunist or a chaotic intellectual who previously supported Václav Klaus, then spawned an ideological breeding ground for the left in general and the Social Democrats in particular, subsequently sided with Miloš Zeman in his presidential campaign despite already being dazzled by Andrej Babiš, and in spite of that went on to run unsuccessfully for the Senate on behalf of the Greens and the ČSSD. Looking for logic or some unifying thread in these twists and turns would defy reason. It would be like looking for a common "school of thought" or even "doctrine" in Bělohradský's philosophical texts! I would say there is something far deeper and more fundamental to Bělohradský's overt enthralment with charismatic leaders, and that is distrust of what we might call the moral legitimacy of politics. This is why he has always argued against Havel's concept of politics and, even more so, against all the trivialised portraits of Havel and his thoughts that, alas, have become so popular in today's Czech society and, in many respects, are a follow-on from the objectionable "father-of-the-nation" portraits of Masaryk. This resistance to political moralism, however, is perhaps the greatest paradox in Bělohradský's thinking because he himself embodies the classic type of moralising public intellectual and philosopher who criticises and inveighs against what you yourself have described as "empire".

Let's stop and think about that term. The American John Perkins, in his *Confessions of an Economic Hit Man*, says that there are four pillars of empire: fear, debt, insufficiency, and the divide-and-conquer mindset. What's your take on empire?
Criticism of empire is not a purely modern posture plotted by critical theory and philosophy in response to the clashes of civilisations and the crimes of modern European civilisation. No, this is an archetypical moral and social mentality familiar from early Christianity, which has also been defined as the "parallel polis" of the Roman Empire. By the way, four centuries later, as the Goths were plundering ancient civilisation, this led Saint Augustine of Hippo to make his philosophical and theological distinction between the earthly city (*civitas terrena*) and the city of God (*civitas Dei*). In this light, I don't view Bělohradský's writings and public performances legitimising the opinions and programmes of the charismatic leaders of post-November Czech politics as the speeches of a would-be functionary, but as a paradoxical counterpoint to his own philosophy, which is saturated with a moralistic element and even directly builds on Patočka's critique of modern civilisation. Václav Bělohradský is a direct continuator of *Heretical Essays'* line of thought and ethics and, while he is a philosopher born out of the spirit of critical theory, he systematically agitates against every theory and even directs his criticism, up front, against all he has

said and has yet to say. I would go so far as to say that his thinking presupposes not only a political or sociological, but also – bearing in mind his criticism of "empire" – a theological reading of "problems". Some of this probably has to do with the fact that, in his inimitable style, preacher meets ironist and his ideas are both unbearably light and heavy. He shoulders the Central European weight of absurd history and, simultaneously, is lifted by the refreshing lightness of the European South, which may come across as chaotic sometimes, but without it we here in Bohemia and elsewhere, choked of culture and civilisation, would have drowned in all kinds of metaphysics of morals.

So what, then, is the difference between the "intellectual" and the "spiritual person" as defined by Jan Patočka?
Patočka's distinction between the intellectual and spiritual person was relevant to critical and ethical debate among political dissidents. While Patočka considered the intellectual a sophist skilled in words and logical arguments, a spiritual person, he claimed, was someone who realises the fundamental drama of freedom in modern times, the drama of the struggle against the pressure of modern civilisation, which constantly marshals and shackles us so that we fear for our bare lives. In his *Heretical Essays*, Patočka goes down the perilous route of interpreting the contradictory works of Ernst Jünger and Pierre Teilhard de Chardin precisely because of their absolute experience of the battlefront, where human existence presents itself for sacrifice. What is particularly heretical about these essays is the ability to expose war masquerading as peace, along with the denial of life by the daily economic and political routine of assured survival, suppressing the possibility of resistance and a real life that recognises the transience of human existence and is therefore also capable of spiritual conversion and solidarity – the *solidarity of the shaken*. It is not only totalitarianism, but also the routine of modern life – that iron cage of modernity – that, for Patočka, poses a chal-

lenge intensifying the state of war against which no alternative ideology or political manifestos and standard political resistance can
be pitted. This makes it all the more necessary to warn against this
warlike state masquerading as peace, public and private well-being,
or the social order, and to resist it with Socrates' *daimonion*, which
can say "no" to all of these warlike states of modern civilisation and
its absurd sacrifices. This is a struggle that is waged against illness
without promising any healing, and a warning against threats and
crises that offers no solution. Nevertheless, this negative warning is
of fundamental importance because it shows how all forms of "constructive criticism" are encapsulated into the all-round defence of
modern civilisation.

**According to Patočka, Socrates showed people that the world was
a dark and problematic place we were unfamiliar with. This path
leads to conflict with society and sticking to it means there is a bor-
derline possibility of going to your death. In contrast to this, you
have Plato's withdrawal from the public in the hope that philosophical knowledge will help to transform the political community.
Or, according to Patočka, you become a sophist, i.e. an intellectual,
the shadow of a spiritual person, relying on skill alone to make
a living. Do you agree with this division?**
I think that these ideal types fashioned by philosophical speculation
need to be supplemented with real historical events if we are to ob-
tain a more accurate and, most importantly, a less rosy picture of the
philosopher's function and teaching in society. Before cloistering
himself in his Academy, Plato had active political and intellectual
ties with the tyrants ruling Syracuse. At the invitation of his dis-
ciple Dion, he returned here to make Dionysius II a philosopher
king who, based on Plato's philosophy, would establish a fair community governed by reason and justice, where political life would
not give in to the temptations of tyranny, oligarchy, or democracy.
In his autobiographical *Seventh Letter*, Plato utters the well-known

sentence "do not enslave Sicily or any other State to despots [...] but put it under the rule of laws." However, as the worlds of philosophical ideas and political practices do not understand each other very well, instead of building his dream utopia Plato is ultimately forced to leave Syracuse in dramatic circumstances. It is only after this experience that he stopped writing constitutions for the mighty of this world and began to devote himself entirely to philosophy. This relationship between philosophers and tyrants permeates human history. Interestingly, in every generation and society there are philosophers who succumb to the illusion and desire to make philosophers out of tyrants, even though history is riddled with real examples of how philosophers become the servants of tyrants. We need to be constantly on our guard to avoid this "Syracusan lure". In fact, I even view Patočka's concept of the Socratic *daimonion*, for example, in this sense, by which I mean primarily as a rejection of any philosophy aspiring to become a "constructive criticism" of politics or civilisation *per se*. For this reason, I have always mainly regarded political dissent as the disruption not only of political, but also moral, schemes, rather than as some sort of moral vanguard that would liberate the country from tyranny and restore its moral legitimacy and political ideals. This makes me all the more irked by today's trivialised descriptions of political dissent and how, after the event, they reduce this historic struggle to a fight between the forces of good and evil.

In this context, we cannot overlook *Filosofie a politika kýče* [The Philosophy and Politics of Kitsch] by Petr Rezek, the philosopher and fiercest critic of the dissident thinkers who was a dissident himself. This criticism spares no one, not even Havel, and lays bare the circularity of dissent, the primary subject of which is not an idea, but a quote containing a quote. He literally writes that the power of big names gets in the way when we are thinking about what they are actually saying. To provide a contrast, Rezek singles

out Milan Kundera, who calls this method kitsch and defines it as an attitude inhabiting the domain of feeling, emotion and self-indulgence...

Kundera's criticism of lyricism in general and kitsch in particular is also a critical rethink of his own aesthetic and philosophical thinking. We need only compare the original *The Art of the Novel* from the early 1960s, in which Kundera lauds the lyricism of Vančura's novels, with the later famous edition of his identically entitled book from the mid-1980s, by which time he devotes himself to his completely non-lyrical favourites, from Cervantes and Stern to Musil and Kafka. Only in this inner tension and these contradictions of a single work can we fully grasp the significance and power of Kundera's criticism of political kitsch. In my opinion, what is most important here is the description of the immaturely narcissistic obsession with the self, which continues to constrain and restrain – if not downright humble and humiliate – today's Czech culture and society. Running to the authority exercised by heavyweights and getting sentimental over their fate continues to weigh Czech public life down heavily. Also bound up with this is the paradoxically distinctive relationship with the intellectual elite. On the one hand, they are uncritically attributed with paternal authority and the ability to rescue society from its moral decadence, but at the same time there is a childish rebellion against them that targets knowledge itself. The pathological desire to identify moral conscience with a particular person on whom we can pin political hopes is thus accompanied by the ignorant notion that everything is already rotten and mendacious beforehand, so it is pointless to become involved in the public world of politics at all. As though the meaning of life should be either bare survival or, on the contrary, criticism thereof from higher moral echelons accessible only to the chosen few. This invariably results in disdain for politics as a morally and culturally repugnant activity. Czech society remains bogged down in this quagmire. We need to respond by grappling with Czech prejudice about the morally avant-garde function of intellectuals and scholars in national history and attribute to them only the role they deserve – not ethically, but on the strength of their own education and knowledge. This is just as essential as the rejection of the very term "treason of the intellectuals", which is mainly employed by intellectuals as a way of branding one other and excluding each other from some sort of spiritual and cultic community that is supposedly indigenous to them, and in doing so they try to wrest a larger public role for themselves than what modern society can offer them. Anyone who bemoans the treason of intellectuals is more often than not an adherent to their cult. However, this is an archaic, rather than a modern, stance.

Rezek's analysis of Havel's well-known *The Power of the Powerless* is also remarkable. Here, he defends citizens who have refused to "live in the truth" and points out that the tipping point is their willingness to "live in conflict with political power", which is not to say that these are people who have decided to "live within a lie". Would you defend them along those lines, too?
Civil ethos and pathos had a tremendous impact not only on Havel when he was writing *The Power of Powerless*, but on dissidence in general. The dissidents did not, in fact, constitute political opposition. Instead, they formed a polyphony that had what it took to say "NO!" to the then political system. The distinction between the intellectual and the spiritual person tempts us to start regarding dissidents as functionaries of humankind who, truth be told, never really wanted to get mixed up with politics because – looking down from their unblemished towers that they had built up with the ivory of thought and culture – it seemed too murky to them. So what we have here, once again, is that more general distinction between "clean" culture and "dirty" politics that is so fatally destructive to Central European thinking. That is one of the reasons why Petr Rezek came down so hard on *The Power of the Powerless*. At the heart of his very harsh criticism is this admonition that dissidence is not a substitute

for politics, and therefore, even in circumstances such as these, it is impossible to wriggle out of practical political responsibility simply by regarding oneself as a spiritual being whose cultural interests and moral life are on a higher plane. In other words, political criticism and dissidence cannot be pursued by the paradoxical gesture of turning a deaf ear to it. Rezek encapsulated a more general problem with Havel's concept of "living in the truth" when he argued that an authentic standpoint could not be put in the same category as a political standpoint. A lot of philosophical detail is bound up in this argument, but the general thrust is that a relationship with the truth cannot replace political will and activity, and that authentic living is not the same as truthfulness or the ethics of virtue or duty. To put it another way, Rezek critically recalls that political dissent has found itself caught in a typically romantic trap where being genuine and authentic is purported to be a key criterion in determining what is fair or unfair, and where higher culture is based on living in the truth as though it were again to lay bare the lowness and squalor of politics.

I get the impression we are tiptoeing around something essential without actually naming it. Could you try to identify the problem in more detail?
We keep coming back to a peculiar suture that exists in the modern history of thinking and culture between the Enlightenment and Romanticism. We have shown how often the difference between the Enlightenment and Romanticism is overrated and overstated, and how, in fact, these are intertwining and complementary strands of our intellectual traditions and patterns of thought and behaviour. We could claim that the Enlightenment placed more of an emphasis on thinking and the correctness thereof, whereas Romanticism was more intent on the deed and the genuineness thereof. Nevertheless, in Kant's philosophy there is a very close link between correctness and genuineness and between the thought and the deed. The three

fundamental questions of the Enlightenment formulated by Immanuel Kant, i.e. *What can I know?*, *What should I do?*, and *What may I hope?*, still provide us with basic guidance in the world and establish conditions for us to understand our own existence. These conditions are as intellectual as they are historical, so moral principles and hopes take on both an individual and social form. In this sense, all of politics raises intellectual expectations, and all politicians are responsible not only for taking specific decisions, but also for rationally explaining and justifying them. This holds true for both early modern and late postmodern times.

But that is precisely where we are falling down. Can this be blamed, up to a point, on the fact that the nation was born of a tradition steeped in the classroom and the lecture hall?

The peculiarities of the Czech national revival are common knowledge and, personally speaking, I would say that the way life was breathed into the nation from school desks and university departments is a historical virtue. Understandably, though, we are reducing a complex historical progression, which started with the national revivalists' vision and ended with an independent nation and autonomous state, to its bare bones. On the other hand, it does explain, for instance, the social prestige attached to certain vocations in Czech society. When you look at opinion polls, it is always the same professions at the top of the pile – besides doctors and nurses, you've got your university professors and lecturers, primary school teachers, and scientists. This is no coincidence! It makes sense, of course, that the standing enjoyed by physicians and nurses can be attributed to modern society's general cult of health and the body, but what is specific to all of these professions is their high level of education. This learning contrasts with the disgraceful economic status of teachers, although here, too, we can identify a cause, what with polls consigning politicians to the lowest rung of the professional ladder, which they share with cleaners. That absolute antithesis between learning and politics is a strange form of social pathology as it exposes a disdain for politics and the romanticisation of education which is not then reflected in economic worth. This pathology, too, is part of the Czech nation's intellectual history, and I think it also explains our unrealistic expectations of the intellectual elite on the one hand and our sardonic contempt of politics on the other. To be sure, though, these expectations have also been moulded by the prevailing role that intellectuals play in modern society, which we could couch as an exploration of how much room I have for hope and what I can hope for even when I appear to be in dire straits. And modern Czech history is heaving with such situations.

I would go back once more to the word "betrayal" in a Czech context, where this term tends to be reflexively linked to the "Munich Betrayal". The question is, who betrayed whom and what is actually meant by that phrase?
Yes, let's move on from the imaginary treason of intellectuals to the plane of practical politics mired in contradictions and tragedies. What we have here is generally considered to be betrayal by our Western allies and a colossal international injustice inflicted on the then Czechoslovakia. This failure by our allies on both the security and diplomatic fronts is an undeniable historical fact and its consequences have been etched into the collective memory of Europeans so deeply that "appeasement", commonly used in the second half of the 1930s for the Western powers' conciliatory political approach to Nazi Germany, is still used in a negative and disparaging sense. With Britain and France reluctant and ill-prepared to take up arms against Nazi Germany, there was nothing to halt the military occupation of the Rhineland in next to no time, i.e. by 1936, with the Anschluss and then the break-up of Czechoslovakia's First Republic following in rapid succession. It wasn't just Nazi Germany that benefited from the Munich Agreement; it was also a godsend to Poland and Hungary at the time. The flip side of this international political

and legal tragedy was the political situation that took hold in Czechoslovakia's Second Republic between October 1938 and the definitive occupation in March 1939. After Beneš quit first his post, on 5 October 1938, and then his country, a hate campaign was unleashed against the First Republic's democratic and intellectual institutions. Within weeks, politics in Czechoslovakia – now naked and shorn – mutated into an internal life-and-death struggle in which hatred and pack behaviour prevailed over the civility of the former democratic public. Animosity towards democracy and its ideals, a backlash against freedom, and a craving for a strongman leader that had been fuelled by nationalistic and racist hatred, it all oozed out with a vengeance at the turn of 1939. Second-Republic Czechoslovakia was an authoritarian regime in which the Enabling Act made it possible for the government to govern without parliamentary involvement, party pluralism was replaced by a system in which the Party of National Unity governed with the National Labour Party's loyal opposition, public debate was crippled by censorship, and Jews faced discrimination. The First Republic and the civic culture it had worked so hard to build up fell victim not only to Nazi Germany's policy of aggression, compounded by the incompetence of our then allies, but also to Czech society's internal hostility towards the ideals that had given life to this modern independent and autonomous republic. It turned out that the Czechs were not a nation of enlightened and tolerant democrats, but that they were capable of betraying their own ideals just like any other nation. Aside from showing that any system of international security is vulnerable and transient, the Munich Betrayal robbed us most of all of the illusion that, in the struggle for "world revolution", the Czechs had always been – and would always be – inherently and unquestionably on the democratic side.

What do you think of Petr Zelenka's *Lost in Munich*, a film that ironically built on a remarkable book by the historian Jan Tesař called *Mnichovský komplex* [The Munich Complex]?

Zelenka's movie is an attempt at deconstructing film narrative by exploring moral prejudices and excuses. In this sense, it is an original crack at dealing with Tesař's book and the idea of the "Munich complex", which casts doubt on the established interpretation of events surrounding the Munich Agreement and, above all, analyses the general formula often employed by Czechs to interpret "moral sacrifice" as they define their own existence and role in modern history. Tesař describes the cliché of "betrayal by allies" and the closely associated cliché of the "the nation wanted to defend itself" as historical and political fabrications grossly distorting the reality of the time. He shows that this was a battle for world public opinion which Czechoslovak diplomacy was doomed to lose if it insisted on armed confrontation in a dispute that was perceived at the time as a territorial disagreement associated with the rights of national minorities. Of course, this is a simplification, but the fact of the matter is that it was only the subsequent aggressive policy pursued Nazi Germany which legitimised – after the event – Czechoslovakia's stance and its status as a "victim of betrayal". Tesař also demonstrates how, instead of showing fighting spirit, the Czechs responded to the Munich Agreement with mute resignation and by surrendering their armaments and other resources to Nazi Germany without much resistance, either telling themselves that they were doing this for the sake of preserving the nation's existence or thinking that there was money to be made by working for Hitler's Third Reich. The idea of a nation betrayed not only by outsiders, but also from within by its own elite, is merely a moral fiction and a pathetic presentation of tangible failures written by politicians, historians, philosophers and public intellectuals in general. The moralistic interpretation of a nation that, though brave, has been betrayed and sacrificed cloaks the passive, wait-and-see mindset that Tesař considers to be one of

Czech society's most fundamental patterns of behaviour. As a result of this attitude, we usually mark time, waiting for some external intrusion in our domestic affairs – a superpower's intervention, perhaps, or a rescue mission undertaken by an enlightened and courageous group of politically active intellectuals and brave individuals belonging to Maffia, or the anti-Nazi resistance, or the dissident movement surrounding Charter 77, or whatever comes next. Elsewhere, figuratively speaking, people fight at the barricades and tear down walls; we in the Bohemian basin pettily crow about how deeply democratic we are and gamble on having the "smarts" to avoid conflict and to bow to the situation before us, which we justify by citing the need to preserve our own existence, cohesion and togetherness. After all, the Second Republic may have been small, but it was ours! After analysing this pattern, Tesař concludes that it is a result of our failure to absorb democratic virtues and practices, and that faith in authoritative external intervention – a belief so typical of authoritarian and monarchical societies – lingers on in us. This explains why Czechs compensate for this by painting a moralistic self-image of ourselves as an island of democracy in Central Europe which – as borne out by the Second Republic, the building of a Stalinist society accompanied by political trials in the 1950s, and the universal cynicism of 1970s "normalisation" – is historically indefensible. I would add the caveat, though, that even in these contexts we should not just be referencing historical patterns of collective behaviour and moral criticism of them because then we would lapse into historical reductionism. You see, the Munich crisis of 1938 is also inherent to and a product of the political and economic crises that other European societies were going through in the first half of the last century. The Great Depression triggered a crisis of economic and political liberalism and was a disaster for the international order, which, when it collapsed, took Czechoslovakia's First Republic with it. These historical contexts also paved the way for the post-war popularity of the Communist Party.

The post-1968 normalisation era eroded our relationship with the state even more and demoralised the nation. People from institutions, the authorities, and schools were forced to say, before commissions, that Czechoslovakia had not been occupied and that it had simply been benefiting from brotherly help. It was not until the mid-1980s that Gorbachev came along with his perestroika. You were living here at the time. How did the people react?

When Gorbachev attempted to reform real socialism with "perestroika" and "glasnost", he was dipping into the Prague Spring playbook and plagiarising its concept of "socialism with a human face". This was instantly recognisable to Czechoslovak society in the 1980s. Of course, this had the party leadership running scared because, all of a sudden, absolute obedience to the Soviet leadership would have meant spurning the entire ideological and political basis of their rule. But before we discuss this period, we should run a critical eye over the importance and significance of the Prague Spring and the whole of 1968. Ten years after the invasion and the violent suppression of the reform process, the political scientist and dissident Petr Pithart published his *Osmašedesátý* [Sixty-Eight] under a pseudonym. This samizdat book caused quite a stir inside and outside the dissident community because he ruthlessly took issue with the entrenched interpretation of this brief – and hence all the more symbolic – period of Czechoslovak history. Pithart questioned the universally accepted assumption that, though our nation had been defeated militarily, it was still morally triumphant before the whole world because once again – as on several occasions in times past – it showed all of humanity the general fortitude of the humanist tradition and a specific political vision in which socialism and democracy could allegedly live alongside each other, thus creating a happier society for the future. As though the traditional prejudice that the Czechs are weak politically but strong when it comes to culture and civilisation were intended to assure us that we had endured the test of history and thus, borrowing Kundera's words from *Czech Destiny*, the Czechs had "again placed themselves at the centre of world history for the first time since the Middle Ages". Pithart lambasted this widely shared national feeling and notion of "national disaster" and wretched historical fate as the dangerous tradition of a "cultural nation without politicians", in which, in the absence of capable and practical politicians, it is left to the intellectuals to explain, through the "triumph of the spirit", our political defeats. These days, we can observe the whole controversy with the luxury of hindsight, at a time when, mercifully, the edge has sufficiently been taken off the various arguments. Sure, *Czech Destiny* is not one of Kundera's most potent texts, as it was overly influenced by the abnormal situation following the Soviet invasion and the atmosphere of despair in the face of more than half a million Warsaw Pact troops occupying our country. Havel and Pithart criticised Kundera's stance and yet, rather than fatalistic politics or cultural illusion, he was far more focused on gesturing sceptically at the historical incompatibility of real socialism with freedom and its existential dependence on the omnipotence of the secret police and universal fear. This is also why Kundera eschewed subsequent political debate and, unlike Havel, for example, communicated everything essential about socialism, including the original and fundamental idea of its lyrical spirit, through literature.

Petr Pithart reminded us that Kundera's essay was a continuation of Czech efforts to experience defeat, in retrospect, as something magnificent and, in doing so, to shrug off responsibility for any further outcomes.

Yes, a much more general and more important argument comes to light in Pithart's *Osmašedesátý* that is merely prefaced by his criticism of Kundera's attitude in the autumn of 1968. It is premised on the idea that the dearth of career politicians means that Czech intellectuals have had to step into the breach, but they fail in this political role and the responsibility derived from it because, by tradition, they interpret political losses as a victory for culture and civilisation. According to Pithart, in 1968 there was also a conflict between the system of real socialism, with its brutally repressive power, and Communist intellectuals, who tried to reform this system at a certain point in its crisis of legitimacy and thereby preserve it in some form or other. While these reformist Communists were betrayed by the Soviet leadership in August 1968, this paradoxically relieved them – like the generation of Czech intellectuals before them – of responsibility for further political developments and, again, they were able to resort to fashioning, out of political defeat, a myth about the virtue of moral and cultural victory. Instead of political revolution, 1968 entered Czechoslovak history as a "revolution of resolutions", in which heart-wrenching rhetoric failed to camouflage political incompetence. The crushing defeat of practical politics is a fixture of modern Czech history, so 1968 simply joined a long line of like political incidents. According to Pithart, with the myth of human-faced socialism having flown around the world, when the subsequent political tragedy bore down on them the silenced Czechs and Slovaks, headed by the reformist Communists, consoled themselves that their desire for good had been broken by the violence of an evil system. In reality, however, the reformist Communists, apparently underestimating the power-play and volitional factors of politics, concentrated on the illusion of the word and the ideological struggle for socialism. Pithart also provocatively asks whether "in the end, should improved socialism truly belong to everyone, or should everyone belong to improved socialism?" Ten years down the line, history answered the question for him when Gorbachev's attempt to democratise socialism ended with its disintegration.

But this was also history grinning ironically. Those who thought they were at the helm of history assumed the rhetoric of the defeated after just sixteen or seventeen years. Gorbachev's democra-

tising reforms mobilised a process that would see the entire Soviet Bloc crumble. Yet Czechoslovakia was perhaps the most sceptical about how events would play out. Why was that?

Pithart had the benefit of hindsight when he wrote his critique of reformist Communism as another in the long line of examples of the traditional non-accountability of Czech intellectuals for political developments. This enabled him to observe normalisation realpolitik's decay once the self-assurance of the nation and its leaders that their culture and civilisation prevailed over that of the occupiers had faded. Just as Kundera could not have foreseen the rapid collapse of the Prague Spring's ethos in 1969, Pithart could not have predicted in the late 1970s that, in the mid-1980s, the occupier would appropriate the very same policy against which it had deployed tanks to Czechoslovakia in 1968. History once again scoffed at the naivety of those who thought they were history-makers! In parallel with this, history paradoxically confirmed Kundera's hypothesis about the incompatibility of real socialism with democracy and freedom, which simply exists or does not. Democratisation cannot be a permanent state. It is merely the vehicle of transition to a democracy that excludes control of politics and society at large from a single centre of power and a monopoly one-party government. The Prague Spring and Gorbachev's perestroika were, historically, a final attempt at having philosophers remould tyrants into righteous rulers. It didn't work for Plato in Syracuse, and it didn't work for the Marxist philosophers who were constantly trying to transform the political monster their teachings had created into a political community that would not only be legitimate, but would also be morally superior to all other forms of government. The end of real socialism is thus not automatic justification of the market and representative democracy, as some conservative or liberal thinkers believe, but proof of the inability to legitimise politics through philosophical ideas or a proclaimed knowledge of the objective laws of society and its history. Anyone who seeks metaphysical laws in human history betrays the critical role of the intellectual. This is how we could literarily bend and reformulate Benda's idea for a situation where the distinction between universalism and particularism has lost its former moral appeal because universal ideas led to the worst forms of particular violence.

Two Totalitarian Regimes

Let's start by recalling that, over the century that Czechoslovakia and then the Czech Republic have been in existence, we have only been able to take decisions for ourselves for 48 years, and not even that long if we subtract the years it took to build the state, then the late 1930s, and ultimately the complications surrounding the split of the republic. The two totalitarian regimes that left their mark on us evidently influenced us more than Masaryk's democracy or the post-1989 building of democracy. That's why democracy is still incomprehensible to us and is constantly questioned, and why the work of our politicians is so amateurish. How would you define a totalitarian regime?

"Totalitarianism" is a peculiar word that has retained its potency. We can all infuse personal, family, national and global history into it. It is a word in which the monstrous cruelties of modern civilisation are presented as part of the routine of everyday life. It is hardly necessary to point out that "totalitarianism", though a nebulous term, is symptomatic of modern history. The actual concept of a totalitarian state is not problematic in the slightest – it surfaced in the political vernacular and in literature on law and political science in the 1920s and is well summed up by Mussolini's motto of "all within the state, nothing outside the state, nothing against the state". A totalitarian state controls and regulates all the material and spiritual goods of society and is the antithesis of a liberal state, which is based on the separation of the private and public spheres and on the civil rights and freedoms that precede all state power. A totalitarian state, as opposed to a liberal state, relies on unlimited power capable of encroaching on any area of social life, thereby erasing the boundary between the public and the private sphere. The way in which it intervenes is defined not, primarily, by laws, but by the ideology of the ruling party, which governs social reality. Party will dictates and determines how the state functions, and this is enforced in particular with savage machinery driven by the secret police, who transform legitimate state power into the terror of Party leadership and dictatorship.

When we hear the word "totalitarianism", what typically springs to mind is that famous work _The Origins of Totalitarianism..._
... by Hannah Arendt. The book falls short on political analysis in many respects, but it does contain two important ideas that remain valid today: totalitarianism is not an excess, but is one of the faces of modern civilisation, and it is a historically distinct and completely new form of government typical of two states – the Stalinist Soviet Union and Nazi Germany. Arendt differentiates totalitarianism from older forms of tyranny or other authoritarian regimes on the basis of their ideology, which is able to mobilise the masses by offering them answers to metaphysical questions about the meaning of the past, present and future. Class conflict or the struggle for racial purity becomes not only the state's initial imperative, but also its final justification. Unlike other forms of state, totalitarianism does not limit itself to persecuting its opponents, but also engages in reprisals against its own supporters, ordinary citizens, and entire swathes of the population. One of its particular features is the concentration camp, which serves as a repressive institution on the one hand, and as an instrument of economic and ideological mobilisation on the other. For a long time, advocates of world communism in particular were unable to accept this direct comparison between Stalinism and Nazism because they considered themselves to be at the vanguard of the bright tomorrows of humankind, and for humankind Nazism was the sworn enemy. And yet we need only look at the art of National Socialism and socialist realism to see how aesthetically, ideologically and politically similar the two regimes are. Communism had symbolically ended not with the fall of the Berlin Wall, but back in 1987, when Neue Slowenische Kunst, the collective of young Slovenian artists, won a Communist competition to

design the best poster for the Yugoslavian Youth Day Celebration. The poster was based on a painting by the Nazi artist Richard Klein, a favourite of Hitler, and simply replaced the Nazi flag and the eagle with a dove and the Yugoslav flag. Although there was still time for the Yugoslav regime to respond to this "joke" with censorship, effectively the poster was recognition of the aesthetic, ideological and cultural defeat of the entire communist movement at a time when Gorbachev was still trying to reform it.

How would you say the Nazi totalitarian system differed from its Communist counterpart? In other words, what set National Socialism apart from international socialism?
Obviously, a typological comparison is not going to tell us that there are no differences or that we could put a simple equals sign between the two systems. I think that one of the fundamental differences is the glorification of violence itself, which became a perverse virtue and value for the Nazis, while the Communists always justified it as a means of progress and a historical necessity that would pass if post-revolutionary developments followed the right path. The fact that the Nazi leaders were of the chosen race led to an aggressive war aimed at conquering Europe and enslaving its "inferior races". At the same time, it led to a policy of racial purification that built extermination camps instead of concentration camps in order to implement the Holocaust. This constant mobilisation of violence, combined with internal and external aggression, eventually resulted in world war and the subsequent fall of the Nazi regime, which, in the twelve short years of its existence, completely destroyed all the ideas and illusions that Western civilisation may still have entertained about itself up to then. Trains, previously symbolising humankind's industrial progress and the revolutionary transformation of modern society, came to denote bureaucratically organised, industrial-scale mass murder! By contrast, the Communists' status as chosen ones and the violence this engendered was always justified by

universalist ideals of modern revolutions and the objective laws of history, so that quite a few people may have had the impression that even labour camps – where millions of people, stripped of all dignity and exploited as economic resources, met their deaths – afforded the vision of a garden of Eden for a classless communist society. For example, as late as the mid-1990s the prominent British historian Eric Hobsbawm, asked whether he would still have supported the Moscow Communist regime if he had been in possession of all information about the scale of Stalin's crimes, said yes, he would, because even amidst such suffering a new world can be born. This difference explains not only the much greater humanist seductiveness of communism, but also the ability to progressively branch into different forms over the course of history while preserving a single ideology. This is also why, for instance, Václav Havel referred to Communist systems in the 1970s as "post-totalitarian". He was thinking of this difference between the mobilised violence of the Stalinist regimes and the relative stasis of normalised Communist societies. Post-totalitarian does not mean, then, that these regimes were no longer totalitarian, but that they were totalitarian in a different way and that, in order to remain in existence, they no longer needed naked terror, concentration camps, a ubiquitous atmosphere of fear and the cold sweat of clinging to life.

In this day and age, is there still any point in discussing totalitarianism or totalitarian society?
I think that, when we look at the history of totalitarianism and totalitarian systems, we can say that the past is a story we tell ourselves primarily to understand our present. The Czech philosopher Zdeněk Vašíček's phrase that "the past is what has been, of course, but some of it is in the here and now", applies here more than elsewhere. We can talk about whether totalitarianism is actually an appropriate term because historians, whether studying Nazi Germany or dealing with Soviet Russia, have doubted its usefulness.

For example, the German historian Hans Mommsen argued that the Nazi regime was too arbitrary and chaotic for a totalitarian order to effectively take hold in it. Mommsen even claimed that Hitler was, in fact, a weak dictator. Similar criticism has been levelled at Stalinist Russia by historians pointing to the existence of, say, the various power-broking and interest groupings within the Soviet leadership. On the other hand, this is something Arendt also wrote about, and in her work the subchapter devoted to the state is called "The So-called Totalitarian State", which is the author's way of emphasising that she has analysed what the National Socialists or the fascists themselves described as a total or totalitarian state. In this context, it is interesting to see Arendt quoting Hitler's dictum, addressed to lawyers in 1933, that "the total state must not know any difference between law and ethics". In other words, this means that positive law must correspond totally to Nazi morality and conscience. I have yet to come across a more precise definition of totalitarian law than this subordination of laws to a single ethical version of the world that is proclaimed to be totally valid in society. We can add to that Vašíček's definition of totalitarianism as an artificial and anti-historical complex that swept away the questions and left only the answers. As soon as you do away with the questions, you also cancel history, because from then on history is controlled by the political machinery of a system producing a single politically binding truth. While a liberal democratic state with a valid constitution expects and even defends moral pluralism, the totalitarian state deliberately abolishes this private sphere and nationalises not only the economy, but also, and most importantly, ideas and morals. Arendt goes so far as to claim that the essence of totalitarian systems lies in the complete lack of a system and the possibility that the arbitrary will of the leader and the party could intervene in any matter at any time, anywhere. Thirty years before Havel compares socialist legitimacy to the façade of the regime in *The Power of the Powerless*, Arendt is also describing the totalitarian government machine as a mere "powerless façade" which hides the real power of the party, and even notes that "totalitarianism uses its power precisely to spread... complicity through the population until it has organised the guilt of the whole people under its domination". The first sign and, at the same time, the worst crime of totalitarianism is its ability to turn its victims into accomplices. Anyone who questions the very notion of totalitarianism should first read Arendt's work to avoid trivialising the thoughts of one of the most important philosophers of the last century. In particular, this work ought to be read by those who today swim against the current of established interpretations to argue that the population actually cooperated voluntarily with the regime and that the Communist regime's politics were therefore shared and *de facto* legitimate.

But, considering how the methods changed over time, can we regard the whole period between 1948 and 1989 as totalitarian?
There is a difference between opinions that starkly challenge whether totalitarianism is a term suitable to denote Communist regimes, and opinions seeking a more nuanced view of the different periods of Communist rule. The former only relativise communism, while the latter compare different periods of Communist regimes, which, from a historical perspective, is right and necessary. You don't have to be a historian or a political scientist to see, for example, the difference between the Stalinist period, with its political trials and labour camps, and the second half of the 1960s, when living conditions in Czechoslovakia came close to a benevolent autocracy, which is also why so many interesting books were published and films were produced here that now belong to the golden archives of European cinematography. I am always reminded of the Spanish director Carlos Saura, who once remarked that he had fought the Franco regime and its censorship all his life, and yet he was artistically indebted to it. Repressive power piques the

imagination of the artist and viewers alike, and intensifies their ability to read figurative images and allegories. However, this is very different from saying that, even in Communist regimes, people lived their everyday lives, made merry, furnished their homes, went on holiday, and, while their lives were perhaps more limited, they were certainly not qualitatively worse off than in Western democracies. This is not a value-relativising judgement, but terrible self-abandonment! Here, you get all these historical peculiarities and differences mixing together, blending into some indistinguishable mush that resembles, at best, meat loaf in a normalisation-era butcher shop right next door to Havel's imaginary greengrocer's. It is akin to saying that there is no significant difference between a concentration camp and a hotel because both have showers. This approach reminds me of a recent lecture delivered by a Chinese professor at our university's Confucius Institute who, responding to a comment condemning the Maoist era and mass murder, condescendingly said that, while Chairman Mao was vilified by Western propaganda, he did so much good for his country that many prisoners heaped praise on their time in labour camps because they had lost weight and got into better shape! Anything at all can be relativised, so in today's garrulous and information-saturated age some people may feel like they have to provoke as much as possible and, most of all, take a stand against established interpretations and terms. As a rule, every such relativistic provocation harbours moral fundamentalism and the desire to "slug it out" with other historians or with history *per se*. Instead of striving for scientific accuracy and clarity, there is a desire for momentary attention, ending in an embarrassing race to come up with the biggest media guff. These people do not realise that they are turning into the flip side of these ideological systems.

We have set up the Institute for the Study of Totalitarian Regimes, and we have legislation on the unlawfulness of the Communist re-

gime and on resisting such a regime, but we have not banned the Communist Party. Isn't that a paradox?

It is not a paradox, but a consequence of the way communism collapsed. When the opposition accepts a round-table invitation and, for example, Lech Wałęsa and Jacek Kuroń shake hands – on behalf of all of Solidarity – with the Communist Generals Jaruzelski and Kiszczak, the very people who had imprisoned them, it is unlikely that, when they come to power, they will simply outlaw their partner in political negotiations. While the Czech situation was much slower in the making, when political change did eventually take place it was faster and more revolutionary, but here, too, there were round-table discussions, a basic political agreement on the country's democratisation was hammered out, and therefore revolutionary justice could not result in a ban on the Communist Party. In this context, there is a paradox, but it lies elsewhere: in the former GDR and the Czech Republic, where the changes were much more revolutionary, the Communist Party assumed the mantle of an anti-systemic political force and cloaked itself in nostalgia for the old order, while in neighbouring Poland and Hungary the Communists transformed themselves into social democratic parties that were only destroyed by the corruption they practised in their attempts to exploit the new system, thus paving the way for populist right-wing parties pursuing anti-democratic and anti-liberation programmes. In the Czech Republic, the Communist Party's dominant position as an anti-democratic force did not end until the parliamentary elections in 2017, when the anti-systemic parties and movements accounted for the majority in the Chamber of Deputies.

That may well be true, but the new premier, Andrej Babiš, was the first post-1989 prime minister to legitimise – through his comportment and his own past – the Communist Party as a democratic party and the SPD's fascist inclinations. Consequently, this also distorts our view of the Communists, who have never entirely dis-

owned their bloody past. In this context, I am interested to know how you view the functioning of the Institute for the Study of Totalitarian Regimes.

Any attempt by official state power to codify and narrate history seems anachronistic today, as shown by the recent example of the controversial Institute for the Study of Totalitarian Regimes. Originally, the political right wanted to set it up as a vehicle to legitimise itself at a time when the transition of post-Communist society was coming to an end. By the time political circumstances changed, the left no longer wanted to shut down the Institute, but appointed political affiliates to it. I have always voiced my opposition to the very idea of creating such an institution because what sort of a society feels the need to bang up its collective memory in some state-constituted institution?! Unlike Poland and Slovakia, in the Czech Republic we were quick to introduce lustration in the early 1990s, carried out the most extensive physical restitutions in the post-Communist bloc, rehabilitated and compensated political prisoners, laid bare the State Security archives, and so on, so when the right-wing government established the Institute for the Study of Totalitarian Regimes in 2007, no one could have viewed it as anything but an attempt to impose a binding interpretation of the past on the public. Twenty years after the democratic revolution, and at a time when we could rely on smoothly functioning and independent academic institutions such as the Institute of Contemporary History, and when there were immensely stimulating and original studies by a new generation of historians, including Jiří Suk, Michal Kopeček and Pavel Kolář, we witnessed an attempt to abuse academic history for political legitimation. When the political situation changed, the left exploited it to exert counter-pressure and guide the Institute for the Study of Totalitarian Regimes towards cultural and social studies. While this opened up the exploration of history to other disciplines, it also confirmed the political nature of the institution and in no way increased its social legitimacy or academic prestige. The Institute needs to be appropriated by historians, regardless of whether their concept of history has a conservative, liberal or socialist political undertone. But in order to gain legitimacy among historians, it must first be wrenched from the political grasp of the post-Communist era.

What moral responsibility do historians have for their work? Aren't historians and sociologists public intellectuals who are meant to shape society's values?

Behind the mask of historical revisionism, moral fundamentalism filters through. When some historians these days criticise, for example, Hannah Arendt and her concept of totalitarianism by arguing that, supposedly, no regime can control society totally, and, on top of that, such control would mean complete passivity, which would exclude, say, the Germans' responsibility for Hitler or the Holocaust, they are simply betraying that they do not know this work because Arendt said nothing of the sort and spent her whole life addressing the subject of moral responsibility and guilt. Note that the point here is not the explanatory power and accuracy of the term totalitarianism, but mainly the need to provoke moral controversy. This approach, however, is by no means limited to the people associated with the Institute. It conceals an intellectual laziness or incapacity, reducing complex issues of history to the problem of moral guilt and accountability. When the notion of totalitarianism cannot be called into question as a category within the historical or political sciences, it is simply labelled as moral subterfuge. On hearing colleagues who consider themselves part of the academic community spout such statements, a famous sentence by the sociologist Max Weber always springs to mind: "the prophet and the demagogue do not belong on the academic platform." And if these historians wanted to deal with the prescriptively political and moral context of the concept of totalitarianism, they would find that, for instance, the deeply conservative (and even, for a while, National Socialist) philosopher and jurist Carl Schmitt viewed the notion of the total state, in a non-judgemental sense, as a consequence of modern society's development towards the bureaucratisation and instrumental use of the law. For him, fascist Italy and Bolshevik Russia were nothing more than specific examples of this general trend in modern society. In contrast, the always critically thinking and radical Hannah Arendt asked the question about the origins of totalitarianism simultaneously as a normative question about the intellectual and cultural origin of evil and its political organisation. A large dose of ignorance and cynicism would be needed for someone to consider her concept of totalitarianism morally flawed or to classify it as part of the ideological struggle between the right and the left. And, by the way, criticism of totalitarianism was one of the basic principles of neo-Marxist and post-Marxist critical theory and philosophy.

Is there any way of studying totalitarianism without judging it at the same time? Here I would once more recall Hannah Arendt, who wrote that the transformation of reality, initiated and facilitated by ideology, again also carries with it the transformation of ideology, and its content is voided by the gradual totalitarianisation of society, with ideology increasingly losing its content.
I think that, most of all, people need to jettison ideological schemes and the assignment of political apparatus in order to still be able, in this day and age, to say something meaningful about the origin and history of totalitarianism, including its transformations. This does not mean shying away from ethical questions in the name of non-judgemental historical science, but clearly separating the subject of study from the political and moral implications of information obtained by the historian, philosopher, jurist or political scientist. However, many philosophers from Arendt to Popper, sociologists from Aron to Horkheimer, and lawyers from Neumann to Schmitt have already dealt with this topic in the past century. We can hardly expect someone to come up with some revolutionary discovery or interpretation of totalitarianism today. In this sense, I think that the

theme has been exhausted and, for example, the history of everyday life in Nazi, fascist or communist societies serves more as an ethnographic supplement.

Now we are touching on the eternal question of "dealing with the past". A linguistic problem of the Czech language is also bound up with this. The Germans, who faced a similar issue, use the word Schuld in this context, which means not just blame, but also debt. The Czech word for guilt, *vina*, does not possess a future dimension calling for "remediation", the "repayment" of debt, and "atonement" for evil...

Already in the 1990s, when "dealing with the past" was far from a historical issue, but mainly a political and legal matter, I proposed that the past is not something that we can definitively come to terms with, but something we need to confront again and again. This holds particularly true for the period of totalitarianism and, legally speaking, it was right for the new democratic regime to use the usual triad of rehabilitative, restitutive and retributive justice, i.e. it civilly exonerated the persecuted, corrected the worst wrongdoings and injustices of the Communist regime, and tried to punish the perpetrators of that regime's crimes. These are typical practices in most societies transitioning from an authoritarian or totalitarian system to an open democratic society built on constitutional rights and the rule of law. The civil rehabilitation of political prisoners and persons persecuted by the Communist regime included financial compensation, but criminal justice in our country, just as in other post-Communist countries, was seldom successful in punishing perpetrators of political crimes. Restitution was primarily physical, and gradually expanded as the 1990s progressed to include the confiscation of Jewish property during the Nazi occupation. I would just point out that the Church restitutions of 2012 were not part of this original process of dealing with the past, as these came about as a result of a political pact between the then right-wing government and Church institutions.

Considering the array of laws we have, including on lustration, on the unlawfulness of the Communist regime and on resisting such a regime, and the restitution we have just mentioned, we should be able to confront that Communist past well enough, shouldn't we?
When we look back at the process of dealing with the past, we discover that the collective memory is always selective, rather than cumulative, and that we more happily and readily deal with one particular past than another past. Even in laws designed to be completely pragmatic, such as restitution in the 1990s, we find a symbolic differentiation between the unjust past and a present seeking to remedy these historical wrongdoings and injustices, including the punishment of political crimes. At the very beginning of the transition from communism to democracy, for example, Poland's first non-Communist prime minister, Tadeusz Mazowiecki, proposed following the example of Spain by drawing "a thick line" splitting the recent past from the present. However, he did not have his way, as the post-Communist countries sought to punish crimes and even came up with preventive decommunisation measures to deny selected representatives of the former regime access to certain public offices. This gave rise to the general term "lustration". When we talk about today's Institute for the Study of Totalitarian Regimes, we should not forget that, as far back as 1995, the Office for the Documentation and the Investigation of the Crimes of Communism was established not only to archive the activities of the Communist regime, but also to identify and investigate its crimes, and in 2002 it became part of the Criminal Police. Unlike, for example, South Africa's Truth and Reconciliation Commission, political crimes were generally brought into the open in post-Communist societies with the idea of exposing them to criminal justice. Consequently, in cases where it was still possible under applicable legislation, those who had committed crimes in the past were prosecuted. So when people compare today's Institute for the Study of Totalitarian Regimes and its functions straddling historical science, politics and law with,

say, the Polish Institute of National Remembrance, founded in 1998, or the Slovak National Memory Institute, established in 2002, it is worth recalling that many of these institutions' activities were already being carried out in the Czech Republic by other bodies at that time. From the very beginning, then, the Czech institute's main role was to mould our collective memory and archive recollections, and this was meant to result in the constitution of our political identity. However, in an open society collective memory is always a live issue that cannot be administratively organised, codified by law, or guaranteed by any public institution. In other words, political institutions and laws cannot codify a politically correct and morally desirable collective memory in a free society.

Besides, isn't forgetting a part of every memory?!
Exactly! Since antiquity, every policy of collective memory has included a policy of active forgetting. Take Cicero. Two days after the assassination of Caesar, he was in the Senate demanding *oblivione sempiterna delendam*, i.e. saying that the murder should be buried in eternal oblivion. In 1946, Winston Churchill said much the same about the crimes of Nazism in his famous Zurich speech, in which he spoke about the need to punish those who had been guilty of war crimes and, in the same breath, about the obligation to turn our backs upon the horrors of the past and to achieve what his predecessor, prime minister Gladstone, called a "blessed act of oblivion". As you can see, any dealing with the past is bound up with some form of not dealing with it, hence we have history that always needs to get to grips with the past, but requires no official bodies to do so. I think "institutionally" dealing with the past by setting up the Institute for the Study of Totalitarian Regimes proves, above all, that what we have here is still this post-Communist neurotic collective memory instead of the free pluralism of historical narratives.

As Karl Jaspers wrote, "That condemnation by the victorious powers became a means of politics and impure in its motives – this fact itself is a guilt pervading history." So I would ask: what, then, continues to make totalitarianism so interesting for historians, lawyers, philosophers and social scientists?

Today we are inundated with studies on transitions from totalitarian or authoritarian regimes to democracies, but the same attention should be paid to transitions from democracy to authoritarian or totalitarian regimes. By describing and understanding these changes in society, we can have a good grasp of how the totalitarian regime itself functions. In these transitions, something is both broken and shaped, so in Czech conditions, for example, our understanding of the totalitarian era of the Nazi occupation must be investigated, among other things, in close connection with the post-Munich development of the Second Republic, where authoritarian features were already in evidence. The deep-rooted image of the Czech nation as a victim of the totalitarian despotism of Nazi occupiers is oversimplified because subsequent collaborative patterns of behaviour were preceded by the authoritarian regime of the Second Republic, which in some respects resembled Italian fascism. While a certain degree of opposition was tolerated, the Party of National Unity emerged at this time, and prime minister Beran was highly critical not only of liberalism, but also of democracy itself. Though the Communists paradoxically remained in parliament, their party was dissolved. There was heavy censorship and the government was able to rule without parliament, which effectively spelt the end of Czechoslovak parliamentary democracy. Add to that the discriminatory action taken against our Jewish fellow citizens and suddenly you see that, while it is true that previously constitutive values and ideals disintegrated in an internationally and diplomatically extreme situation, the Czech political representation and the people of this country were not just passive victims, but also actors. From the National Unity Party, it was a slippery slope to the Protectorate's National

Partnership, and when Hácha placed the fate of the "Czech nation and country, with complete trust, into the hands of the Führer of the German Reich" on 15 March 1939, this was nothing more than the culmination of the tragic progression of those few months.

How did the Nazi occupation and the later Communist dictatorship skew our relationship to statehood and politics per se?
Perhaps we could turn this question around and ask how much our traditional relationship to statehood and politics affected even such an extraordinary and cruel period as the Nazi occupation or the formation and internal transformation of the Communist regime. The Nazi occupation was an extreme period during which the occupying power deployed instruments of warfare and terror to mow down any manifestation of political defiance and cow the civilian population. The resistance movement became the only possible form of opposition. Incarceration in concentration camps, the Nuremberg Laws and the Holocaust inflicted on fellow citizens of Jewish descent, mass murders to avenge the successful assassination attempt on Heydrich... All extreme times like these necessarily raise the crucial questions of who has passed this extreme test of moral integrity and how they did so, who is considered a hero in such a situation and why, and what society makes of such people. And heroism is not a virtue particularly appreciated by Czech society because we attach more symbolic importance to the victims of Nazi terror than to the heroic deeds of the resistance. These days, hardly anyone talks about the Protectorate prime minister Alois Eliáš, who was secretly a leading figure of the resistance movement at the same time, and in our collective memory the Lidice tragedy overshadows the courage of the Czechoslovak paratroopers who, despite knowing they were going to their deaths, pulled off an exceptional feat in the pan-European context of anti-Nazi resistance. And yet it is interesting how these fates intersect. Eliáš assumed the office of Protectorate prime minister as a symbol of patriotism and a guarantee that the Czech

fascists – openly collaborating with the Nazi occupiers – would not be able to usurp power. Eliáš, on behalf of the government, managed to avoid swearing allegiance to Adolf Hitler, was involved in the domestic military resistance, cooperated with Beneš's government-in-exile, and, despite the limited room to manoeuvre in the Protectorate, sought to minimise the pervasion of the German occupying authorities and, especially, intelligence services into the Czech government administration. Despite the circumstances, he even successfully set up his own intelligence network, and Beneš, from his place in exile, implored Eliáš's government not to resign. The classic political and legal question of where the boundary lies between occupier-enforced obedience and open collaboration was of secondary importance between 1939 and 1941 because Eliáš's government had the support of Beneš's government-in-exile and there was a general consensus that the final word in the liberation of the country would rest with the exiles, while the domestic Protectorate government would actively coordinate and spur on the national revolution, even though the situation in the Protectorate was deteriorating all the time and the domestic fascists and collaborators were carving out more and more space for themselves. It is also worth recalling that, on 27 September 1941, the date of Eliáš's arrest, Heydrich declared a state of emergency and then, on the following day, martial law. This only goes to show that Nazi repression and terror had been escalating long before Heydrich's assassination. It was Eliáš's death sentence that prompted Beneš, from his place in exile in London, to demand that Hácha step down, but he refused. Eliáš was executed by firing squad on 19 June 1942, the day after Jozef Gabčík and Jan Kubiš perished along with other paratroopers – Adolf Opálka, Josef Valčík, Josef Bublík, Jan Hrubý and Jaroslav Švarc – in the Church of Saints Cyril and Methodius. It would not be true to say, then, that the Czech nation has no heroes, but it is not so fond of them because it prefers victims. Not active resistance, but passive resistance, that is the pattern of behaviour permeating our modern history. And, as we know from Škvorecký's novels and short stories, the problem is not just that we live our lives as cowards, but, above all, that these cowards take the right to historical retaliation into their own hands and hypocritically compensate for their former failings by engaging in revolutionary violence and sadism.

But is this cowardice not related to the fact that, even when the situation had quietened down, or immediately after the war, there was a prevailing lack of trust in democratic institutions here?
To this day, quite a few people reproach President Beneš for being a weak democrat who, after 1945, did not hesitate to eliminate his rivals by restricting democratic competition. However, we need only think a bit about what the post-war Czech political scene would have looked like had it been a free-for-all, and what influence those who liquidated the First Republic and supported authoritarian – even totalitarian – occupying politics would have had on it. The political moves made by Beneš were not a foretaste of the Communist dictatorship, as some supporters of the ultraconservative right are still trying to maintain, but a futile attempt to keep it at bay in a situation where the Communist Party had successfully mobilised a large swathe of the population to win the first post-war elections in 1946. The transitional period between 1945 and 1948 has now been historically explored in detail, and even the figure of President Beneš has been the subject of a political biography by Zbyněk Zeman and, more recently, an exquisite work penned by the French historian Antoine Marès that is free of the homespun stereotypes clouding the way we look at our national history. Let's not forget that Beneš was a politician at a time when the Western democracies were weakening and Hitler and Stalin were divvying up spheres of influence on the continent between them. In these circumstances, international diplomacy was the only possible way of preserving the Czechoslovak state, but Marès goes beyond that and cleverly analyses Beneš's theoretical approach to domestic- and foreign-policy issues. You see,

Beneš believed that scientific methods could be applied to politics, as borne out by his early sociological studies of partisanship, democracy, international diplomacy and war. Interestingly, it took a French professor of history to convey to Czech readers this important and unique side to the second Czechoslovak president.

Okay, let's move on from 1948. But what interests you, as a legal philosopher, in this regard?
It really makes no sense to keep revisiting the events in the run-up to the Communist coup in 1948 and the subsequent installation of the Stalinist dictatorship because these have been described *ad nauseam*. What interests me more in this respect is the more general link between domestic political culture and the Communist vision of a society that is liberated from politics and enjoys abundance and prosperity, where everything seems to manage itself solely by virtue of the fact that the people govern themselves as though in some fairy tale. The Communists' triumph in the free elections in 1946 was exceptional in Europe, comparable perhaps only to the French parliamentary elections in the same year, in which the Communists captured almost thirty per cent of the vote. And yet, when we consider the traditional local support for left-wing parties and the post-war popularity of the Soviet Union, whose soldiers liberated most of our country, the victory of the Czechoslovak Communists stands to reason. This was a variation on the theme of the social question, which crops up again and again in Czech modern history and is one of the constitutive elements of our political culture and imagination. The vision of a society no longer divided into social classes, delivering the ideal of the *de facto* equality of all people, has always been popular in Czech society. In parallel with this, the Communist Party's popularity was boosted by another traditional element of our political culture: fundamental distrust in the state, public institutions and politics *per se*. Let's not lose sight of the fact that the total political mobilisation of the Bolshevik Revolution was presented as

both a historical and social necessity because this event was simply effecting the absolute norm of a law of history which the Marxists claimed to have discovered, meaning they had the right to be its sovereign and sole interpreters and implementers. An absolute political event, such as a revolution, is thus legitimised by the promise that it is simultaneously the end of politics. Czech voters were therefore being offered liberation from the politics they had traditionally distrusted. I think that this promise to redeem society from its political existence, combined with the opportunity to fantasise that we are only bystanders in a spectacular historical struggle that has been decided in advance, was just as important for the legitimacy of the Communist Party as the traditionally egalitarian values of the modern Czech nation.

Although, for the most part, our cultural avant-garde backed away from the Communist Party very early on, this had no effect on the public. Perhaps because of that, the fate of the avant-garde simply served to illustrate Czech history of the second half of the last century. Or do you see things differently?
It's not quite true that the vast majority of the Czech artistic and intellectual avant-garde distanced itself from the Communist Party as early as the interwar period, specifically after the Gottwald wing took control of the Party in 1929. In 1929, *Manifest sedmi* [Manifesto of Seven] was signed by Olbracht, Malířová, Seifert, Majerová, Neumann, Hora and Vančura. With the exception of the latter, they were viewed by the then "avant-garde", headed by Teige and Nezval, as artistically more conservative authors. These two figureheads, along with František Halas, Julius Fučík, Jiří Weil, Karel Konrád, Bedřich Václavek, Ladislav Novomeský, Vladimir Clementis and others, made this abundantly clear to them in *Zásadní stanovisko k projevu „sedmi"* [Fundamental Opinion on the Manifesto of the "Seven"]. In this retort, one of the harshest manifestations of Stalinism from the First Republic, these mouthpieces of Czech avant-gar-

de art decried their fellow artists for stepping "out of the line that we must all toe". Not even the Stalinist trials in Russia in the 1930s persuaded Teige, for example, to revise his political stance, so he did not fall victim to Stalinism until after 1948. While the avant-garde came to a definitive end in Soviet Russia after 1932, and Fifteen Years of Artists of the Russian Soviet Republic, an exhibition in Leningrad, was the last public outing of the modernist avant-garde, with Kazimir Malevich at the helm, after which Soviet art and literature was dominated once and for all by the totalitarian canon of socialist realism, in Czechoslovakia illusions about Stalinism were popular even among the avant-garde. Only with the arrival of the Communist regime did it transpire that the avant-garde would not be tolerated by the official cultural policy and that all art – entirely in keeping with the Stalinist model – would bow to the needs of the political dictatorship. Figuratively speaking, after that the former Czechoslovakian avant-garde could only choose between Vítězslav Nezval and Karel Teige, i.e. between the paths of servitude and suicide. Writers, philosophers, and artists in Czechoslovakia had to wait for Stalinism to pass before they could tentatively reassume the critical role of public intellectuals. It is nothing short of ludicrous that, while the Hungarians and the Poles associate de-Stalinisation with the turbulent year of 1956, we identify it with the 1963 Kafka Conference in Liblice. But it is somewhere here that the seeds of the Prague Spring were sown, and it is also somewhere here that we should seek out the original inspiration for domestic criticism of totalitarianism, as represented, for example, by Kosík's 1968 study *Our Present Crisis*. This is based on general criticism of the technical rationality unfolding in consumer culture, political manipulation in the name of pragmatism, and the merging of the economy, technology, and science. However, such criticism of modern civilisation targeted the then technologists of Communist power and their bureaucratic apparatus, ideological schemes and elitist behaviour, contrasting with the mass of the controlled citizens. Here we also find a completely new form of Communist self-criticism that is the opposite of Stalinist public rituals because in it Karel Kosík, our most influential Marxist philosopher, declares: "We are not bearers of truth, and nothing – youth or old age, origin or social status, dogma or belief – entitles us to cloister ourselves in the complacency that the truth is already ours. We distance ourselves from the truth if we live under the illusion that we have it in our hands and that we can play with it or dispose of it at will." If Stalinist political totalitarianism ended with the dictator's death, Communist totalitarianism could not survive 1968 ideologically, as evidenced by Kosík's sentences. Everything that happened after 1968 could only ever have been a cynical play for power by the Party elite, who clung to power by more or less repressive means, but had also entered into a social contract with citizens under which the elite would provide economic benefits on the understanding that the public would not interfere with political governance and rituals. Nobody could embody this corruptly repressive system better than the proven political and ideological manipulator Gustáv Husák. That is why we must examine the normalisation era both in terms of the development of Communist regimes over time and by comparing them with the then Western democracies, whose normalisation after the stormy end to the 1960s took place in the atmosphere of a unifying European market. Although the prominent German philosopher Jürgen Habermas posed the question of the crisis of legitimacy in late capitalism in the early 1970s, in the end it was actually the late-socialism systems' crisis of legitimacy that led to their total collapse. From the second half of the 1970s, European development progressed towards the increasingly articulated voice of political dissent in Communist Europe, which, after the Helsinki Process, could rely more and more on human rights arguments. While the world at this time was still split into East and West, dissidence was already speaking the language of global politics and asking questions to which the Communist regimes were unable to provide convincing answers. So, faced with a choice between the martial law offered by the Polish model and democratisation according to the erstwhile Czechoslovak model, the leading party ultimately, and mercifully, opted for democratisation and, by dismantling its own dominion, definitively brought its historical role to completion.

From the Disintegration of the State to the Disintegration of the Regime

From 1918 to 1989, our main threats were external, first Germany and then the Soviet Union, but today the biggest danger seems to come from within. Do we have the strength needed to defend our democracy?

At the start of this book, we discussed historical relativism on a general level, and now, at the end, we have returned to this subject in the very concrete historical context of the post-1989 building of our democracy. The way we want to deal with totalitarianism paradoxically proves that we are unable to accept the basic premise of life in a free, open society: a plurality of values and opinions. We view value pluralism as something dangerous, something that threatens us, but in reality freedom is most at risk from the monistic notion that there is only one truth and one good, and therefore politicians and everyone else are duty-bound to reassert this good and truth over all who have somehow strayed from them. Pluralism, however, is not relativism. On the contrary, it is the ability to find an Aristotelian middle way between the extremes of monism and relativism.

So you would say that value pluralism is not relativism, as we sometimes hear. Can you expand on that? In what circumstances could we talk about relativism?

It is not, because relativists are content with the subjective view that we all profess our values and, in the event of a conflict, the might-is-right principle prevails, i.e. the side that is able to assert its values by force wins. Political and value pluralism, on the other hand, recognises the objective nature of values because they form part of our humanity. People share different values, but despite their diversity and the conflicts between them, it is values that determine our human existence and therefore they are not just a figment of the subjective imagination or random social constructs.

We must also approach the Nazi or Communist system of values in this spirit because the fact that some people are able to accept, say, race as a criterion of humanity does not make them inhuman beasts. Rather, this is an extreme and perverse manifestation of the general human desire to impose a code of values on the world, even if monstrous crimes are the price that has to be paid. Understanding society's plurality of values and the fact that my values may differ from those of other people, without this meaning that my values are true and theirs are false, is a first step on the way to grasping the principle of tolerance, in the absence of which a modern open society and a constitutional democratic state are inconceivable. When the two of us got down to the brass tacks of national identity and nationalism, we came across many cases in history where patriotism and national pride, as positive mindsets and values, rapidly descended into the inflamed rhetoric of hate-fuelled nationalism and slogans in the vein of "my nation's better than yours". These curious transitions, in which positive values become volatile substances while noble ideas lead to the gallows, are also part and parcel of value pluralism. In this respect, value pluralism is a form of defence against the pathological extremism that would assure its followers they are the sole elected protectors of values (whether national, universal, religious, or anything else), hence all crimes committed on their behalf are amnestied before they even happen. A monistic image of society in which everything needs to chime with the greatest good and truth is the enemy of a pluralist democracy. Within such a society, at the very least since the writing of Plato's *The Republic*, those who know this have also arrogated to themselves the right to rule and to determine not only how society is to be organised and managed, but also how individuals are to live their lives and what culture society ought to be cultivating and developing. As you can see, this threat extends far beyond totalitarian ideologies. We can find parallels, for example, in the modern notions of a "government of experts" that is geared towards efficiency and profit, to which all political institutions, including the state, are meant to be committed. It is interesting how relativism often lends support to these ideas that there are simple solutions to complex problems. Pluralism, on the other hand, is well aware that social problems have no simple solutions, so it is necessary to find procedures whose legitimacy does not rely on the duty to eradicate "improper" values and opinions. The point of democracy is not to exact any obligation to stamp out other values or opinions. On the contrary, democracy gives us the opportunity to refute and reject opinions in a civilised manner by engaging in honest debate.

But how do you want pluralistic democracies to defend themselves against totalitarian ideologies when people are clamouring ever more insistently for simple solutions in a globalised and bewildering world?

A constitutional democracy stands or falls by this paradox: it must convince citizens that it is the best possible political system and, at the same time, it must – by coercion, if necessary – fight against any political monism and ideology arguing that only its values are right and proper and that all those who do not recognise them are people of inferior order and must conform. The German constitutional judge and legal philosopher Ernst-Wolfgang Böckenförde formulated this very precisely in the 1970s with the phrase "the liberal secularised state lives by presuppositions that it cannot itself guarantee". This *Böckenförde Dilemma* is clear, precise, and simple, yet informed by the Nazi past, and states that the prerequisites for the functioning of a constitutional and democratic state lie outside its power apparatus, in the field of human morals, ethics and the rules of social behaviour and values.

Democracy is a culture that defines the framework of what is acceptable, but the protracted absence of a political elite and two totalitarian regimes heave meant that this tradition of high culture is lacking in our country...

The state, even one as young as our own, has a duty to stand up to evil, but must not dictate what is good because that is beyond its authority and competence. In the Czech Republic, however, we choose to interpret politics as a conflict between good and evil, so some people feel that the state is here to uphold what is good. This is incompatible with the idea of a pluralistic democracy and open society because politics can only give a definitive answer to the question of what is right, not what is good. We have to look for good in society and in the human mind, not in the state, and not at all in constitutional bodies.

Are we even able to build a functioning democracy based on liberal values, about which the likes of Ralf Dahrendorf wrote in the early 1990s, in the situation today, where constitutional democracy is crumbling in both new and old Europe?

The current situation is completely different, but I'd like to keep to a general plane for a while longer. The Slovak sociologist and politician Martin Bútora called his book of articles and essays from the period from 1967 to 2004 *Odklínanie* [Breaking the Spell]. Everyone, of course, immediately makes a connection with Weber's sociological theory that the process of modernising society is linked to its gradual disenchantment and the growth of rationality, purposefulness, materiality and functionality. We had the same sort of idea about the Czechoslovak post-Communist transition in the early 1990s, i.e. that we would carry out economic reform by introducing a market economy, and political reform by amending the Constitution (and, building on that, other laws), and that society would begin to function and adopt democratic and liberal values gradually and, obviously, as its own. Dahrendorf warned about this simplistic view in his memorable quip from the early 1990s that new laws and constitutions could be adopted in months, and economic reform in years, but that the transformation of civil society would last for decades. Bútora's book stands testament to that. What's more, it shows that the process of disenchantment also breathes life into new and old demons: in our particular case, nationalism and national populism. Instead of constitutional reform, we lost a common federation within two years of the fall of Communism; instead of a functioning market economy, a tribal economy was created, with the state nothing more than a clientelistic institution and political parties trade organisations. The past quarter of a century has shown how, in political and economic structures and in the deep subconscious of society, the demons of modernity slumber yet. As society wakes up to the rationality of modern state bureaucracy and the market economy, so those demons of irrational nationalism, too, are awakening. This is how we must view not only the emergence and extinction of the Communist regime, but also the ineffectual building of a federal republic as a common state for the Czechs and Slovaks. The collapse of the federation was opposed by civil society, but even this was unable to hold off the actions of the new political elite, whose inexperience and disinclination inhibited any constitutional and political alternative after the 1992 parliamentary elections.

One of the paradoxes of our most modern evolution is that we dissolved our federation with the Slovaks in 1992, at the very moment Europe was really starting to integrate politically and the European Community was remodelled as the European Union. Masaryk's idea that the nation states in Central Europe, once created, would be federalised was defeated entirely in Czechoslovakia at that time. How deep a role was played in this respect by the totalitarian concept of federation between 1968 and 1989?

The tragedy of the Czechoslovak federation was that the Constitution adopted in 1968 may have guaranteed the wide-ranging decentralisation of power and the delegation of authority to each republic on paper, but in reality it held no sway at all. The federal Constitution was adopted in an occupied country where power was concentrated not in constitutional institutions, but in party bodies, so the Slovaks felt that this sort of federation wasn't working and didn't allow them the right to self-determination, whereas the Czechs thought the federalisation of the state and the decentralisation of power were incidental matters. If we are to understand the constitutional crisis and the subsequent break-up of Czechoslovakia, we must therefore return to the classic socio-legal distinction between law in books and law in action. The text of the 1968 federal Constitution guaranteed the two republics equality and far-reaching powers, and assured them that they were members of the common federation voluntarily. Constitutionally speaking, these republics were viewed as sovereign nation states, from which the Czechoslovak federation's sovereignty – which also required the respect of both republics – was then derived. The written federal Constitution was thus a treaty on the creation of a common state based on shared sovereignty, that is, on the very same principle now upheld by the European Union! Such a constitutional document was intended not only to dovetail with the Slovaks' notions of the common state's constitutional architecture, which we can trace all the way back to the Martin Declaration, but was also deeply rooted in the general idea that federalisation is inextricably linked to democratisation. And yet democratisation fell to the wayside as, under the occupying power, the normalisation era dawned and reduced federalisation to a bureaucratic and party-controlled process. Consequently, after the fall of Communism we had a dead-letter Constitution and this idea of a federation that was regarded by the Czechs – influenced in part by normalisation – as a trivial administrative change and by the Slovaks as a promise that had not been kept.

But as soon as the revolutionary changes were under way in 1989, there was talk about how this promise needed to be fulfilled!

You're right, but this lapse, prompting the division of Czechoslovakia, exemplifies how politics can never be fully bound by constitutional rules and how the essence of every constitutional regime or constitutional reform lies in intercourse between political will and legal norm. We can't simply assume that rewriting the Constitution will automatically resolve political conflicts and crises. By the same token, political will cannot ride roughshod over the letter of the Constitution. In the post-1989 political transition, this tension between political will and constitutional norms ought to have been resolved by constitutional reform ending in what was then referred to as an "authentic federation". The basic mistake that Czech and Slovak politicians made after 1989 was to believe that constitutional reform is essentially the same process as economic transformation, i.e. that it can be managed administratively and translated into a profit-and-cost calculation. Following the 1992 parliamentary elections, however, this constitutional process was eventually narrowed down to bargaining between Václav Klaus, who viewed further federalisation as nothing more than a political millstone, and Vladimír Mečiar, who believed that being authentic meant the opportunity to say and demand what happened to be best for him at any given moment in order to strengthen his grip on power. It was clear that this project had hit the skids.

When all is said and done, though, didn't the disintegration of Czechoslovakia benefit both nations in various respects?

These days, Czechoslovakia's break-up serves as an example of an amicable split between two nations who have always been close and never harboured hatred towards each other, but were never able to find a constitutional way of co-existing in free conditions. The 1968 federal Constitution was a dead letter, yet the new democratically elected representations failed to breathe life into a common state which, at various times, had been of existential importance for both nations. For the Czechs, the disintegration of the Czechoslovak federation confronted them with the need, above all, to passively come to terms with their autonomous state. Initially, they could not even bring themselves to call it by the unofficial name of *Česko*, so we spent ages using the awkward Czech Republic, and at international sports events we resorted to "Czech Team" emblazoned on our kit or even, ludicrously, just "Czech" instead of the simple Czechia. The Slovaks, on the other hand, were thrust into very turbulent politics. In the second half of the 1990s, they found themselves once again fighting an authoritarian regime, this time engineered by Vladimír Mečiar, which even temporarily isolated Slovakia. Subsequent governments managed to iron everything out, so in the end Slovakia achieved the admirable feat of joining the European Union together with other post-Communist countries as early as 2004.

In hindsight, aren't these differences also proof that the common state was prevented from functioning by the dissimilar political culture and priorities in the Czech Lands and Slovakia?
They aren't evidence of anything because then we would be thinking consequentially and deriving causes from the consequences of a particular act. However, there is another fundamental difference lurking in your question, namely the difference between the written constitution of the state and the living constitution of society. And unless we grasp this difference, we really can't understand the break-up of the Czechoslovak federation. In the post-1989 period, we thought that it would be enough to write down and approve the new text of the Constitution, and that the democratic context would then emerge spontaneously. In fact, we only managed to adopt the Charter of Fundamental Rights and Freedoms and the closely related Constitutional Court Act. To be sure, this was important, but, considering the need to hammer out a completely new constitutional contract between the two republics and nations, it wasn't enough.

Nowadays, no one ever talks about how the fate of the federation was hanging by a thread, but that it could still have been saved. In this context, it is also worth remembering that, in March 1992, the praesidium of the Slovak National Council, i.e. the Slovak parliament, was a single vote short of approving the negotiated text of the state treaty, with voting tied at 10:10. And the federation was split, with no referendum, on the basis of a constitutional law passed by the Federal Assembly, again with a single vote making the difference! Opposing this official voting machinery of the constitutional bodies was the unofficial living constitution of a society in which most Czechs and Slovaks wished to stay in a common state and did not recognise the struggle for power and influence being waged among those that politically represented them as their own. A referendum, that most legitimate means of fulfilling the right of nations to self-determination, and I emphasise "self-determination", was not allowed to be held as it would have confirmed the legitimacy of the living constitution of society and the illegitimacy of the political will of the political representation at the time. The fact that these legislators won the parliamentary elections because their political parties and movements did not campaign for the break-up of the Czechoslovak federation does not alter this. In other words, the citizens of Czechoslovakia overestimated the fledgling political elite's prowess and its respect for the virtues and ideals of Czechoslovak democracy and statehood.

Is this contradiction between the official constitution of political power and the unofficial constitution of political society common to all political communities?
Definitely! Though I'm not thinking of any academic speculation or retrospective civic soul-searching. What interests me is a more sweeping description of the difference between political decision-making and its social context, which was positively chasmic in the case of the Czechoslovak federation's split. For one thing, I fully realise that,

in the face of the *Constitutional Declaration of the Slovak National Council on the Independence of the Slovak Republic* of 17 July 1992, President Havel could do nothing other than step down because this document, unilaterally manifesting the will of the sovereign authority of the Slovak Republic, effectively tore asunder the constitutional order of the then federal state. The break-up was stoked by the paucity of political will to negotiate and compromise. In parallel with this, it has to be said that, where political will has overwhelmed the constitutional norm, democracy itself has paradoxically become helpless. Yet it is impossible to draw a line beyond which any further negotiation will be pointless. In particular, negotiations on the constitutional form of federal co-existence between democratically established nations can be a protracted, open-ended process. We need look no further than Quebec, or Scotland's status within the United Kingdom, to see that politics in an open and democratic society hinges, above all, on the ability and willingness to persistently address political crises, including constitutional crises. However, when Czech prime minister Petr Pithart proposed partitioning off the home of the Czechoslovak federation to make two "semi-detached houses", he was derided by most engineers of policy at that time. Yet this was one of the few realistic attempts to hold off and deal with the constitutional crisis in a way that wouldn't undermine the country's economic and political transition. Take a look around the world and you'll find many such semi-detached houses and other structural solutions in democratic societies. Sometimes the buildings look like they're crumbling – witness Catalonia. Other times, you get the impression that a massive extension is being built, with the odd hammering on the neighbour's wall, such as in Quebec. When you're laying the foundations of these structures, you need to mix courage with patience, and restraint with the active ability to negotiate compromises that may seem disadvantageous at first but can prove effective in the long run. In 1992, however, no such foundations of constitutional legitimacy had been laid in Czechoslovakia, so we clung to the authority provided by the letter of the then constitutional architecture and dissolved the state in a legality of procedures, without anchoring these fundamental state-destroying and state-building processes in the democratic legitimacy that could only be guaranteed by a referendum.

This tension between legality and legitimacy was also typical of Czechoslovakia's First Republic, or am I mistaken?
This tension exists in any modern state, be it democratic and republican or autocratic and monarchical. We can even trace it back beyond the First Czechoslovak Republic to the Habsburg monarchy. The fundamental paradox of this monarchy was that it was able to create general laws, but failed to harness them as a way of organising a multinational community in which the desire for freedom and democratic government also took the form of a struggle for national self-determination. Austrian bureaucracy was meant to cool the heads of revolutionaries and separatists in the various nations, but was unable to justify itself through any leading political idea or values. In other words, it had this surfeit of rational legality embodied in legal norms, but was starved of the legitimacy of values, as the countries lacked democratic institutions and, on top of that, were deprived of civic virtues and skills. In point of fact, First-Republic Czechoslovakia – despite officially pursuing a policy of "de-Austrianisation" – continued to cultivate the Austrian spirit of public administration and state organisation. Czechoslovakia was an attempt to transform the Habsburg spirit of legalism into a legitimate republic with a functioning democratic system and freedoms for all citizens and nationalities. That is why Czechoslovakia's First Republic, much like interwar Austria, boasted exemplary legality and a working constitutional regime, even while it had to battle constantly for legitimacy, which required superhuman effort and was a daunting task given the then multinational structure of society, the international situation and, particularly, the transformation of neighbouring states into racially profiled societies. Post-war Czechoslovakia

was unable to restore this spirit. With the Communist legal school having labelled legalism a bourgeois hangover, we did not view the post-1989 tension between legality and legitimacy as a normal manifestation of an open and democratic society, but as a pathological situation that needed to be resolved by the division of the state along ethnic lines. Czechoslovakia fell apart because we mishandled the aspects of both legality, in the shape of constitutional reform, and legitimacy, in the form of the democratic manifestation of the will of the people, robbing them of the chance to decide on the existence of their own state. This is why the Czech Republic is today more ethnically homogeneous, and all the more politically cloistered as a result, than the actual history of Czech society and the political ideas of its erstwhile democratic statesmen would suggest.

In this context, I would like to quote part of the speech Václav Havel delivered in the Rudolfinum on 9 December 1997, when he discussed our resistance to joining an integrating Europe and NATO: "We would all be infinitely guilty if we were to squander this chance. However, if we do not want to squander it, then we have to start with our souls. By this, I mean the need to declare a war without mercy on Czech provincialism, isolationism, and egoism. On all illusions of some cunning neutrality, our traditional short-sightedness, and all types of Czech chauvinism. Those who today decline to shoulder their share of responsibility for the fate of their continent and the world as a whole seal the doom not only of their continent and the world, but, first and foremost, of themselves... Identity is a deed, a piece of work, an accomplishment. Identity does not stand apart from responsibility; on the contrary, identity is an expression of responsibility." It seems to me that this identity is mirrored in how we perceive our statehood, how we are ignorant of what statehood means and implies. What is your opinion?

That speech was important not only because it captured contemporary society's state of mind, and the risks wrapped up in that, but also – and mainly – because, in parallel to the economic recession and political crisis at the time, Havel highlighted how the Czech Republic was at sea internationally and what dangers were thrown up by questioning our involvement in the European integration process or NATO's defence structures. In this speech, Havel described precisely how Czech nationalism, craving to isolate itself from the outside world, posed the gravest threat to the Czech nation. His words still hold true today. Some political scientists are fond of recalling the German legal and political philosopher Carl Schmitt's basic tenet that politics exists where people distinguish between friend and foe, and sovereignty is the ability to determine who the enemy is. I would say that this definition does not apply, simply because politics is a much more complex process than working out who the enemy is. It also presupposes the reaching of a consensus, the negotiation of compromises, and the forming of coalitions. Similarly, sovereignty is defined not by political will alone, but also by the responsibility and the ability to take on commitments in domestic and foreign politics. That's why I also like Havel's definition of identity not as an existential state, but as a living, breathing endeavour and enterprise, creating the basis needed for a political community to define the meaning of its own existence.

This brings us back to the very beginning of our discussion on Czech identity and statehood. Does that mean that the questions are still the same and just as topical as they were two hundred years ago?
I'd say there are some questions we have to ask ourselves time and again, simply because the Czech state exists and finds itself in a place on the European continent where all kinds of political influences converge and intersect, and where, as history teaches us, there are frequently major political clashes and conflicts. To parody Schmitt's definition of politics a little, I would say that today we are our own biggest enemy, as you remarked in the question introducing

this chapter! And we are most imperilled by our historical prejudices and political constructs that can genuinely be traced all the way back to the early days of the national revival. Take, for example, the construct in which the classic "them-and-us" attitude, as defined by every social group, including large imaginary national societies, is reflected in the "nation-versus-state" difference. This is accompanied by distrust in the state and politics *per se*, in contrast to which we keenly foster the idyll of friendly communities and neighbourly "cosy dens" – a place where we like to put our feet up and dream as a way of escaping the reality of the world around us. In the past, Czech politicians protested against the Habsburg monarchy by pitting nothing more than their national culture and sense of belonging against the monarchy's national policy. That lives on today. For us, there is too much contact and conflict in politics, so it is still our preference to build up a cultural idyll to repress it. The main political agenda then becomes the protection of that idyll from all "foreigners." We need to continue fighting these political phantasmagorias because they would cloister and encapsulate Czech politics. Everything "out there" is vilified, while what we have at home is what "counts" and creates the illusion of safety and unity. Yet this is one of the dangers posed by current Czech politics, because here somewhere is the seedbed, for instance, of the opinions that the European Union today is just a variation of the former Soviet Union and Comecon, hence it would be better for us to be independent, sovereign, etc. I believe that this fanciful antithesis of an internal idyll and external danger is a great risk deeply engrained in the Czech political tradition.

Can this be ascribed to the predilection of politicians for winning over voters with an outdated nationalist policy that shepherds us away from the state when it should be building up our constitutionality and statehood?

The paradox of modern Czech politics lies in the fact that, in 1918, it succeeded in creating a state that was autonomous for a nation that wasn't autonomous. This nation still clings to authority and views the country's presidents as a monarchical majesty. It has fashioned this meretricious image of Masaryk as the daddy of the nation, an informal title that sums up precisely the desire to escape and shed the burden of the public world of politics, replacing it with the cosiness of the private world of one big family. We witnessed something similar, though not on the same scale, with the posthumous image of Václav Havel, even though what was admirable about both Masaryk and Havel was their ability to place ethical idealism at the service of real politics. Besides attempts to transform public goods into private profits and the need to make "daddies" of constitutional actors, there is another much more dangerous aspect to this prevailing distrust in the state and politics: a dream of the end of politics, whose conflicting world it is impossible to inhabit in harmony. Dreaming of an end to politics opens up the way to a preference for non-political solutions, the spectrum of which could now include the current promise by Babiš, the leader of the ANO movement and prime minister, to establish a new technocratic government that would govern our pockets. He has offered citizens not political ideas and ideologies, but the non-political principles of profit and efficiency.

But the political steps taken by Babiš fly in the face of our constitutional regime, do they not?
It goes without saying that *We're going to get the job done, with or without your confidence*, the Babiš government's mantra, is a flagrant violation of the principle of parliamentarism, in which no government can govern in the long term if it does not enjoy the confidence of the Chamber of Deputies. Topolánek's government in 2009 sought parliamentary confidence and eventually gained it at the expense of political corruption, and the Rusnok government appointed by Zeman in 2013 held out hope of winning confidence, but when that did not happen the country found itself headed, five months down the line, for early parliamentary elections. On the

other hand, in December 2017 we witnessed for the first time both the president and his designated prime minister declaring in unison that the government could govern on a lasting basis even in the absence of parliamentary confidence. This is, of course, unconstitutional because the existence and functioning of the government is immediately dependent on parliamentary confidence. And yet not even this naked denial of the Constitution can be explained in the narrowest sense of constitutional engineering, that is, at the level of political structures and constitutional institutions, principles and rules simultaneously permitting and restricting the exercise of political power. Again, we have to look beyond constitutional texts and concentrate on the social contexts in which the Constitution functions. The context we have today unequivocally shows that Andrej Babiš offered citizens a new social contract promising them liberation from politics, even if the cost was that the letter of the Constitution itself would not be respected. Instead of constitutionalism, the technocratic goal of social reform and standardisation prevailed. Andrej Babiš's reforms are bent on reining in social benefits and introducing market logic into public services, such as the health service. In certain respects, this emphasis on "strivers" and the fight against "shirkers" echoes Orbán's vow to create a nation state based on a work ethic, although this drift from constitutional democracy in our country is not as strongly nationalist.

Do you think we can still fend off this trend?
We're going to get the job done, with or without your confidence is effectively a proclamation that changes to the constitutional regime in the country are afoot, heralding the potential end of the First Czech Republic. This republic has certainly suffered from many failings and defects, but at the same time it has chalked up all sorts of success. For example, we have created a constitutional judiciary that is the envy of other post-Communist countries, and despite the privatisation of the economy and all manner of economic reforms in the

last quarter of a century, we have managed to maintain fundamental and important elements of the welfare state, such as free health care and higher education. Without this, citizens' chances in life would have been hurt a lot more by social and economic inequalities. A fundamental failing, however, has been political parties whose leaders and machinery could not grasp that, in an open and free democratic society, their primary task is to create a counterweight to economic power, not be its adornment and extended arm. That is why the party system collapsed in the parliamentary elections in the autumn of 2017, anti-system parties gained a majority in the Chamber of Deputies, and politics as a whole veered towards entrepreneurial populism, with the mobilising force of political movements literally annihilating the party apparatus and democracy.

But isn't it premature to talk about the end of the First Czech Republic? After all, there is still a possibility that, as in Slovakia, resistance to the actions of President Zeman and prime minister Babiš will establish a stronger civil society that will not allow anything of the sort to happen.

I was talking about the possible end that began with the parliamentary elections in autumn 2017 and with what followed, namely the appointment of a prime minister and government that everyone knew in advance would not have the confidence of the Chamber of Deputies. Since then, we have seen how this government, despite having resigned, is carrying out sweeping purges in state institutions while its prime minister, Andrej Babiš, prepares for a second attempt at forming a new government. This is a clear and systematic violation of the fundamental constitutional principles of this country. On top of that, power in the Chamber of Deputies is now divided between populists and extremists, a textbook example of the internal transformation of this constitutional institution. The former mainstream right- and left-wing political parties that have steered politics over the past quarter of a century, i.e. the ODS and the ČSSD, have been decisively vanquished, and today they too have strong factions that support Miloš Zeman's extremist politics and are biding their time until an opportunity presents itself for them to take over the party reins. Thus, on a political level, we are already at the point where we can say that the Czech parliamentarist regime, in which it is the custom for political governments and coalitions to alternate and the government is backed by the confidence of the Chamber of Deputies, is unworkable. Still, other constitutional regime backstops, such as the independent judiciary and the Constitutional Court, continue to function, so we need to keep a closer eye on all attempts at constitutional change, whether this takes the form of a referendum, changes in the election of senators, the direct election of mayors, and so on. Any such incremental change could spell a further and irreversible deflection of power from the constitutional-parliamentary regime to an oligarchic-populist regime.

But what you have described is not just a purely Czech problem because, as we can see, it also concerns Hungary, Poland and, in various guises, other European countries.

Unlike in Hungary, today's extremist populist bloc comprising the Castle, Okamura's SPD and the Communist Party mercifully has no constitutional majority. And, as opposed to Poland, we have a much stronger and more independent judiciary. For example, the Czech Constitutional Court is in a better position because its justices' term will not end until after President Zeman's second term of office has finished. Yet when we see how diatribes against the public-service media, the police and the judiciary are escalating, it is clear that we, too, will be facing a monumental battle for the character of the political and constitutional regime in the immediate future. And we, too, are exposed to the risk of what we might call *benevolent authoritarianism.*

Can you clarify what you mean by that?
This is a regime in which the powerful decide how essential resources and the most lucrative contracts in the country are to be distributed, allocate them to loyal factions, and thereby strengthen their own grip while simultaneously limiting the influence and opportunities of the opposition in the economy, the media and constitutional bodies. This transformation is in no way restricted to Czech politicians; it's just that we've been concentrating on some of its specific domestic manifestations. If we look, for instance, at Hungary, benevolent authoritarianism has created strong oligarchic groups that need to keep Viktor Orbán in power because, were the opposition to defeat him, they would face criminal prosecution for corruption and abuse of power. That is also why we are now witnessing the interweaving of oligarchic interests and the concoction of new variations on the old theme of the nation state, which, for example, Viktor Orbán has artfully formulated as the end of liberal democracy and the ascent of the new politics of a sovereign state legitimised by work carried out to the benefit of the national whole, rather than by constitutional freedoms.

But there is a civilisational conflict here because the intrinsic importance of life within national communities is declining in our global society while its politically symbolic value is rising!
At first glance, this situation is paradoxical. The nation state is a political institution without which a modern representative democracy would be inconceivable and which has historically facilitated political emancipation and the protection of civil rights and liberties. At the same time, however, the political and social problems of today's globalised society can evidently not be tackled solely within the framework of national politics. And this tension, where political issues and risks are global but democracy cannot be globalised, creates a situation in which the state's decision-making capacity is increasingly constricted, but the nation clings to it all the more as the

only institution that can and must take decisions. The state, then, is expected to protect the national community from external risks and threats through bureaucratic and administrative procedures. Paradoxically, this means that the most important function of the political organisation of the state is to perform the non-political task of protecting the nation as a cultural tribe. In this context, one area discussed by Zygmunt Bauman was the end of the nation state and its replacement by the much more inconstant, more volatile, and more rudimentary politics of post-modern tribes. In a global society, even national identity is no longer a manifestation of common traditions, but a momentary eruption of collective emotions that freely spill over and engender the sense of belonging that comes with being in a crowd.

As Bauman would say, today's nationalism is part of "liquid modernity"...
In point of fact, I would say that the current decline of the tradition of Czech parliamentarism, the growth of the tribal concept of nationalism, and the transformation of the Czech constitutional regime can be attributed to a general – and not to mention two-hundred-year-old – idea advanced by the French founder of modern social sciences and engineering, Henri de Saint-Simon, that, in various permutations and forms, accompanies any crisis of modern society. Back at the dawn of the 19th century, Saint-Simon was dismissive of republican and democratic revolutions and instead demanded that the monarchs become the dictators of modernisation and drag society out of its feudal backwardness into a modern industrial age ruled by scientists, engineers, bankers and industrialists. According to Saint-Simon, in that new era everything should be governed scientifically and economically, so politics – with all its feuding, conflicts and protests – would eventually vanish and bow to economic and administrative rationality. Such rationality cannot be protested, only – purportedly – accepted. Saint-Simon published

his industrialism-centric Declaration of Principles, in which a person's value was judged by their productivity, two hundred years ago, in 1817. If you look at today's global society, extending from the United States through to South Africa and on towards India and, ultimately, China, you will find that it is this ideology of industrialism that continues to drive our current post-industrial world and post-modern culture.

Do you think today's chaos can be translated into concepts we use for our established everyday notions of reality? After all, public space is dominated by total chaos, where a lie is called an alternative truth and where it is easy to get completely lost in a flood of information, untruths, nonsense, and conspiracy theories.
Many of the problems we think have only just emerged have their own history and genealogy that we have to address if we are to make sense of them in the current climate and context. This applies as much to "post-truth" as to the social and cultural situation that we have become accustomed to calling liquid modernity. For example, the term "post-truth" in itself invites us to make the erroneous assumption that there was once some sort of truth-based politics that has since been annihilated by evil forces. This is nothing but a regurgitation of the myth of a golden age and of civilisation as the decline of humankind. The merest of glances at history shows that politics has been availing itself of both truth and falsehood since time immemorial. What's most glaringly new nowadays is instant access to information and the speed at which it can be produced, falsified, manipulated and disseminated. To digitalise truth is to make it instantaneous, which is to the detriment of sound judgement because you always need time and a certain distance to make good sense of something.

This has been competently described by sociologists. Most people are now oblivious to information, sensing only the echoes reverber-

ating from specific protest communities made up of people with the same mindset who are seeking not fresh information, but solely the affirmation of their views. This is something not even the inventors of the internet had anticipated. Chamath Palihapitiya, the former Facebook executive, acknowledged this general threat when he said they had conjured up an instrument that was ripping apart the fabric of our society.

But not even these considerations are new: Bauman's reflections on liquid modernity are inspired by Marx and Engels' remarks in *The Communist Manifesto* on how capitalism dissolves everything that has been solid and how it desecrates everything that has been sacred. The difference between the early modernisation of society in the first half of the 19th century and today's globally liquid modernity or post-modernity lies in the fact that, back then, sanctity and tradition were being dissolved, while today what we have gone so far that what we had thought were solid social institutions, including the state, are being liquefied. It is not just business and capital flows that are being globalised, but also media reality, information flows, and, with them, the surveillance and monitoring of people and entire groups, environmental destruction, humanitarian disasters, etc. Many people believe that the territorial sovereignty of a state and its borders are one of the few ways of shielding themselves from these globalisation pressures, even though the state's ability to organise society has generally diminished.

There are no end of anniversaries in 2018: Czechoslovakia was founded a hundred years ago, the First Republic ended eighty years ago, a dictatorship of the proletariat was introduced seventy years ago, the Soviet Union occupied us fifty years ago, and people began their wholesale rebellion against the socialist system thirty years ago. We've just had the national parliamentary and presidential elections, which saw Miloš Zeman re-elected as president. Would you say there's anything to celebrate in 2018?

With a quarter century of the Czech Republic behind us and a hundred years since the founding of Czechoslovakia, we have found ourselves at a critical juncture that, in many respects, resembles the situation in other European countries. Here, as elsewhere, we have witnessed the disintegration of the pluralistic system of political parties, which have been replaced by populist movements. To compound matters, the re-election of Miloš Zeman as president was a triumph for the politics of fear that had been spawned by an overtly extremist and xenophobic campaign. As though the presidential standard were emblazoned not with the motto "Truth prevails", but "Fear prevails", which is hard to comprehend in a country that is safe, economically stable, and prosperous, and where the gaps between rich and poor are narrower than in other EU countries. Consequently, we cannot resort to Marxism and explain the existing differences as economic differences. Nor, though, can we allude to the legacy of Communism. The historical roots of this fear and distrust of the outside world stretch back to the beginnings of the national revival, as we have discussed. In other words, what has prevailed is this political tradition that we will not let Brussels or any other metropolis ruin our weekend cottages and orchards!

But the election results have clearly shown that half of the country's citizens are aware of the danger that comes with the victory of the politics of fear. What role could this play in the future?
Quite a few people are talking about a divided society, but that is a political cliché because every election splits society in some way or another. These differences mould both mainstream opinion and democratic politics. There is nothing pathological about that. And social and political differences are part and parcel of an open society. Having said that, today we are living in a society that is not fractured, but torn apart. This is what makes it so hard to persuade those who have succumbed to the politics of fear that those on the other side are not out to destroy or subjugate them. When fear becomes the

central argument in politics, democratic debate and the ability to thrash out trade-offs and compromises ebb away, while demand for authoritarian government skyrockets. We are teetering on the edge and what is at stake is not just the functionality of constitutional institutions, the state apparatus or public administration; above all, this is a crisis of the values from which the legitimacy of our state is derived and which, as we know, no state can enforce because they are the result of a more general social contract. Yes, the anti-system parties won the parliamentary elections in the autumn of 2017, but what was more noteworthy in this context was that left-wing voters voted for Tomio Okamura's openly racist and fascistoid party, while conservatively right-wing voters backed the Pirates. Faced with this situation, rather than studying possible changes in the constitutional regime we need to reconsider the work of the Austrian writer Hermann Broch and his image of modern society as a permanent and deepening crisis of values. Today, we could say that it is not only the political and constitutional regime of the First Czech Republic that is on the point of collapse, but also the system of values that has been emblematic of this state and its constitutional democracy. On the one hand, we are offered the extreme alternative of a state built on an ethnic community, in which the Czechs are pitted against the whole world and fight for their truths in the spirit of Otakar Vávra's Hussite trilogy. On the other hand, there is the equally extreme alternative of politics abolishing the state as an unnecessary obstacle and replacing it with Saint-Simon's dictatorial industrialists, who will manage society and distribute its resources according to productivity. The worst alternative, however, would be for a nationalist political agenda to tie in with the dictatorship of the new oligarchies. In such an eventuality, we would have to question the "idea of the Czech state". The showdown over that idea would be monumental in determining our national existence and future because, a century after the founding of Czechoslovakia, it wouldn't take much today for the Czech state to fall victim to this "global counter-revolution".

What opportunities do citizens have to prevent this "global counter-revolution" from happening here?

Democracy is more than the act of election; as Tocqueville noted, it is also a form of social life. I believe that our main task today is to give a civic and civil form back to democratic politics. Subscribing to the position that the voters of Miloš Zeman and Tomio Okamura are morally worse or intellectually more challenged than the "other half" would mean accepting their image of politics and society. As we form a single political community, we must treat each other as equals and, for all our political and social differences, respect each other. Despite the immediate threat of a change to the political regime, I think the 2018 presidential election also mobilised citizens to such an extent that, were the newly-forming power to attack the Constitution and its values, there would be civil protests and demonstrations. And make no mistake, political conflicts in the future will be a fight for constitutional values and the very essence of our constitutional regime.

What do we need to do so that we can continue to dwell on our own past and present in a way that also factors in Europe's future?

In the first place, there's no need to think apocalyptically because the Czech Republic did not become a dictatorship in 2018. We still have the opportunity to engage in free and democratic elections, so the future and, with it, the direction taken by Czech society remain open. I remain staunchly optimistic on that front. In our talks here, we have discussed the revivalist myths and historical narratives stretching back to Palacký's concept of history, in which the Czechs have devised this notion of themselves as a deeply democratic and peace-loving nation whose political disasters and misfortunes could always be blamed on someone else. However, this cocktail of perceptions making us out to be historical victims and a bastion of democratism has been toppled for good in the last three decades as no outsiders have threatened us and we have been governing ourselves. At most, we might fall victim to our own democratic choices. We are neither better nor worse than other European nations. Inebriated for so long by our revivalist stories and notions, 2018 was the year in which we sobered up once and for all. A hundred years after the founding of their modern democratic republic, the Czechs entered the post-revivalist period, fraught with risk and fortuity, but also offering opportunities and challenges that require a cool head and civic fervour. As a Czech and a European, I am confident that, eventually, we will successfully cope with this political and cultural watershed, too.

Here's hoping that's the truth, and not post-truth.

Prague and Cardiff, 2016-2018

ABOUT THE AUTHORS

Karel Hvížďala, born 16 August 1941 in Prague, journalist and essayist. In the 1960s, he worked for *Mladý svět*, before joining the Albatros publishing house after the "normalisation" era. He spent the period from 1978 to 1990 in exile in Germany, where he worked with RFE, Deutschlandfunk, and the BBC and wrote radio plays. In 1990, he was appointed the chief reporter and board chairman of MAFRA, which publishes the newspaper *MF Dnes*, and then went on to co-publish and edit the news magazine *Týden* in 1994-1999. He is now a freelancer. He has published more than thirty books of interviews conducted with the likes of Václav Havel, Václav Bělohradský, Karol Sidon, Karel Schwarzenberg, Jacques Rupnik, Eva Jiřičná, and Jiří Přibáň, five prose works, including *Fialoví ježci*, *Raroh*, and *Nevěry*, over twenty radio plays, among them *Vzkaz*, *Rekonstrukce začínajícího básníka*, and *Snídaně na střeše*, five books on the media – *Moc a nemoc médií*, *Jak myslet média*, *Restaurování slov*, *Interviewer aneb restaurování kontextů* and *Mardatu, vzpoury v žurnalistice*, and the essay collections *Uvízlé věty* and *Pokusy*. In May 2015, a selection of his feuilletons was published under the title *Osmý den týdne*, followed in 2017 by a continuation of these memoirs released as *Dobře mrtvý dědeček* and by a book of interviews with Magda Vášáryová and Iva Brožová entitled *Vlčice*.

Jiří Přibáň, born 25 August 1967, legal philosopher. In 2002, Charles University made him a professor of theory, philosophy and sociology of law. He currently teaches sociology of law, legal theory and constitutionalism at Cardiff University, UK, where he was named a professor of law in 2006. He has also taught at New York University, the University of California, Berkeley, the University of Pretoria, the University of New South Wales, Sydney, the Catholic University of Leuven and numerous other foreign universities. Jiří Přibáň co-founded and directs the Centre of Law and Society at Cardiff University. He is the author and editor of many academic papers and books, such as *Sovereignty in Post-Sovereign Society* (2015), *Právní symbolismus* (2007), *Disidenti práva* (2001), *Právo a politika konverzace* (2001), *Sociologie práva* (1996), and *Tyranizovaná spravedlnost*, an interview with Karel Hvížďala (2013). He also addresses the sociology behind contemporary art and literature in the books *Obrazy české postmoderny* (2011) and *Pod čarou umění* (2008).

The Václav Havel Series aims to honor and extend the intellectual legacy of the dissident, playwright, philosopher, and president whose name it proudly bears. Prepared with Ivan M. Havel, and other personalities and institutions closely associated with Václav Havel, such as the Václav Havel Library and Forum 2000, the series focuses on modern thought and the contemporary world – encompassing history, politics, art, architecture, and ethics. While the works often concern the Central European experience, the series – like Havel himself – focuses on issues that affect humanity across the globe.

Published titles
Jiří Přibáň, *The Defence of Constitutionalism: The Czech Question in Post-national Europe*
Matěj Spurný, *Making the Most of Tomorrow: A Laboratory of Socialist Modernity in Czechoslovakia*
Jacques Rossi, *Fragmented Lives: Chronicles of the Gulag*
Jiří Přibáň & Karel Hvížďala, *In Quest of History: On Czech Statehood and Identity*
Miroslav Petříček, *Philosophy en noir: Rethinking Philosophy after the Holocaust*

Forthcoming
Petr Roubal, *Spartakiads: The Politics of Physical Culture in Communist Czechoslovakia*
Martin C. Putna, *Rus – Ukraine – Russia: Scenes from the Cultural History of Russian Religiosity*
Olivier Mongin, *The Urban Condition: The City in a Globalizing World*
Jan Sokol, *Power, Money, Law*
Josef Šafařík, *Letters to Melin: A Discourse on Science and Progress*
Ivan M. Havel et al., *Letters from Olga*